PRAISE FOR *NOT BUYING IT*

"With great wit and spirit, Judith Levine tackles a profound question: Why do we buy and what do we get out of it? Clue: the answer is not just things. . . . If you have to do without, or just want to do with less, Levine is the person to do it with."

—Barbara Ehrenreich, author of *Nickel and Dimed*
and *Bait and Switch*

"One of the Five Best Books on Consumer Culture. Charming [and] fair-minded."

—Paco Underhill, *The Wall Street Journal* Weekend Edition

"Genius."

—*The Times of London*

"Approach *Not Buying It* prepared to confront your own shopping demons."

—*Detroit Free Press*

"What makes *Not Buying It* stand out among the many books about consumerism is the personal approach. By following Levine's progress the reader gets to appreciate the difficult trade-offs and tensions in not consuming. Her entertaining prose also does a good job of integrating a number of important academic works on the subject, making them relevant and digestible. . . . [B]y focusing primarily on the personal choices and consequences of not shopping, Levine may be telling us far more about the mind-set of American consumerism than perhaps she even fully realizes."

—Lee Drutman, *Los Angeles Times*

"Levine joins the ranks of authors who do crazy stuff . . . and then write books about it—in her case giving up buying anything but 'necessities' for a year. But Levine lends her project global implications with thorough reporting about everything from consumer psychology to the decline of public libraries. . . . And best of all, while she makes you want to repent for your greed more than a few times, she also points out the absurdities of 'voluntary simplicity' and recognizes the soul-stirring happiness implicit in finding a perfect new pair of heels, making *Not Buying It* well worth its price."

—*Entertainment Weekly* Editor's Choice

"I so enjoyed [Levine's] new book that I'll be 'gifting' my copy on this Christmas, in turn, to each member of my penurious family. . . . Levine's yearlong VISA-free journey reveals a hitherto-invisible realm. Without the whirl of buying, vast quantities of time open up—and not just from a lack of purchased entertainment; consuming itself takes time. . . . But perhaps Levine's most pointed observations are political. . . . These days, Americans are not citizens so much as consumers; says one friend of Levine's, 'What's left of the counterculture is the counter.'"

—Sandra Tsing Loh, *The Atlantic*

"Smart [and] funny. . . . Even though this fascinating book is more about consumerism than economizing, Levine doesn't take the easy way out and condemn her fellow citizens. Rather, she thinks that, as Americans, we don't desire too much, we desire too little. Compared with what we could want—from the freedom to call a doctor . . . to the time to lie by a lake and dream—consumer desire is a paltry thing. Levine urges all of us to want more."

—*St. Louis Post-Dispatch*

"Judith Levine's account of her year of doing without unnecessary stuff is An Important Book. *Not Buying It* is also kicky and fun to read. . . . Given that we live on a finite planet, consumption may be the issue we need to think about the most. But, given our devotion to consumer culture, it's the one we usually think about the least."

—Bill McKibben, *Seven Days*

"Her probing examination . . . forces readers to examine their own shopping compulsions and what it means to go without."

—*Bust*

"Levine explores with refreshing doses of self-critique the emotional and social impulses that drive shopping, reflecting on how readily we define ourselves by what we do (or don't) purchase. [A] lively, thoughtful look at consumerism and anticonsumerism."

—*Library Journal*

"Perceptive . . . funny . . . Levine is a keen observer . . . An entertaining exploration of personal desires and needs, with larger social and economic implications."

—*Kirkus Reviews* (starred review)

"Other than phenomenal willpower and maxed-out credit cards, what does it take to simply stop purchasing for 12 months? Levine took the plunge—and found it irritating, exhilarating, thought-provoking, and humiliating—among many other conflicting emotions. . . . [H]er secondary sources, from the recently issued *Trading Up* (2003) to federal deficit projections and Socratic pronouncements, add a great deal of depth to a topic that could be perceived as frivolous."

—*Booklist*

"insightful, witty, and well-researched."

—BookLoons.com

"[With] a . . . personal and intellectual approach to her topic, [Levine] has some terrific insights into the psychology of shopping."

—*Kitchener-Waterloo Record* (Ontario, Canada)

"Informative and refreshing."

—*Willamette Week* (Portland, OR)

ALSO BY JUDITH LEVINE

Do You Remember Me?: A Father, a Daughter, and a Search for the Self

Harmful to Minors: The Perils of Protecting Children from Sex

My Enemy, My Love: Women, Masculinity, and the Dilemmas of Gender

NOT BUYING IT

My Year Without Shopping

Judith Levine

Free Press

NEW YORK LONDON TORONTO SYDNEY

FREE PRESS
A Division of Simon & Schuster, Inc.
1230 Avenue of the Americas
New York, NY 10020

First Free Press paperback edition 2007

FREE PRESS and colophon are trademarks of Simon & Schuster, Inc.

For information about special discounts for bulk purchases,
please contact Simon & Schuster Special Sales:
1-800-456-6798 or business@simonandschuster.com

DESIGNED BY PAUL DIPPOLITO

Manufactured in the United States of America

10   9   8   7   6   5   4   3   2   1

THE LIBRARY OF CONGRESS HAS CATALOGUED THE HARDCOVER EDITION AS
FOLLOWS:
  Levine, Judith.
    Not buying it: my year without shopping / Judith Levine.
      p. cm.
    Includes index.
    1. Consumer education. 2. Shopping. I. Title.
    TX335 .L456   2006
    640'.73—dc22   2005055517

ISBN-13: 978-0-7432-6935-3
ISBN-10:   0-7432-6935-7
ISBN-13: 978-0-7432-6936-0 (Pbk)
ISBN-10:   0-7432-6936-5 (Pbk)

To Paul Cillo, partner in parsimony
and to Ellen Willis (1942–2006)

Contents

NOT BUYING IT

Panic

The idea occurs to me, as so many desperate resolutions do, during the holiday season. I have maxed out the Visa, moved on to the Citibank debit card, and am tapping the ATM like an Iraqi guerrilla pulling crude from the pipeline. Convinced I am picking up no more than the occasional trinket—a tree ornament for Howard and Nanette, a bar of French soap for Norma—in just two weeks this atheist Grinch has managed to scatter $1,001 across New York City and the World Wide Web. I am not in the spirit, but somehow I have gotten with the program.

And what a program it is. Through three years of lusterless economic reports and rising unemployment, consumer confidence has barely flagged. The coffins are returning from Iraq: by Christmas, the U.S. body count is near 500. Still, this month America's good guys caught Iraq's bad guy, several employee-starved companies hired several workers, and a "hoo-wah!" rose from the malls of America. Interviewed on the Saturday before Christmas, Everyshopper Barbara D'Addario chuckled as she told CBS what she had spent: "Today, about $75, and I've been here twenty minutes." What is the source of her generosity and glee? "[I have] great hopes that the economy is improving, and we caught Saddam Hussein," said D'Addario. "We're very happy."

We are very happy, and when we are happy, as when we are

sad or angry or bored or confused or feeling nothing in particular, we shop. On Fifth Avenue, luxury watches priced from $1,000 to $200,000 are flying from the shops as fast as time. In the more earthbound districts, although sales are less brisk, the hoi polloi are enlisting in their own campaigns of retail shock and awe. At a Wal-Mart in Orange City, Florida, a woman is trampled by a crowd surging toward a pile of $29 DVD players.

Since September 11, the consumer in chief has been exhorting us to keep our chins up by keeping our wallets open. In his second post-attack address to the nation, he rooted for "your continued participation and confidence in the American economy." Executive Vice President Dick Cheney was more direct, expressing to NBC's Tim Russert his hope that the American people would "stick their thumb in the eye of the terrorists" and "not let what's happened here in any way throw off their normal level of economic activity." In New York only a day after the towers fell, Mayor Rudolph Giuliani counseled his trembling constituents to "show you're not afraid. Go to restaurants. Go shopping."

It was impossible to remember a time when shopping was so explicitly linked to our fate as a nation. Consumer spending accounts for two-thirds of the U.S. gross domestic product, and if the gross domestic product is what makes America strong, we were told, the marketplace is what makes us free. Consumer choice is democracy. A dollar spent is a vote for the American way of life. Long a perk and a pleasure of life in the U.S. of A., after September 11 shopping became a patriotic duty. Buy that flat-screen TV, our leaders commanded, or the terrorists will have won.

All this floats to mind in mid-December as I stoop to fish a glove from one of the little arctic seas that form on New York street corners after a snowfall. In the act I dip my paper shopping bag into the slush, allowing its contents to slump toward the sodden corner and begin to drop through. Frigid liquid seeps into the seam of my left boot.

"Merry fucking Christmas," I spit at a foot pressing one of my purchases to the bottom of the filthy soup. The foot is attached to a leg bulwarked by its own supersized shopping bag. A mass of bags buffets me about the head and shoulders as I struggle to stand. I flash on the Wal-Mart victim. *This is freedom?* I asked myself. *This is democracy?* As I heave my remaining shopping bag to dry land and scramble after it, I silently announce my conscientious objection: *I'm not buying it.*

I know I'm not alone in my ambivalence about consuming. Environmentalists have been warning for decades that unchecked consumption—from mining to manufacturing, shipping to retailing, overusing to disposing—is laying waste our planet. Globally, we gobble twenty times the resources we did in 1900. Since 1950, paper use has risen sixfold, mostly for packaging. Groundwater use is up threefold, mostly for industry, and fresh water is being poisoned worldwide by pesticide and fertilizer runoff, a product of high-intensity industrial farming, as well as golf courses and perfect suburban lawns. Our vehicles are thirstier for fuel than ever, and as development spreads over the earth there are ever more gas tanks to slake, more factories to stoke. The world's scientists are unanimous about the result of all this fossil-fuel burning: the atmosphere has heated higher, faster, in the past twenty-five years than during the entire time records have been kept. Global warming and its co-conspirator acid rain are devastating habitats and species and melting the polar ice caps.

Human profligacy with nature's bounty is not a new phenomenon. For centuries, hunters and fishers massacred herds of whales, bagged whole flocks of birds. Nor is inequality of consumption new. "One has to be a great lord in Sumatra to have a boiled or roast chicken, which moreover has to last for the whole day," wrote a seventeenth-century French traveler. "Therefore, they say that 2,000 [Westerners] on their island would soon exhaust the supply of cattle and poultry."

But the scale and the relative imbalance of our overconsumption are unprecedented. According to the World Resources Institute, "On average, someone living in a developed nation consumes twice as much grain, twice as much fish, three times as much meat, nine times as much paper, and eleven times as much gasoline as someone living in a developing nation." Among the high-income countries, Americans consume the most. Just 4.5 percent of the world's population, we use 24 percent of its resources and emit 23 percent of the greenhouse gases that are dissolving the ozone layer. The environmentalist organization Redefining Progress measures this inequality with a tool called "ecological footprinting," which quantifies how much of the earth's resources any entity, from an individual to a nation, uses. From the planet's current population and total resources (measured in acres), sustainable and just consumption allots each earthling an ecological footprint of 4.7 acres of nature. The average American devours 24. Translate that to more familiar measures of consumption, and in 1998 an American used 1,023 kilograms of oil or its equivalent and ate 122 kilos of meat. In the same year, his Bangladeshi cousin burned a thimbleful of fuel— 7.3 kilos—and ate a mouthful, 3.4 kilos, of meat. A kilo of meat takes seven times the resources needed to produce a kilo of grain.

Our consumer goods grow ever cheaper; each gizmo performs more functions for fewer dollars than the one before it. Optimism is written in the fresh and crispy product names—BlackBerry, Apple, iPod. Our good life, however, requires that elsewhere—generally east and south of here, but also just down the street—life not be so diverting or convenient. Worldwide, workers, some of them children, pay for our cheap consumer items with miserable wages and working conditions, their air and rivers choked with chemicals.

But even as the gadgets shrink and our houses and cities sprawl, we don't have enough room for our possessions. The average North American household tosses four pounds, a national total of almost a billion pounds, of stuff daily. "You can't have everything," the comedian Steven Wright mused. "Where would you put it?" One answer: in a landfill. Another: in someone else's backyard. On a beach north of Salvador, Brazil, the man who runs an organization called Global Garbage has identified rubbish from sixty-nine countries.

If everybody in the world consumed and discarded at the rate Americans do, says the Earth Council, three planets would be required to sustain us.

I wedge my way through the subway turnstile and onto the Brooklyn-bound train, mashing aside several clumps of wet, overstuffed packages to make room for my own. Although it feels as if the entire U.S. population is inside this car, I know there are a few who have opted not to join us. Some have started their resistance on the Friday after Thanksgiving (America's biggest shopping day), joining almost a million worldwide in celebrating Buy Nothing Day, a twenty-four-hour period of abstention from and meditation on the true meaning of the Retail Season. This twelve-year-old "national holiday" from consuming is the mischief of Kalle Lasn and the Adbusters Media Foundation in Vancouver. Along with sponsoring Buy Nothing Day and national respites from driving and TV-watching, this band of self-styled "media jammers" produces a stream of "uncommercials," the best known of which is Joe Chemo, the skinny, sickly twin of the Camel cigarettes mascot.

So as I squeeze into a seat between two members of a wet, over-stuffed, and ketchup-smelling family of Christmas shoppers, a vision appears before me. I see a puffy cartoon heaven suffused with warm pink light; Brian Eno's "Music for Airports" plays in the background. I conjure emptiness—no slush, no family, no ketchup. No credit cards, no shopping bags. No shopping.

And then it comes to me: what if I were to meditate on the true meaning—and economic, environmental, social, and personal consequences—of the Retail Season not just for a day, but for a month? Too easy. I've got enough stuff to last me for three. Okay, three months. Nah, gratification of desire can be forestalled that long without much trouble—at six months, I might start feeling the pinch. What if I resisted for the actual length of the retail season: the whole year? What if I (along with my live-in partner, Paul) undertook an X-treme trial of nonconsumption, a Buy Nothing Year?

We take the vow. Starting January 1, 2004, Paul and I will purchase only necessities for sustenance, health, and business—groceries, insulin for our diabetic cat, toilet paper, Internet access. I am not primarily out to save money, though I'll be delighted if that happens. I make no claims to replicating the daily sacrifices of people who cannot afford to buy what they need, much less want; I won't insult them by offering my "wisdom" on how to stretch a dollar, nor will I preach the gospel of the Simple Life. I have no illusion that forgoing this CD or that skirt is going to bring down consumer culture—and I don't even know if I want to bring it down. And while Paul and I will do our best to conserve fuel, we live half the year, summer and winter, in Vermont, where driving is unavoidable; so I won't personally be rescuing the ozone layer. Big problems need big, collective policy solutions, I know. From distributing the wealth equitably to halting the destruction of the earth, these issues must be on the tables of legislators, economists, and agronomists, with the rest of us yelling to get it done.

Still, I am moved by a sense of personal responsibility, not to say personal panic, about this big, bad problem and the rapidity with which it is getting worse. Consumption is social—that is, it happens inside a structure larger than a single person or family. But it is also personal. And once we've satisfied our hunger and sheltered ourselves from the cold, shopping is emotional. There is no way to approach the problem of overconsumption without investigating the feelings that surround fantasizing, getting, and owning our stuff. My stuff.

On the principle that you don't give a second thought to your water until your well runs dry, Paul and I will drain the well and see how thirsty we get. Will we want more than the clear liquid that comes from the tap, or will we want Evian? And why?

Materially, we will survive. That's the least of my worries. But, I ask myself, can a person have a social, community, or family life, a business, a connection to the culture, an identity, even a *self* outside the realm of purchased things and experiences? Is it possible to withdraw from the marketplace?

These questions are almost entirely unstudied. In spite of mountains of theory and data on what we buy and why we buy it, "little if any research has been done on people's choices not to purchase or to seek less consumptive, less material-intensive means of satisfying a need," writes Thomas Princen, co-director of the Workshop on Consumption and Environment at the

University of Michigan. "The reason may be obvious. It is very hard to get an analytic or empirical handle on an act that entails not doing something." Economists do not walk around the corner from McDonald's at lunch hour to the park bench where a guy is eating a peanut butter sandwich out of a brown paper bag. Until now, says Princen, "market transactions" have been the alpha and omega of models of the economy and people's places in it. But the peanut butter sandwich eater—or Paul and me figuring out what to do for fun, away from the cineplex—may hold answers to some of the big and little problems of consumption that have so far escaped us, including why it's so hard to resist. That possibility, writes Princen, *"makes the nonpurchase decision a critical focus of inquiry."*

I read these words and feel buoyed by the italics. Our project falls under the rubric of "sustainable living," which generalized as social policy holds the key to the earth's survival. That makes me feel noble. Still, I'm already wondering whether the idea of sustainability, even dignified by italics and the salvation of the planet, will sustain me for a year.

The symptoms of my materialism start to show two weeks before D (for Deprivation) Day: panic attacks, anxiety, depression. That DVD player we've been thinking about? We decide to buy it quick. What about the magazine subscriptions? Better renew in advance so we don't run out. My niece is graduating college in May. Would it be cheating to look for a gift now?

I worry, I grieve. My appetite for things gnaws relentlessly. I pass a Korean grocer with a bank of cut flowers outside. My heart is pulled toward the mini-sunflowers. They're so brilliant, so perfectly formed, so convenient for apartment use! I want them!

Upstairs at the food and cookware emporium Zabar's, as I buy Paul a new coffee grinder for Christmas (the one he's got chews the beans only slightly more efficiently than I would), I am distracted—no, *deranged*—by the hundred-thousand products on display. My own kitchen and everything in it suddenly appear hopelessly shabby. Our cloth napkins are soiled. Shouldn't I pick up a half dozen? Or that nasty old teakettle with rust spots inside. Here's a Calphalon on sale for only $49.99!

During the week of December 22, Paul and I go to four "must-see" movies.

On December 29, I shell out $175 for a pair of "city" snow boots to wear when I'm not wearing the other ("country") snow boots.

On December 30, when I need a tablespoon of Grand Marnier for a recipe, Paul comes home with the largest bottle of liqueur I've ever seen.

On December 31, we drive to Vermont. At 9 P.M. we light candles on the kitchen table and send off the old year with our traditional dinner of spaghetti and supermarket caviar. We toast the Year Without Shopping with our second-to-last bottle of champagne.

At 10 P.M. I unearth a Red Envelope catalogue with a turned-down page featuring a small concrete baby elephant. When I found it more than a year ago, we'd been looking for an ornament to place on a jutting rock in our perennial garden. The elephant was just right, and Paul volunteered to make the purchase but never got around to it. "Oh well," I sigh. "I guess we can say goodbye to our elephant."

"There are still two hours left!" declares Paul, surprising me with his enthusiasm. He leaps online and punches his way to the

Red Envelope Web site. "They still have it!" he shouts, reaching for his credit card. A familiar frisson courses through me—the thrill of the perfect gift, the unbelievable bargain, the hat or shirt that is absolutely me.

Paul hits the Send button and a confirmation of our order appears on the screen. The elephant will arrive the day after tomorrow. And after that . . . 363 days will pass without the UPS man brightening our door. Even if we shopped without surcease for the next hour and thirty-seven minutes, there is only so much buying we could accomplish.

The frisson turns to a chill.

Surplus

VERMONT, NEW YEAR'S DAY

I wake to fresh coffee and a forecast of snow. The wood furnace is hot, the windows frosted. As the sun melts the ice from the glass and the orchard and pond come into view, last night's chill starts to dissipate.

If anyone can make it through a non-buying year, I figure, Paul and I can. We're both self-employed and work at home, conducting most of our business by phone and e-mail. We have no office rents, no payroll to meet; our work outfits—pajamas and pajama equivalents—require no dry cleaning. Although we lurch from deadline to deadline, hour by hour we make our own schedules. We're free to rise before dawn and put in our eight hours before knocking off to ski in the afternoon; we can take two hours to mow the lawn with a low-fuel push mower or simmer a big, cheap soup all day.

Because Paul and I were adults with established lives in two different states when we met, we still spend spring and fall in my Brooklyn apartment and summer and winter in Paul's house in the rural Northeast Kingdom of Vermont. Besides building the variety of "travel" into our routine, the arrangement allows me to rent the apartment and save a half-year's housing costs. Paul is a political and energy-efficiency consultant, I am a full-time writer and editor. We are educated, cosmopolitan, self-directing, and childless.

These lives of enviable flexibility are also insecure. Paul consults for the deep-pocketed likes of Texas's low-income advocates and the Vermont legislature. I earn less than the high school graduate in my Brooklyn building who has a union job fixing garbage trucks for the city. We pay our own stripped-down, high-deductible health insurance premiums (including out-of-pocket bills, this comes to about $6,000 a year for me). We have no job security, no workers' compensation or paid vacations, and minuscule savings.

By necessity, we've learned to keep the overhead low, the financial view long, and the gratification delayed. Still, we come to the project of buying nothing with a certain urgency. We are both past fifty. When we're eighty, presuming ordinary human frailty, we will have to work, and spend, less than we do now.

Temperamentally, we are suited to the task. Paul is a non-shopper. A Vermont boy from a penurious family, he'd rather spend a day a month retwisting and soldering the coils of an ancient toaster than purchase a new one with a micro-graduated darkness scale and bagel-size slots. My own shopping enthusiasms are livelier, and my aptitude for brand discernment better honed than Paul's, but in the scheme of things American I am a desultory and uncommitted consumer at best. When the market researcher calls, I'm an outlier in the sample: "Yes, ma'am, I own a television, yes *one* television, about twenty-five years old. No, no electric hedge trimmer, no riding mower, no dishwasher, no cappuccino maker. Yes, you heard right: no microwave oven (and no, I am not talking to you through an orange juice can at the end of a string)." I mostly buy what I need, I tell her politely. Other than that, I don't want much.

And yet somehow Paul and I have managed to amass what can only be described as *a lot of shit.* This fact will shape our strategy for the year. Besides those few pre-project panic purchases, we have decided not to stock up. We will use whatever we have, and if something runs out, decide if we need more of it.

A logical place to start is an inventory. So with pen and yellow pad in hand, I wander through the house in my slippers.

Start with the clothes closets. These are thick with jackets, their floors a stampede of work boots, snow boots, dress boots, barn boots, and ski boots, as well as winter shoes and summer shoes for business and for play, in dry weather and wet weather, for running, walking, hiking, cross-training, mountain biking, and road biking. In Vermont alone, I have twelve pairs. There are probably twice that many in Brooklyn. Our drawers barely close for all the shirts and underwear mashed into them.

The living room shelves bristle with unread books and barely listened-to CDs; the bathroom is a cornucopia of vegetable products crushed and gelled into potions to heal and soothe, smooth and sedate.

Together Paul and I own a federal bureaucracy's worth of office supplies. These, it is agreed, fall into the Must-Have category. But what about the subcategories? Printer cartridges? Absolutely. Yellow legal pads? Probably. Neon-colored Post-its? And what of the dozen computers lying in state under various desks, their dead mice interred in nests of connector cables? Can't really throw these out—they have valuable data on them. Never mind that the data are inscribed in forgotten computer languages on obsolete disks.

I put a pot of organic seven-grain cereal on the stove, and

while it cooks I open the kitchen pantry and count: eight kinds of rice (short-grain white, long-grain white, short-grain brown, long-grain brown, Thai sweet black, Chinese sweet black, basmati, arborio); six flours, three grades of corn meal, two dozen varieties of beans, peas, and whole grains, and an entire section of organic faro. We also have six oils, six sweeteners, and nine vinegars (balsamic, white, red wine, white wine, rice wine, apple cider, raspberry, champagne, plum). There are condiments to cheer any hungry, homesick member of the U.N. General Assembly who happens by, ranging from dried Chinese black mushrooms to a can of Mexican *huitlacoche* fungus. I am not sure the last is a food.

The top shelf is our liquor cabinet, stocked for a prince's bar mitzvah.

And on the floor stands a case of prescription cat food for our diabetic cat, Julius, plus a container of low-ash, nutrient-rich kibbles specially formulated for a feline of his age, weight, and exercise level. Add in insulin and syringes, blood glucose test strips and lancets, regular veterinary visits, Kitty Kaviar, and an endless supply of jingle balls, and maintaining our companion animal in the style to which he is accustomed costs a minimum of $1,000 a year. Ana, a friend who grew up in Cuba, describes feeling "overwhelmed and a little sick" the first time she walked into an American supermarket at the age of fifteen. "What amazed me most," she says, "was that animals had their own food."

JANUARY 6

Our friends are intrigued. Some regard us with the transfixed queasiness of viewers witnessing contestants eating slugs on *Fear*

Factor. Others wish us luck, even thank us, communicating an attitude there's probably a German word for, meaning "admiration for an enterprise you are glad someone else is doing, so you don't have to."

Soon, their doubts surface. Rorschach-like, these reveal their own consumer ids—their fantasies and frustrations—as well as their superegos—their ethics and guilt. One clue is the word that keeps recurring: *allowed.*

"Great idea," says my agent, Joy, on the phone. She calls back an hour later. "So, okay. Let's talk about this. Are you allowed to get haircuts?"

"What about hair gel?" inquires my haircutter. To her it goes without saying that haircuts are in the Necessity category (I agree). But she is stymied by the question of whether the hairs at the crown of the head must, necessarily, stick up just so.

The pledge to buy "only" groceries resolves little. Alison, a cartoonist, wants to know if we're allowed to buy mesclun salad or only "unprocessed" lettuce heads (we nix the mesclun). I serve kale with garlic and olives to Charlie and Kathy. "So, Judith. Olives," Charlie says, fixing me with narrow prosecutorial eyes. "Would you call *olives* a necessity?" To those who ask, Paul and I can offer no excuse for the designation of seven-dollar-a-pound organic French roast coffee beans as essential. We cannot agree on wine. "I'm Italian," Paul argues. "Wine is like milk to me." I raise an eyebrow.

Janice, a sociologist, mulls over the scariest proscription of all: movies. Contemplating a whole year without this nourishing pleasure, she mourns with me for a few minutes. Then she brightens, having discovered a possible loophole: "But you can see documentaries, can't you?"

Vanalyne, a video artist, e-mails me from Chicago, wondering "whether you're allowed to buy paper towels or whether you have to use a sponge." Her question is a slight variation on the discussion Paul and I have been having about Kleenex versus toilet paper. Paul (who is turning out to be more of a materialist than I'd expected) says nose-blowing requires a ready box on the desk or beside the bed. Walk into the bathroom, say I. When I consult with Alison, she suggests cloth handkerchiefs. Hmm, can snot aversion be considered sufficient reason to use paper? I'd tend to rule in the affirmative. But, for the sake of argument, suppose we do buy facial tissues. Must they be the high-quality, anti-scratch variety, or can we make do during ordinary non-cold periods with the stiff, cheap stuff? And while we're discussing paper goods, do we have to purchase the premium Scott toilet paper? Or could we settle for the store brand, which, while cheap, is scratchy. Why not use newspaper? quips Paul. Or leaves? America's embarrassment of consumer products and experiences is producing an embarrassing surfeit of trivial decisions.

JANUARY 7

Paul is in front of the shed, lying on his back in the snow, readying his multiply pre-owned 1983 Chevy S10 pickup for inspection. A few days ago, the guy at Gates Salvage Yard cut the parts he needed off a dead vehicle; Paul paid $60 and got to work. We're recycling and repairing, harvesting local resources. Life is good.

"Let's get rid of my car," I suggest casually as I watch him untwist a coil and weld a joint. We've vowed to cut down on gasoline, and all those hiking boots, running shoes, and walking shoes are at the ready, along with a fleet of human-powered conveyances including five bicycles, seven pairs of skis, two pairs of snowshoes, a canoe, and a Windsurfer.

"Wish we could," Paul answers without conviction. We've outlined the conundrum too many times. We have three motorized vehicles. Besides the Chevy pickup, which takes us into the woods and hauls lumber, trash, and manure for the gardens, Paul owns a 1999 Subaru Legacy sedan and I, a 1995 Honda Civic. The truck isn't reliable enough for long-distance driving. The Subaru, which is reliable, is not fuel efficient, since it has all-wheel drive. The Honda is efficient and reliable and it's a hatchback, which makes it a great car for trips between Vermont and New York, loaded with stuff, including Julius in his box.

But the Honda doesn't have all-wheel drive, so it's a hazard on Vermont's snowy or muddy roads and can't make it up our driveway in snow, slush, or mud. We use the Subaru during moist seasons. If I have to drive the Honda in these conditions and it gets stuck in the driveway, Paul hitches it to the truck and drags it to the house. The trinity of vehicles seems indivisible.

The situation is more than expensive, it's embarrassing. Two avowed environmentalists who spend six months a year in the most ecologically efficient city in the country, we are doing our part in making America a country where four-wheeled residents outnumber the two-legged ones with drivers' licenses.

JANUARY 15

The rules are shaping up, and we are starting to adjust. No processed or prepared foods except the most basic, bread. No cookies or crackers, then. For hors d'oeuvres, we toast bread and cut it into small pieces. No restaurants, we tell our friends. Come to dinner, they reply. No movies or video rentals. We pull the unread books from the shelf and each week I take my green paper borrower's card up the road to Greensboro, whose patrician summer residents have kept the white clapboard Free Library well stocked. I'm reading a book every three or four days.

What I want is what I've got—more than once in the last two weeks I've found myself singing Sarah McLachlan's lyric to myself.

Still, dilemmas are presenting themselves. We are invited to a blues jam at the Town House, a nonprofit arts center in Hardwick, $5 suggested donation. Should we go? Should we purchase no entertainment or just no commercially produced entertainment? The five bucks covers the heat and upkeep of the space, so that neighbors can play music or see an old movie together. How is this cash donation any different from a casserole brought to a potluck supper? Maybe by going to the blues jam, we'd actually be supporting the anticonsumer culture, I suggest to Paul. Then why not go to the Film Forum or La Mama Theater in New York, he counters—they're nonprofits, too. It occurs to me that by partaking only of homemade spectacles, we might be accomplishing nothing more than condemning ourselves to a year of third-rate entertainment. Since I'm not a blues fan, we opt not to go. But the question remains.

JANUARY 16

My lack of a hedge trimmer or a microwave oven may qualify me as an enemy combatant in George W. Bush's book, but as I start to read about income, spending, and debt, I learn that I am Jane Q. Consumer, the typical American. I earn about the median income for a New Yorker (a bit under $45,000 before taxes and business expenses); my perennially unpaid credit card balance (about $7,500) is average, too. Even my attitudes about spending are normal. Research shows that just about everyone thinks she needs the things she buys and considers almost everything she wants a necessity. A life of "reasonable comfort" appears, always, just a little out of reach. Surveyed in any given year, people peg the resources necessary for such an existence at one to two thousand dollars above the median income for that year. Half of Americans—not just poor ones—say they can't afford all their "needs."

We're not greedy, we say. It's *everyone else* who is acquiring useless stuff. In one study conducted by the economic sociologist and author Juliet Schor, 78 percent of respondents stated that most Americans are "very materialistic." Only 8 percent considered themselves very materialistic. Typical of this attitude is a couple of Texans profiled in *Trading Up: The New American Luxury*, by Michael Silverstein and Neil Fiske. The husband, a real estate developer named Charles, owns a BMW 325 and a Jaguar X-Type. His wife, Judith, bought a Thermador six-burner range and other "premium appliances" when they renovated their kitchen. Nevertheless, Charles and Judith say "they don't like to overspend and don't believe in status buying." For instance, "Charles scoffs at the idea of buying a fancy watch."

I don't consider myself materialistic, either. Like Charles and Judith, I don't like to overspend and don't believe in status buying. I'm a vegetarian; I eat at the "low end of the food chain," as the enviros say. I sneer at the *New York Times* travel section piece about retreats where people sleep on cots, rise at five, eat some gruel, an apple, and three almonds, and pay $4,000 a week for the privilege. I buy generic tampons and three-dollar shampoo.

And yet . . . I think nothing of forking over ten bucks to view any obscure French film that passes through New York or $15 for an hour and a quarter of yoga instruction, half of which time I do little more than breathe. I buy the no-name tampons, yet I unswervingly maintain that the 200 milligrams of pure ibuprofen in an Advil capsule cures my headache faster than a 200-milligram capsule of pure ibuprofen in the bottle labeled Ibuprofen, which costs half as much.

In the pantry, Paul and I have three kinds of salt.

JANUARY 20

What I want is what I've got. Unfortunately, what Paul's got, I don't want.

Reader, it is time for a confession. Paul and I have two homes, my small but ample apartment in Brooklyn and his house, cellar, shed, and forty acres in northeastern Vermont. In addition, I've got a cabin in a birch grove a hundred yards from the house, the Platonic writer's space, built from salvage materials six years ago. Together, we have literally acres of space.

And yet we did not have enough of it. What Paul's got was spreading across our bedroom, down the stairs to the kitchen, a glacier of stuff carving out its own indoor geology: buttes of newspaper, sedimentary layers of credit card receipts, archipelagos of boxes, fliers, spreadsheets, and every While You Were Out memo that has entered his life in the last two decades ("See you Thursday"). The landscape was so mature that it had spawned an ecosystem. Spider webs knit together leaves of disintegrating paper, flies swarmed on window sills inaccessible to swatters. The spiders ate the flies, the paper turned to dust; the fly carcasses collected on the sills and fossilized.

We fought. Paul called his stuff need, I called his inability to part with it desire—neurotic desire. We had been fighting about it since we started living together, fourteen years ago.

At first it seemed a room with a door would solve the problem. All I wanted to do was open the door, toss the stuff into the room, and close the door. If the door became impossible to close, Paul could rent a backhoe and shovel the stuff out. It would no longer be my problem—our relationship's problem.

But as we measured and sketched, there was no place for a room in our house's long narrow layout. The impossibility of a small change morphed into the possibility of a big one. Possibility transformed into desirability and, as these things go, to necessity, which became inevitability. I "needed" a winter office (my cabin is cold in the winter months, so I work in the hall). Our guests "needed" a private place to sleep (not the living room couch) and a bathroom of their own. Our boots were piled behind the kitchen door, our skis were waxed while balanced between a sawhorse and a plastic garbage can on the subfreezing back porch; we needed a mudroom. And since Freud himself could not make of Paul's neurotic hoarding a case of ordinary untidiness, besides an office for him we needed, desperately needed, more closets.

Six months before we started downsizing, we began to scale up. Our cute 1,300-square-foot house with curling clapboards, a bedroom and a bathroom, a torn-screen porch, and a gravel-floored cellar prone to flooding will become 1,800 newly sided feet of floor space incorporating a large living room and library, master bedroom, guest room, two offices, two baths, insulated porch/mudroom, wine cellar, and many, many built-in cabinets, shelves, and closets.

The renovation will add $25,000 to the mortgage and $1,000 to the property tax bill. An additional $5,000 or so will come out of pocket for furniture, lighting, and accessories. After that, the new rooms will need perpetually to be heated, vacuumed, painted, and repaired.

All we wanted was productivity in work and tranquility in love, an end to the fight. Perhaps we should have sought counseling. Perhaps, if we'd known about him, we could have engaged Ron Alford of Disaster Masters Inc., provider of crisis intervention for people suffering from what he calls "disposaphobia." If we had had a name for the disorder, maybe we could have found a less radical therapy.

Instead, we came up with a home remedy, which, alas, was a homeopathic one. For the problem of having too much, we self-medicated with the American cure-all: *more*.

JANUARY 30

"This is cozy," I say, as we snuggle under two down quilts on a 30-below-zero night. "It's like a studio apartment." Paul opens his eyes. "I mean, we only have guests about four weekends a year," I continue. "And I use the winter office for two months."

In preparation for rebuilding the walls and sanding the floors upstairs, we have packed Paul's things into dozens of boxes and mashed them into a corner. Two truckloads of detritus went to the recycler and the dump and a derelict sofa to some newlywed friends with three large dogs. While our house is under construction, we are living in the former living room on what's left of our furniture, with our clothes in Hefty bags beneath the bed. A bookshelf separates the living space from my workspace, and Paul has set up shop in the hallway.

Paul cocks his head thoughtfully, gazes across the expanse of floor. What we are calling the "new living room" is still a warehouse of lumber and Sheetrock, though elegantly lit by $2,600 worth of tall, argon-filled, low-emissivity insulated-glass Andersen casement windows. "So remind me," he says, as much to himself as to me. *"Why* are we building all this?"

Only a month of Not Buying It has made our old space feel almost sufficient.

Visiting a young country full of ancient emptiness, Alexis de Tocqueville observed that its inhabitants had humble tastes. They rejected the "sumptuous depravity and splendid corruption" of the aristocrats on the other side of the Atlantic. Still, they had a penchant for "physical gratifications," among which he named a bigger house with a few more rooms.

Could Tocqueville have foreseen the empty spaces filling with 40,000-square-foot private homes equipped with gyms, movie screening rooms, and restaurant-grade kitchens? Did I, a woman of birdlike domestic-consumer appetites, imagine I would be feeding the collective obesity of the American home with a two-person living and storage space weighing in at over 4,000 square feet—all so one of those persons could have a room of his own?

"I want space," people say when intimacy strains. Did my beloved and I believe that given enough two-by-fours we could build a wall between ourselves and the stresses and disappointments of the partnered life? From design sketches to window trim, the renovation is likely to take five years of our labor. We have been fighting about it since before the foundation was dug.

I pull the quilt up around my neck as the cold air blows through the still half-insulated new living room. "You could have rented a self-storage unit," I suggest. "There's one on Route 14, you know, right next to the Knights of Columbus."

"Self-storage," Paul snorts. "Store this."

As we move into a year of defining our needs and monitoring our desires, the house-in-progress gives cautionary new meaning to the term *self-storage*. "[F]or our houses are such unwieldy property that we are often imprisoned rather than housed in them," wrote Thoreau. "And the bad neighborhood to be avoided is our own scurvy selves."

Consumer Psychology

FEBRUARY 3

Shit, I've lost my SmartWool socks. They're not in my drawers or Paul's drawers. Not in the laundry basket or under the bed. My socks are lost. So am I.

I discovered SmartWool while buying new boots at the Ski Rack in Burlington two years ago. Over my silk sock liners, I'd pulled on the thick, pilling purple polyester $3 tubes that had served me for a decade. The salesman, whose tanned face and snowpack abs told me he was a Super-G racer when not selling shoes, looked away. He seemed embarrassed, as if catching his mother wriggling into a girdle.

Then I asked to see the Rossignol X-ium Classic cross-country racing boots, which run about $250. He became confused. How could this purple-polyester customer be interested in these high-end silver boots? (Answer: by not fitting into any other boots.) He became attentive, almost respectful; he explained the X-iums' technology, the plastic liners that are heated up and cooled to the contours of the wearer's feet. "You want them as tight as possible," he said. "You'll want a thinner sock. A real *athletic* sock." On the word *athletic,* I thought I heard a note of skepticism as he looked me over again.

I mustered my self-respect. Naturally I will want a thinner sock, I thought. I will *need* a thinner sock. We athletes, the kind who buy $250 boots, do not wear purple polyester tube socks.

And that was when I met SmartWool. The salesman took a pair off the rack. They were a cool gray, not exactly thin, but lean; they were hardworking but efficient, sleek but muscular—yes, these were some truly *athletic* socks. I skimmed the user's manual hanging on a plastic tab from the sock's edge. It told me how SmartWool wicks moisture away from the skin, keeping it dry and warm in winter, dry and cool in summer. SmartWool, said the testimonials at the end of the care instructions, delivers consistent "high perform-ance."

They cost $15, about $12 more than I'd ever paid for socks. I did not hesitate. Along with the boots, I bought two pairs of SmartWools, brought them home, put them on, and went skiing. I couldn't wait.

Within days I developed an unwholesome relationship with the new socks. The old ones were rolled in a ball at the back of the drawer, not to be withdrawn until spring, when I needed some-thing to protect my feet while staining the upstairs floors. Pimply as a teenager's face, purple as the Sixties, the old socks became more than expendable. They were despicable.

Which brings me to the current crisis.

I am barreling through the house, throwing small pieces of fur-niture out of my way and myself onto larger pieces of furniture, crying out in exasperation. "I can't find my SmartWool socks! Where are my SmartWool socks?!"

Paul tries to help. "Are they in your boots?"

I ignore him.

He presses on. "Maybe they're in the laundry. Did you look in my drawer?"

I turn on him. "Did you do something with my SmartWool socks? Are *you* wearing my socks?"

He ignores, then reassures me. "Don't worry. You'll find them later."

When this doesn't work, he hectors. "Come on. Just put on some socks and let's get out of here. Look at that perfect snow!"

I am immovable.

He threatens. "Okay, I'm going without you." But he doesn't.

I am as bummed as he is. I mean, how can I look at the perfect snow? Its perfection only renders me, in my sockless state, even more imperfect. Without my socks, how can I ski? How can I expect high performance, or any performance at all? I sit on a pile of flung clothes and sulk.

If you ask a neoclassical capitalist economist, the free market is the epitome of Intelligent Design. Yes, investors fall prey to occasional paroxysms of panic or irrational exuberance. The indicators sometimes behave weirdly and must be interpreted by the oracles at the Conference Board. Interest rates or currency supply want a little nudging by central bankers now and then, and prices and wages may ask for a little bullying by legislators and regulators. But these are adjustments around the edges. For the most part, Adam Smith's Invisible Hand guides itself.

Inside this rational system, claim these economists, the consumer—*Homo economicus*—is also rational. He is well informed and good at balancing his current needs and desires against those in the long term, then deciding where to put his money. *Homo economicus* lives in the economy, not in, say, a San Fernando Valley suburb or a neighborhood of Delhi. That is, he is abstracted from the social: he is not exactly a person, but a consumer, and as such he is motivated by one thing, self-interest. Neoclassical, or utilitarian, economists argue that all these individual self-interests, working together and in conflict, keep prices low and wages reasonable, demand in balance with supply, and the economy prospering, enhancing everyone's lives. It may be a system based on greed, but, many theorists say, greed is natural. The system works, they say.

Back at our house, the day is waning. Paul stares at me. He is out of ideas, out of time, out of what could have been a glorious ski. He slouches into the kitchen and makes the motions of starting supper. I follow him and flop down at the table.

"I don't know what could have happened to those socks," I mumble, redundantly. "Why can't I find them?"

Paul closes the refrigerator and turns to me. His face is blank, then sympathetic. Now he offers consolation: the one obvious shortcoming in SmartWool's perfectly consistent high performance. "If they're so smart," he says, "why can't they find themselves?"

The same question might be asked about me.

And here's another question: *you call this rational?*

FEBRUARY 5

Ann, one of my dearest friends and political comrades, and a feminist intellectual and New School University professor, calls to tell me about a lecture on consumer desire she heard this week, in which the speaker mentioned the Apple Computer logo. "There's a bite taken out of the apple," she quotes the lecturer. "Something you are missing, something the computer will supply."

"Or something you've tasted, that you want more of," I add.

Ann tells me a tale of two tablecloths. Someone cleaning up

after a party at her house mistakenly threw them out. Like me at the loss of my socks, Ann was inconsolable. "Oh, Judy, they were the perfect thing," she moans, just the right colors, the right size, and washable! "A triumph." Greatly increasing the pleasure and value of the tablecloths, though, was "the hunt," the time and perseverance invested in their capture. Ann had traipsed from store to store. Nothing was quite right. She pored over the catalogues. Then, finally, under a heap of teacups and saucers, so to speak, she found them, in the Anthropologie catalogue.

Not only wanting the thing but getting it—the excitement of the hunt—"is pumped up and socially mandated," says Ann, describing the engagement and pleasure that economists call "transactional utility." A long, hard chase does not necessarily mean a lower price. Indeed, wrote the German philosopher Georg Simmel, "we call those objects valuable that resist our desire to possess them." The tablecloths were expensive. Ann describes Anthropologie, in which items chintzy and classy, cheap and costly are displayed in a meticulous hodgepodge, "like a yard sale."

"Only you don't have to drive to rural Illinois," I say. Instead, Anthropologie "finds" the kitschy, cool collectibles for you, ships them to your mailbox, and charges you for the feeling of having discovered them yourself. The job of consumer capitalism is to make things both resistant to possession and irresistible, both distant and attainable.

Ann sighs. "Consumer culture is a machine for dissatisfaction," she says. "You could get a facelift, you could find the perfect dress, you could be beautiful, you could be youthful. I have to admit," she continues, "it has been deeply instilled in me. It all depends on people having a lot of yearning. That excitement is offered in lieu of."

In a *New Yorker* cartoon, a woman stands at a department store counter and inquires of the salesperson, "What would you suggest to fill the dark, empty spaces in my soul?"

FEBRUARY 7

Saturday is chore day. Paul and I drive to the recycling center a mile outside Hardwick, then back to the food co-op and the supermarket. Our basket is full of basics: bread, milk, onions, rice, kale, biodegradable dish soap. Even if we wanted to, we'd be hard put to buy anything fancier here.

Our little town is one of the few spots between the shining seas where commercial temptations are few. The ads in the *Hardwick Gazette* stick to the goods and services that can be bought around here: asphalt roofing, front-end alignments, Reiki. In keeping with local small-britches mores, merchants keep their pitches modest, almost self-effacing. The Village Laundramat offers a "FREE Wash with Our Frequent Washer Club!" The ad for the nearby community college resembles a carpet retailer's: "Convenient. Affordable. And so many options." And on Main Street in Hardwick the owners of the Chinese takeout Wok 'n' House (a branch of Wok 'n' Roll, in nearby Morrisville) draw attention to the restaurant's one indisputable attraction: it is usually open. The electronic advertising that Paul and I hear is no more tempting. On public radio, the sponsors sell intangibles, if not incomprehensibles. One underwriter is "promoting the enhancement and diffusion of knowledge and understanding." Another (courageously?) "believe[s] in early defibrillation."

Purchasable entertainment hereabouts is sparse. The nearest decent restaurant or "art" cinema is thirty miles down the winding Route 14. The former hasn't changed its menu in a decade, and by the time we arrive here from New York we have usually seen whatever is playing at the latter. That leaves the local video rental, which has a fairly good, but thin, selection (and how many times can you watch *Run, Lola, Run*?).

With the nearest mall sixty miles away, our only "emporium" is Willey's, a huge, old-style general store in Greensboro, which sells everything you need. Everything, that is, if what you need is ammunition, steel-toed boots, birdseed, or muffin tins in any of five sizes. They also carry a knockoff SmartWool sock.

Still, Hardwick has its hot consumer products. Its most conspicuous consumption is of new vehicles, each of which enables the driver to traverse a distance in a different kind of weather over a different terrain, preferably while burning maximum amounts of fuel and creating maximum amounts of odor and noise. You can purchase a straight-off-the-conveyer-belt mega-pickup truck, a 90-mile-an-hour state-of-the-art snowmobile, a terrain-shredding all-terrain vehicle, a Jet-Ski (an aquatic snowmobile/ATV), or most recently, an ultralight, a kind of motorized hang glider.

A similar new-product hunger is fed by weapons that enable a person to kill a different kind of animal at a different distance using different skills in different seasons. There are shotguns for birds and small game; traps for slightly larger, wilier game; rifles in a range of calibers for coyote, deer, and bear; along with muzzle loaders and high-tech bows and arrows, and hundreds of rods, reels, lines, depth finders, and fish finders for every piscine species. In Vermont, you are also allowed to shoot fish.

Why do people buy all these things? Hardwick's Economic Man, living in seclusion, would surely want something to transport him from here to there, as well as something with which to kill something to eat. But he probably would not feel the urge to trade in the 2005 Yamaha RX Warrior snowmobile with the 145-

horsepower Genesis Extreme engine for the 2006 Yamaha Apex RTX with the 150-hp Genesis engine or to clutter his hut with another 30-30 rifle boasting a slightly better scope.

Classical economics, which assumes he does live in seclusion (inside the marketplace), advances the tautology that he wants more because it is human nature to want more. In the depths of the Great Depression, John Maynard Keynes posited a widespread "pent-up demand" for consumer goods that was being suppressed by worries of joblessness. Once unleashed into the marketplace, consumer demand would end the country's woes, Keynes promised. Some help might be needed to transform a deeply rooted cultural ethos of thrift into one of gratification. Among other things, he recommended widely available consumer credit.

But once people fulfilled what he called the "essential" needs, Keynes didn't worry that they would stop buying and stall the economy again. The "second-class wants" would never abate; indeed, they were likely to be "insatiable, for the higher the general level [of wealth] the higher still they are." At the turn of the 19th century, Thomas Malthus had defined the good life as a piece of meat and a glass of wine at dinner. What Keynes was counting on was the escalation of these simple pleasures to a fillet of Japanese kobe beef and a 1949 Domaine de la Romanée-Conti. Or a 2005 snowmobile to a 2006—all charged on the credit card. Consumer credit resolves a fundamental dilemma of capitalism: how to pay workers as little as possible while making sure they can buy as much as possible.

If you step back, it would be hard to describe the purchase of an $8,000 snowmobile on the credit card of a person earning $35,000 as rational (though judging from the chat around Brochu's garage, it is highly informed). As for self-interested, this goes without saying; the purchase of a snowmobile or a high-tech firearm cannot be construed as altruism. But that begs the question of what this interest is. The deer is self-interested, too, after all, and she's not buying a 9-millimeter rifle to make it a fair fight.

Utilitarian economics does not go far in explaining consumer behavior. Consumer psychology has its limits, too. You can find twenty-seven libraries full of market research on why the guy buys the Yamaha instead of the Ski-Doo. What it doesn't clarify is why he wants either of them.

FEBRUARY 12

Paul and I drive north through a swirling snow to hear the story writer and poet Grace Paley read to benefit the tiny Glover Public Library. Every writer in the state has made the trek, in twos and threes arriving inside the plain town hall and stomping the snow from their boots into puddles on the wooden floor. Here, too, is a good part of Glover, many of whose residents, including the librarian, are current or veteran members of the political theater troupe Bread & Puppet. The event is redolent of B&P, whose ramshackle farmhouse, barn, and museum of giant props and puppets are just up the hill. A folding table is stacked with homemade brownies, carrot cake, cookies, and vegetarian samosas; on a stool by the door is a tall, papier-mâché hat for donations.

Grace, getting tinier and wilder of hair as she ages, is both incongruously Jewish here in the Northeast Kingdom and precisely in place among Glover's *haimisher* peaceniks. She reads some poems and two stories about her father, and several poems by her husband, Bob Nichols. After the satisfying reading, I drink some chamomile tea out of a paper cup and eat a brownie. I drop $5 in the papier-mâché hat. As we leave, Paul adds $20.

Why do we put this much money in the hat? Is it just because we are generous individuals? Why does the guy buy the $8,000 snow machine? Because he is selfish and greedy?

Neither, say sociologists and anthropologists. Our personal tastes and personalities explain only a small part of why we buy. All exchange, from gift-giving to barter to money-based commodity purchases, is *social,* they stress. People generally behave in ways that are rewarded and avoid doing what is punished in their societies. Why does the guy want the Yamaha? For the same reason every seven-year-old wants a Hello Kitty lunchbox one year and a SpongeBob Square Pants lunchbox another year: *Because everybody else has one, Mom!* The phenomenon is called emulation.

Emulation can stoke desire for goods or indifference to them, purchase of a snowmobile or donation to a library—or any other attitude or behavior. A person isn't even greedy or generous in isolation, for what is called greed in one culture may be parsimony in another; generosity here is profligacy there. This goes not just for cultures, but also for subcultures. I look inside the tall hat—it's full of bills. We poets and puppeteers don't tend to have snowmobiles.

As a group, even if we may have similar values to some snow-mobilers', we inhabit what sociologists call different taste cultures. Still, like the snowmobilers, we library donors are emulating someone.

FEBRUARY 14, VALENTINE'S DAY

At the convenience store and Texaco station on the corner of Routes 14 and 15, the red-foil-covered chocolate roses are selling well. A man in line in front of me buys two. The clerk approves. "Aren't those pretty?" she says, ringing them up. "I got six for my mom." I pick up my *New York Times* (a necessity) and leave the store thinking about a Valentine's gift for Paul.

When I get home, I empty the matches from a small, thin matchbox and wrap it in iridescent purple paper. I glue an elongated, striped heart, also iridescent, onto one side and a striped red, green, and gold one onto the other. Then I gather up whatever old magazines I can find and cut a couple dozen tiny hearts of different sizes from them. I stuff these inside the box. The whole thing has taken about an hour, the same time I'd have spent driving to the bookstore and picking out a card.

When Paul gets home, he opens the box and the hearts tumble out. He kisses me.

Later in the evening, Linda, the bookseller in town, stops by for a beer on her way home. I show her the matchbook valentine on the kitchen table. "Cute!" she says. I'm proud of my matchbox, proud as I am of our Chevy S10 held together with welding compound and Bondo. I'm proud, moreover, of what these things are not: *not* the brand-spanking-new zillion-hp extended-cab Dodge Ram, *not* the foil-wrapped rose.

I'm not keeping up with the Joneses who drive the big trucks, but the Joneses who grow organic carrots and drive beaters like ours. My funky valentine could hold its own beside the papier-mâché hat in Glover, winning the admiration of the people—and the person—whose opinions matter most to me. In our little subculture, not consuming gives Paul and me cachet. Soon *our* Joneses may be keeping up, or down, with us.

FEBRUARY 20

Paul and I have been spending our days doing more or less what we have always done, minus shop. We work at our desks, go to the food co-op, engage in local politics, help friends with their projects (Charlie has started baking eight loaves of bread a week in the outdoor clay oven he built with Paul's help last summer). For entertainment we visit friends, read, ski, and walk. Our Scrabble games improve. For surprise and spiritual uplift, we look around at deer, fox, and owl, snowdrifts and stars.

In this way Not Buying It has thrust us back to the nineteenth century, when amusements were non-mechanized, non-electronic, and non-mass, enlivened not by speed or special effects, but by direct human contact. We are not, however, purged of the desire for speed or special effects.

We're taking a walk up our road, Bridgman Hill. The mountains are mauve, the air dry and sharp. "You know, I'd really like to get DSL," Paul says. He's not sure he can get it here, but he wants it in the city.

"Is that a necessity?" I ask.

"It's for work," he answers. I know his complaints about his current Internet setup, which he rehearses now: the pokey modem, the minutes—hours!—wasted waiting for his e-mail to appear on the screen, the documents lost, the frustration of getting bumped offline in the middle of a download. Neither of us knows how DSL works, but he reasons that his getting it is not going to sully the New York cityscape. "Whatever the infrastructure is, it's already in place."

I get irked. So the infrastructure for DSL is in place, I say. Once he gets it in New York, won't he want it in Hardwick? And if he wants it here, doesn't he think other people will simultaneously be wanting it, and doesn't he think other infrastructure will show up—a cell tower, a paved road—on Bridgman Hill once everyone starts wanting, and having, and . . . I'm working up a bit of a rant. Paul turns silent, his standard defense against such harangues. I forge on. No matter how slow his Internet connection is, it's a hell of a lot faster than the U.S. Postal Service was, which was fast enough until FedEx and faxes and e-mail demoted it to "snail mail." DSL doesn't reduce work time, I conclude. It contributes to speedup. "You'll just end up working more."

"I'm not going to work more," Paul says. "I'll go skiing or play tennis. I'll read, I'll make maple syrup. I'll clean my room." A saccharine smile. "I'll spend more time with *you*, honey."

Having no impact except to smudge the infrastructure-free landscape with discord, I walk on without responding. "Well, I don't want DSL," I say after a while. "I don't think fast enough for high-speed Internet. I'm a 56-Kbps thinker." Don't worry about me. I'll sit here in the dark.

Why am I arguing? I'm also frustrated taking twenty minutes to download every little video or PDF file. Am I trying to prove that Paul is behaving irrationally? That DSL is not necessary? That it isn't useful? Must a thing be useful to be necessary?

I pull myself back from the World Wide Web to our beautiful hill, and this focuses me on our walk, and then on my own body. On the snowy road, my feet are warm, dry, and comfy. As it happens, I am wearing my SmartWool socks (they were in my drawer all along, nestled beside their purple sisters). SmartWool continues to realize the promise of its propaganda. The socks are soft, they don't itch. They're machine washable and fast-drying, durable and, yes, excellent wickers. In fact, I have come to adore SmartWool so much that I've purchased ski pants and a jacket made of a similar fabric, along with an entire wardrobe of Polartec, Coolmax, Capilene, and other similarly science fictional–sounding natural-synthetic hybrids. These fabrics outperform the ones they've replaced—cotton, silk, ordinary wool—by fifty kilometers. They outperform me.

Now I see what worries me about Paul's high-speed Internet access. Will the same thing happen to him as happened to me with

SmartWool? As soon as I bought these socks, a perfectly adequate product (my purple polyester socks) became an inadequate product, and shortly thereafter a hateful product, by virtue solely of the appearance of the new product. The useful new thing became indispensable. My affection for it became an *amour fou*. SmartWool became what Saatchi + Saatchi Worldwide CEO Kevin Roberts calls a "lovemark," a brand that inspires "loyalty beyond reason."

Aka, a fetish.

When I'm back in the house, I look for Freud's essay on the sexual fetish. The relevant passage concerns cases in which a person requires a fetish object—a shoe, for instance (or a sock?)—"if the sexual aim is to be attained." The condition "becomes pathological," says Freud, "when the longing for the fetish passes beyond the point of being merely a necessary condition attached to the sexual object and actually *takes the place* of the normal aim."

I replace the word *sexual* with the word *athletic* (sports having supplanted sex in the American erotic imagination anyway), and yikes, I am looking at myself in the mirror. The SmartWool socks became necessary to the attainment of my athletic aim. Then passion for the socks replaced the aim itself—I opted *not to ski* rather than ski without the product purchased to make skiing more enjoyable.

Ja, meine leibe, remarks Dr. Freud. This is the point at which "mere variations of the . . . instinct pass over into pathological aberrations."

FEBRUARY 21

Am I sick? Are we all?

In spite of the plenitude of products, many of us are not happy. We are wealthy; even America's poor are wealthy compared with the rest of the world, which shows that wealth is relative. "Men do not desire to be rich," wrote John Stuart Mill, "but richer than other men." And thanks to U.S. tax and corporate policy, some men and women are getting a whole lot richer than other men and women, and this, say critics, is driving quite a few of us crazy.

A century after Mill, as the postwar suburbs filled with houses and the houses filled with kitchen appliances and matched bedroom sets, the economist James Duesenberry observed the Smiths scrambling to "keep up with the Joneses." If they didn't look much further than the end of the block, Mr. and Mrs. Smith might even succeed. A half-century hence, thanks to a widening wealth gap and the media-enhanced visibility of the extravagantly fed, clothed, and sheltered, argues Cornell University economist and public policy professor Robert H. Frank, we feel obliged to keep up not with the Joneses but with the Zeta-Joneses or the Gateses. He calls what ails us "luxury fever."

Most of us can only attempt emulation; it usually can't be realized. Juliet Schor describes an "aspirational gap" leading to an "upward creep of desire," a cycle of seeing, wanting, buying (with or without ready cash), then having to work more to pay for it (an average of nine weeks more per year than Europeans). Documentary filmmakers John de Graaf, David Wann, and Thomas H. Naylor have declared an epidemic, "affluenza," which they define as a "painful, contagious, socially transmitted condition of overload, debt, anxiety, and waste resulting from the dogged pursuit of more."

Just this year Erzo F. P. Luttmer of Harvard's Kennedy School of Government studied people who move into better neighborhoods hoping for better schools, prettier surroundings—in short, happier lives. But whereas in the old community they may have *been* the Joneses, now they are the Smiths. Their spirits sink to the level of their new social position. Luttmer calls the effect "Neighbors as Negatives."

One of the things I like about Hardwick is that my neighbors are not negatives. I have almost nobody to envy. No one has a lot of money, almost no one has a big house. I have few writers in my circle (writers are notorious enviers of other writers who are even marginally better paid, better reviewed, or better looking than they). Other potentially enviable accomplishments more plentiful in these parts do not concern me, since I don't consider myself skilled enough even to be in the running. Gardening or skiing, for instance, I just enjoy.

So here I am, sailing along enviably free of envy and, out of the blue—out of the white—skulks the green-eyed beast. I've arranged with Lucy, a persevering, competent skier, and Grace, a former racer from a family of ski instructors and Olympic athletes, to take the afternoon off for a twenty-kilometer trek from Greensboro to Craftsbury. It's snowing softly and the temperature is hovering around 32 degrees. Since these are almost impossible conditions to wax for, I put on my oldest pair of skis, some flat, white Trax no-wax touring skis (a $90 starter kit, complete with poles, if I remember), and my first pair of boots, which fit their bindings.

The day is magnificent. We have the trail to ourselves, except for the occasional chipmunk or white-winged crossbill. We push along at a sprightly but not tiring pace, moving mostly in silence. From time to time one of us alerts the others to the song of the crossbill or exclaims about how cute a chipmunk is. We keep congratulating ourselves for taking the afternoon off.

It is, in short, a near-perfect experience. With the emphasis on *near.*

I progress smoothly for several kilometers. Then after a while I find myself falling slightly behind Grace and Lucy. Soon I can't hear their voices, and when I call out to them, they don't hear me. I feel a little abandoned and a little klutzy, though I am still having a good time.

A few more kilometers and I am starting to feel dissatisfied. Things aren't working. My gators, the Gore-Tex chaps that strap under the shoe and extend up the shins to keep the snow out, are scrunching down and falling under my heels. My toes are pushing against the front of the old soft boots, the skins of which are beginning to flake off. My heels are sliding off the sides of the old-style bindings. Dissatisfaction with myself is attaching itself to my equipment.

Now I am mentally enumerating the sporting goods I will buy (next year) to improve the experience. I'll get a pair of nylon snow pants, which will be light and windproof and tuck neatly into my boots. Then I won't need gators. I'll need new boots and bindings, too, so my heels don't fall off the skis. The poles I have, racing poles with only a suggestion of a basket at the bottom, are punching through the deep snow. Put a pair of touring poles with wider baskets on the list. And while I'm at it, why not a pair of new backcountry skis, rather than making do with these old things?

I'm falling farther behind. From a distance I watch Grace's muscular butt tighten with each strong kick. When I get my new boots and bindings and pants, I won't be wobbling off the skis and stopping to shake off the clotted snow. I'll get thinner and stronger, like Grace (who, by the way, is on twenty-year-old skis).

The snow is getting too deep and the weather too warm. I'm trudging. Snow is sticking to the bottoms of my skis and clumping between the bindings and the boots, feeling like tennis balls beneath my arches. How many more kilometers? The distance between me and Grace and Lucy is widening. I imagine they are still chatting happily about the snow, the sky, the chipmunks, the little chirping birdies.

I'm trying to be happy, too. But if only I had . . . I'd be keeping up with Grace and Lucy. If only I could buy . . . I'd be a better skier. Better skis, a better skier. If only I were more like Grace and Lucy, I'd be a happier person. If I had better skis and were a better skier, I'd be a happier person. I'd be like Grace and Lucy. A better person.

FEBRUARY 24

I receive in the mail a large, glossy textbook put out by the American Psychological Association. *Psychology and Consumer Culture: The Struggle for a Good Life in a Materialistic World* is an anthology of academic articles on "acquisition-related disorders," which, the writers argue, are marked by depression, anxiety, impulsivity, compulsivity, shame, guilt, perfectionism, narcissism, self-loathing, fear of intimacy, "cognitive narrowing," and magical thinking. Like this list of contradictory symptoms, the book is a strange hybrid. On the one hand, it recognizes the social and historical nature of our relationship to consumption (the materialistic world). On the other, as psychiatrists have done with shyness, shortness, mourning, indifference to sex, and other former eccentricities and unpleasant facts of life, this book declares overconsumption a medical disorder. The diagnosis carries with it a great boon to their profession and its allies in the pharmaceutical industry. Now, shopping can be treated by psychotherapy (and hopefully, reimbursed by insurance) or (like shyness, shortness, etc.) with drugs. Indeed, in 2003 a study published in the *Journal of Clinical Psychiatry* announced an "effective treatment" for "compulsive acquisition disorder": the antidepressant Celexa.

The news may not be good for General Motors. But it has been good for Celexa's U.S. licensee, Forest Laboratories. Thanks in no small part to the happy little pill, Forest last year achieved an 84 percent rise in profits and became a darling among Big Pharma investors. Overconsumption may cause misery. But drug companies love misery.

FEBRUARY 26

Another ski-related trouble offers another clue about consumption.

Paul has meetings in Montpelier today. He gets up early and before leaving removes my skis from his car and puts them into mine, so I can go out when I'm finished working. Then he drives off with the wax kit in his car.

At two, I am ready to get up from my desk. I put on my ski clothes, warm up the car. Soon, I'm on my way to the Craftsbury Sports Center, widely regarded as the best place for cross-country skiing in the Northeast, and I'm psyched. Halfway there, this time with my good, waxable skis, it occurs to me that I didn't see the wax kit in the back of the car. I pull to the side of the road, open the hatchback, riffle through the bag. I'm right. I get behind the wheel again. Traversing some of the most breathtaking landscape in the northeastern United States, I am locked in a windowless cell of anxiety.

Here's what I'm worried about: I'm going to have to beg a few swipes of wax from the guy in the warming hut. "Can I borrow . . ." "May I have . . ." "You see, Paul drove away with . . ." "I'm doing this project and . . ." I devise various strategies, compose and rehearse appropriate lines. I don't want to sound too demanding, but I don't want to be too nonchalant, either. A note of apology might be appropriate, but abjectness is over the top. Basically, I want to ask for help in such a way as to prevent anyone from noticing I'm asking.

I shouldn't fret. The people who work at the center are friendly. I ski practically every day; they know me. But I am fretting. They are friendly, they know me, but that doesn't mean they are my friends. They are employees of a business, and I am a customer. Customers buy things. It's unfair to ask them to break the rules for me, a friendly person they know, who is not really a friend. The twenty-five-minute trip takes about twenty-five hours. Every one hundred yards I consider turning around and going home.

This feeling throws me back twenty-five years, to my late twenties. I had come out of college with a $5,000 government-guaranteed National Defense Student Loan and was advised by numerous friends and former NDSL recipients that no one had ever paid back one of these loans. For two years I didn't. Then Ronald Reagan was elected and sold the debt to Citibank. The bank promptly jacked the interest to the going rate and got serious about collecting, but try as they did, they couldn't manage to collect from me. This was the era before credit companies discovered that bad debtors are (for the companies' profits) good debtors. Until I paid off the loan and gave the banks a decent interval to reconsider me for a credit card, I could not buy a plane ticket, rent a car, reserve a hotel room, or purchase a winter coat without greenbacks on the counter. I had few greenbacks, so I bought almost nothing. On the rare occasion I traveled, I slept on couches and got around by thumb.

On one such trip, to California in 1975, as I stood on a roadside outside Los Angeles, a motorist informed me of the rung on the American social hierarchy where my credit-unworthy ass had landed. He slowed down as he came close to me. I thought he was going to pick me up. Instead he rolled down his window and practically spat. "Hey, you! Why don't you get your own goddamn car?"

Approaching the hut at the ski center, I am again my hitchhiking, pad-crashing, cash-economy self, about to rely on the kindness of strangers—or collide with their unkindness. And then I realize it's not ski wax that I want, not even the convenience of having the ski wax ready to use.

What I want is autonomy, the sine qua non of Western commercial citizenship. To be creditworthy is to be worthy of respect. To buy is to be an adult. A person without money is a child, and all children are beggars.

What to do now? My friend Debbie, an editor, has recommended staying undercover, employing a "don't buy, don't tell" policy. "If you're a journalist writing about homelessness and you dress in rags and don't bathe for a week but tell everyone 'I'm writing about the homeless,' people will treat you like a journalist." When Paul and I tell our friends that we are not going out to dinner because of a yearlong project, they congratulate us. "If you dress in rags and don't bathe and keep your mouth shut," Debbie continued, "people will treat you like a homeless person. You might learn something about what it's like to be homeless."

Inside the hut, a hot fire is burning. Business is slow and Nick is alone behind the counter. Though an aggressive racer, off the trail this lanky young Buddhist would be flat on the floor were he any more laid back. His demeanor gives me courage. "Um, could I borrow a little blue wax, just a few swipes?" I ask, assuming the identity of a person who has arrived at a ski center without ski wax and without money.

Nick smiles. "Borrow it? You can have it." He takes a ski, bites the plastic cap off a stick of wax, and starts applying it himself.

As I glide down the long hill at the start of Ruthie's Run, I realize that while envy may mobilize consumer desire, it's not the things other people have that one necessarily envies. I mean, how many people actually *like* Rolex watches? What we want from things is what we want from other people, and from ourselves—whatever it is we want. I want to be a strong, competent athlete, one of the athletic crowd, like Grace and Lucy. Advertising offers images of product-enhanced bonhomie—tan volleyball players guzzling Pepsi; cool-looking slackers helping their pals load used furniture into Volkswagens. But I also want to feel independent. And just as it promises to buy us love, the marketplace also frees us from relationship, releases us from needing other people. As long as you've got a credit card in your pocket, you can go it alone: call it a form of consumer confidence.

Not buying has forced Paul and me to feel vulnerable and to ask for help, an almost un-American behavior. But the ability to ask for help might be a good skill to cultivate. Today I asked, and got service and a smile. As I ski up the next long hill, I tell myself that what I need is some non-consumer confidence.

FEBRUARY 28

The Ten Commandments of the Old Testament prohibit coveting not only thy neighbor's wife but also his house, his servant, his handmaiden, his ox, his ass, "or anything that is his." Will the Lord smite me for coveting Grace's ass, its flexing muscles propelling her forward over the snow? Need, envy, desire: these problems have vexed not just economists and anthropologists, but poets and philosophers for a long time.

In Plato's *Dialogues*, Socrates and his students describe an ideal city-state, wherein material necessities are satisfied and a just social balance is achieved. The sage loosens his toga and spins a fantasy of citizens relaxing on their pallets, feasting on loaves of plain barley meal and wheat, enjoying homemade ordinary wine. Bedecked in garlands, their children gamboling about them, they praise the gods who have bestowed such good fortune. They do not abandon good sense, though, do not run up their credit cards or buy new cars with home equity loans. These are the rational, prudent men a utilitarian economist would recognize. Says Socrates, "They take care that their families do not exceed their means."

Not so fast, the student Glaucon pipes up. What the teacher is talking about is a base society, he says, in which people eat just to fill their stomachs—a "City of Pigs." But people do not want to live like pigs. If they have enough, they will want more. "People who are to be comfortable are accustomed to lie on sofas, and dine off tables, and they should have sauces and sweets in the modern style."

As is his method, Socrates carries Glaucon's critique to its logical, perhaps ironic, end. Not just sofas and tables, he replies, but "also dainties, and perfumes, and incense, and courtesans, and cakes, all these not of one sort only, but in every variety." To make the fancy furniture and decorate the beautiful rooms, embroiderers and painters will have to be employed, and gold and ivory procured. These needs will in turn necessitate the conquest of more territory, as well as the protection of the state from its equally voracious neighbors. The taste for sauces and sweets leads to imperial ambitions, in other words, and Empire necessitates war.

From Proust to BG, the rapper who coined the term "bling," our bards remind us that desire is rarely satisfied by satisfaction. Possession affords a flicker of warmth, which almost inevitably cools. Then we want something else, something different, better, something less attainable. The more pressing that desire, the harder it is to distinguish from need.

We are left with a conundrum. Our economy is fueled by desire, ignited and fanned by advertising and easy credit. Yet the satisfaction of our desire by the relentless production and marketing of goods is depleting the earth of its air and its animals and putting some of the world's people under the others' boots. We have enough stuff; most Americans have more than enough. Yet capitalism needs us to want what we do not have, and desire for what we do not have is an infinitely renewable resource.

Plato suggests that the tide of expectations rises as surely as the sea is pulled by the moon. But the philosopher of balance believed that a surfeit of personal desire was the enemy of social harmony. Indeed, the very name that Socrates gives the city of sauces and sofas and armies to defend them connotes illness and madness. He calls it the Feverish City.

New and Improved

MARCH 1

Into the city we drive. City of George Smith sofas and vintage Formica kitchen tables, of rosemary ginger sauce from Vong and champagne chocolates from Jacques Torres. City of cakes and courtesans of every variety—and then some. Behold the Feverish City, New York!

Over the Whitestone Bridge and through the streets of Brooklyn we travel. Arrive at Third Street. Carry our luggage up four flights. Unlock the door to the apartment. Let the cat out of his carrier. Pull up the shades.

"What's that smell?" asks Paul.

Walking from room to immaculate room, we find them everywhere. Plugged into electric outlets and stuck on closet walls, under sinks, beside garbage cans, even in Paul's clothes cabinet: Air Wick Wizards and other plastic . . . gosh, I don't even know what they're called . . . fragrance discs? . . . each emitting Forest Glade or Wildflower Meadow or Ocean Breeze, simulacra of natural scents as close to the real thing as a Barbie doll is to an adult female body. The Wizards, one of which has muscled my plastic Jesus nightlight from the living room outlet, are turned up to 5, the highest level of . . . again, words fail me . . . velocity? humidity? . . . pumping out spritzes like a perfume lady at Bloomingdale's. No wonder the electric bills have been so high.

In the hall closet, I find a Swiffer mop and a plastic tub of Wet Thick Mopping Cloths ("Open-Window Fresh"), along with some classic Dry Disposable Cloths, which, I read, "use electrostatic action and Lift & Lock Pockets to attract and trap dirt, hair and 93 percent of common allergens on contact—instead of just stirring them up." Wow. Ninety-three percent. On both bathroom and kitchen sinks glow dispensers of orange Dial Anti-Bacterial Hand Soap. My $3 toilet brush has been replaced by a Johnson Scrubbing Bubbles Fresh Brush toilet cleaning "system" and a plastic pouch of detergent-soaked paper cleaning pads (12 for $4.69) to insert into a claw at the end of the Fresh Brush and toss after one use ("It's so easy . . . Just Clean! Pop off! Flush!"). The pads are biodegradable, says the label. So biodegradable, I learn while wiping the toilet bowl with one, that they begin to degrade halfway through the job.

The label also warns: "Do Not Use For Personal Hygiene."

Paul translates: "Not a vaginal douche."

My tenants were a couple of tall beauties from the Czech Republic. Milosz works as a distribution coordinator for a large orchard that sells fruit at New York's farmers' markets. He wears camouflage pants and ties his coal-black hair in a ponytail. Magda teaches English to Czech businesspeople; she tosses out American slang enunciated with British precision. Both effervesce with an American-style friendliness, more Peoria than Prague.

Milosz had told me that his girlfriend is a "clean freak." That was an understatement. She is a devotee, worshipping at the shrine to Procter & Gamble that she has made of my apartment.

I ask Ann, whose political work takes her frequently to Eastern Europe, how far consumerism has gotten in the Czech Republic since the collapse of the Soviet Union. "When I first started going there ten years ago, I had to carry everything with me—contact lens solution, dental floss, extra tights, everything," she says. "In Prague you could not find a single consumer product. The stores would get in one item, everyone would hear about it, and, magically, there would suddenly be lines in the streets. Then weeks would go by with nothing in the stores, until some other thing showed up—and the lines would appear again." So bereft of consumer enticements was the city that there were no glass storefronts to look into. But since then Prague has been filling with foreigners and other imports, from contact lens solution to couture, and my tenants are of the class that can afford them.

Still, I can tell that Magda is a neophyte consumer. I mean, she's excited about *soap*. She has not yet developed the genius for discernment of the second- or third-generation shopper. If the cleansers and air fresheners give her life meaning, that meaning has not yet squeezed itself into a narrowcast demographic. Nor has she pledged the brand loyalty that is instinctual to any American six-year-old. Ocean Breeze, Forest Glade, Fragrant Gingko—whatever, she'll take it. As a gift, she has left me a box of Caswell-Massey soap without *any* identified essence. It is merely lavender-colored. Did she not notice that my apartment's aesthetic (midcentury modern / flea market / global South / contemporary recycled) is, semiotically, the *anti*-lavender?

There is one distinction this couple is clear about, however. On my office door I had tacked a huge poster given me by a friend in Paris, reading "NON à la guerre en Irak," in red letters over a massive black exclamation point. In the circle at the bottom is the name of the poster's sponsor, Partie Communiste. Milosz and Magda have taken the poster down.

Now, I'm no fan of the Communist brand—er, party—but I

liked this message and design. To me, the placard was an aesthetic product, a work of political art of which the party was, at best, a merchant. I could display it with a kind of ironic nostalgia, an attitude possible only for someone who has not lived through the real thing. My tenants, on the other hand, are survivors of Soviet communism (Milosz tells me his generation was the last to learn Russian at school). To them the Communist Party was a merchant of misery. As noxious as I find the unregulated market of cloying scents forced under my nose in my own home, so Milosz and Magda must have found the daily sight of the party's name. Newly naturalized capitalist entrepreneurs, they have embraced Brand America with their hearts and their dollars. They are unconditionally in love with consumer culture.

Back from the real forest glade, I breathe in Forest Glade and cough. It's a bracing welcome back to life in the Feverish City, breeding ground of the delirium affluenza. I can already feel my temperature rising—and my brain addling—with its temptations, and contradictions.

MARCH 3

"One hears a great deal about the role of the town in the development and diversification of consumption, but very little about the extremely important fact that even the humblest town-dweller must of necessity obtain his food-supply through the market," writes the historian Fernand Braudel. Last night Paul and I finished off the falafel mix and put together a salad of vegetables cleaned out of the crisper in Vermont. We won't buy more mix; processed foods are nixed from our shopping list. But the cupboard is bare and we are hungry. Even if we do not live to shop, we humble town-dwellers must shop to live.

We hoist our canvas sacks for a hike over the Manhattan Bridge to Chinatown's groceries. Out the door, past a row of brownstones, we are thrust into the bazaar that is our neighborhood, Carroll Gardens. "Consumption is the very arena in which culture is fought over and licked into shape," write the sociologist Mary Douglas and the economist Baron Isherwood in *The World of Goods*. In Carroll Gardens, this is literally true. Two blocks over, Court Street still tastes like a little Italian village. This main artery is larded with pork butchers and delis boiling fresh mozzarella twice a day, with bread bakeries and sweets bakeries, which are further subdivided into dry-cookie bakeries, buttery-cookie bakeries, and gooey-pastry bakeries. Old men drift into d'Amico's after their bocce games to sip espresso from tiny paper cups and gesticulate emphatically in Sicilian. Marco Polo Restaurant offers red sauce and valet parking; outside, men with large bellies and thin legs, impeccably garbed in black shirts and thin-soled shoes, discuss business *sotto voce*. Their ringed hands hold the door for their wives, whose hair is coiffed in the brilliant helmets that are the specialty of Chic Élégance.

But it is one block nearer our house, on Smith Street, where the old merchants were poorer and darker-skinned and the rents cheaper, that the fighting is fiercest and the licking most furious. Here, in the seemingly benign shifts of taste, class muscles out class, which means that some people muscle out other people.

In 1997 came the first fashionable eatery, Patois, with its "Brooklyn-French" cuisine and its newly created patina of age, and before you could say *tarte tatin* the street was *the* "restaurant row." Soon hip diners from Manhattan picked up the scent, with reviewers from *TimeOut New York* on their heels like hunters behind the hounds. Young designers joined the young restaurateurs, European guidebooks started starring Smith Street as an off-the-beaten-track destination, and now every weekend droves of tourists are beating the F-train tracks to the Carroll Street stop, prettifying the air with their French and Italian accents.

Nearly gone are the Puerto Rican *cuchifritos;* these shops, where steam tables of fried foods melted from crunchy to sodden, have been supplanted by places serving more refined, if not exactly authentic, Latino fare in impeccably authentic ambiance: Cholito (Peruvian), Pacifico (Mexican), Café Cubano. A "diner that's about being a diner," as a *New Yorker* cartoon once described such establishments, is drawing clientele from the decades-old Smith Street Diner on the corner of Atlantic. Both serve the same moussaka, but you pay a premium at the new place for irony. A dingy Puerto Rican–Brooklyn social club, a bar with a pool table, has been displaced by Brooklyn Social Club, a bar with a pool table, aspiring to dinginess.

For residential tenants, such "revitalization" is both good news and bad news. The neighborhood used to be patrolled by casual bands of working-class white vigilantes. The good news is that, these days, people of color can walk the streets at night unmolested. The bad news: most people of color—or for that matter, most of the former vigilantes—soon won't be able to afford to live here. The first time I passed Patois and read the menu taped to the window, I said to myself, "Finally, a good local restaurant." My second thought, instants later: "There goes my rent." Sure enough, within three months my landlady had tacked 50 percent to the cost of my top-floor brownstone apartment.

This year, the parks and schools teem with children of all classes, but it is only a matter of time before the gracious houses and roomy apartments will be too expensive for any but the wealthiest families. My walk-up four-room co-op, purchased in 1998 for $116,000, was reappraised in 2002 for $299,000 and almost monthly I receive a plea from a realtor to sell my place, promising prices at least $100,000 higher than that. I could sell my apartment for a fortune, but where would I move? To an equivalent apartment nearby, though probably not quite as nice. Or I could "pioneer" another "frontier" and play my small part in running out the natives.

Commercial tenants suffer the same fate. The storefronts whose low rents drew young Manhattan sous-chefs now command—thanks in part to their restaurants—four to five times the rents they did in 1997. In the shops, well-designed quasi-useful items have replaced utilitarian ones—housewares pushing out hardware, shoe stores stepping over shoe repair, "vintage" clothing hanging on the racks where plain old used clothing could once be bought for a song. The scruffy miscellany that filled every third storefront a decade ago has been packed up and moved farther into the boroughs, or sold by the pound. Among the victims of this process is an intermittently open business, run by an intermittently attentive purveyor of Brooklyn memorabilia, old sheet music, and vintage posters with the emphasis on grade-C monster movies and racy women's prison films. A fixture on the street since the early 1980s, the shop was called Main Street Ephemera.

Consumption, say Douglas and Isherwood, is an instrument that both confers social privilege and effects social exclusion. On Smith Street, consuming is fun and funky, tasteful and tasty. But the system inside which it works can also be powerfully cruel.

Paul and I emerge from the diesel fumes at the other end of the Manhattan Bridge pedestrian walkway, and the air turns redolent of pork. I am excited, but also a little sad. Sad because our weekly jaunts to Chinatown for greens, fish, dried mushrooms, and soy products have always been forages for street food, too. We have sampled all manner of fried and stuffed dough, as well as a less appealing class of edible featuring gelatinous substances inside inedible grasses. But the all-time prize, which we seek out on each visit, is what we call the "green bun," a spongy white-flour roll stuffed with mustard greens fried in hot sesame oil. There is only one Green Bun Lady, stationed in front of the mall tucked under the Manhattan Bridge, selling everything on her cart at the low, low price of $1. In fact, almost everything in Chinatown can be had for $1—a pound of long beans, a windup bathtub frog, a plush slipper ($2 a pair).

Usually we buy two green buns, share one, eat it in haste, then put the other away to avoid repenting of our impatience later. Now, having eliminated street food as Not Necessary, we pass the Green Bun Lady's table without stopping and make our way to the supermarket at the back of the mall. I feel in my stomach a wistfulness where the green bun would have been.

Inside the noisy supermarket, my mood brightens. As always, we are the only Caucasians in the store. No one speaks English except the schoolgirls working the cash registers, and many of the food labels on the shelves are in Mandarin, Korean, or Vietnamese. We skip the zillion prepared sauces that baffle our Western palates with minutely differentiated grades of heat and what sometimes tastes to us like spoilage. I select one of the soy sauces, which are equally numerous and varied, on the basis of its attractive yellow label. We pay $19 and haul out three bags of food (the bill never comes to more than $25). It's as if we've just flown to Beijing, but saved the $900 airfare.

Walking westward, we stop at the Thai Grocery on Mosco Street for hot basil, lime leaves, lemongrass, sweet black rice, and fresh-frozen coconut milk. My consumer desires this year are all channeled into food. I hope I don't get fat.

Well, I think, as we approach tourists' Chinatown, one thing I

won't consume: "bubble tea," cafés dedicated to which have prolif-
erated since our last expedition. Bubble tea originated in Taiwan,
but it resembles a sweet Southeast Asian milk drink; it is served hot
or cold, with or without a scoop of tapioca pearls, or "bubbles"—
pronounced "bobos" by the waitstaff—that float to the bottom like
rubber-cement roe and are sucked along with the drink through an
extra-wide straw. The bubbles appeal to the pan-Asian taste for
savorless, toothsome culinary elements. The teas' colors are the soft
pastel of Japanese teen apparel; their flavors are named for a catalogue of the teas, beans, and fruits of the northeast Pacific, many of
which are exotic to Western drinkers—but bubble tea is as comfort-
ingly bland as frozen custard from an American roadside stand.

The arrival of this odd and delicious beverage is one more bit
of evidence that the worse things get for the rest of the world, the
better they get for this city's diners: each famine, war, or economic
catastrophe abroad brings a new food or cuisine to New York. But
unlike the stews of sauced gristle and chicken feet being served to
the elderly Chinese along East Broadway, bubble tea is a global citizen. It poured into town with the latest, immense wave of Asian
immigration. And like the kids clustering around these café tables,
sporting post-punk haircuts and tattoos, text-messaging cease-
lessly and chattering in Spanglish, Korenglish, and Chinglish
spiked with words like *chill* and *mad,* bubble tea assimilated in a
New York minute.

After two months in Hardwick, it's exhilarating just to be on
the street. Around us commerce clangs, spices sting the nostrils.
Inspecting the merchandise overflowing onto the sidewalks and
hanging from the awnings of the souvenir shops, I note this year's
Thing, an embroidered silk handbag in any of a hundred fabrics
and color combinations, available in every store for $10 to $15. I'd
love one of those handbags, which would add just the splash to

refresh my spring look. But I can't take the street home with me today. There will be no spring look for me this year.

We pause to wait for the green light on the median halfway across Confucius Square. "So how are you feeling about the project so far?" Paul asks.

I put down the canvas bag, which suddenly feels heavier for the plainness of its contents. Part of me feels relieved not to be indulging thoughtlessly in the fruits of the world's poverty (though we have already gathered groceries whose prices depend on cheap immigrant labor). An equal part feels severed from my city, not to say from the world. The traffic is loud; I wait for a lull in the honking. "So far," I answer, "I'm appreciating all the wonderful things there are to buy."

MARCH 7

For vicarious pleasure, or perhaps in anticipation of next year, I clip restaurant reviews and take them out from time to time to reread, returning like a regular to my favorite spots. Marian Burros praises Bread Tribeca: "Every neighborhood would be lucky to have a place like it, where the dress code is immaterial for patrons and waiters alike, and people who linger over a cup of coffee and the paper in the middle of the afternoon are not shooed out."

Not patronizing cafés, bars, or restaurants has made social life, and especially business life, awkward. In Vermont in winter, with two feet of snow on the ground, you can't exactly hold a meeting on a park bench. Paul has timed get-togethers not to coincide with meals and engineered the occasional brown bag lunch in a conference room. I don't have much business to conduct there, but I'll have to face the problem here. I'm not looking forward to finessing this aspect of Not Buying It.

But reading the review, I realize I'm forfeiting more than con-venience. I'm losing conviviality and communion, which is a lubricant for dealmaking both professional and personal. Without the glass of wine or cup of coffee, the meeting—and its partici-pants—can't help but be all business. At the same time, if forced to meet at someone's home, which Paul has sometimes done, it's hard to maintain any businesslike distance; the level of intimacy can feel too high.

The café is a uniquely urban amenity, offering a uniquely urban pleasure: to work, eat, read, daydream, or observe others doing the same, unknown but seen, private in public. The city allows anonymous intimacies of every intensity—from sidewalk glances to barroom confessions to backroom sex. This version, coffee and the newspaper among friendly strangers, is safe and solitary; compared to sex in a bar, it is frigid. Paul doesn't partic-ularly miss it; not being a city native, he's enjoyed transporting our country custom of at-home dinners with friends to the city. Yet I find myself yearning for the time I'll again sit at a side table and sip, consuming cool intimacies.

MARCH 13

Organizing our cultural life around one primary criterion—"Does it cost anything?"—we seize on a too-little-tapped venue of enter-tainment, the Central Branch of the Brooklyn Public Library at Grand Army Plaza. The library, where I'm already a regular patron, has many things to recommend it besides being free. It is ten min-utes by bike from our house. It is open late almost every night. And you don't have to dress for events there. Due to underfund-ing of both library and users, the look is shabby chic, with the emphasis on shabby.

Today, Saturday, the place is ababble with immigrants from even more severely underfunded countries, lapping up America's comparative plenty. They are using the computers, reading to or scolding their kids or helping them balance circus-act stacks of children's books on the way to the checkout counter. In the Multilingual Room, languages from Swahili to Croatian are represented on the shelves, and from the round wooden tables rise shy and halting conversations in accented Spanish and English. Next week, Paul will join the free Italian group.

Like the room's bookshelves, the library's films and reading series are themed by identity: last month was Black History Month; March is Women's History Month; April, National Poetry Month. The turning carousel of honored identities and genres constitutes a kind of fashion—first African-Americans are "in," then women—if a somewhat dowdy one. But it also allows the library to introduce patrons to the likes of James Baldwin and Dorothy Dandridge. For me this year, hungry for any fashion whatever, it offers a series of "new seasons."

I browse the French section and come across Michel Houellebecq's *Les Particules Elémentaires,* which caused a scandal in France a few years ago, not for its graphically misogynistic sex but for its finger-flip at the Sixties generation. I also check out *Austerlitz,* by W. G. Sebald, named one of the best books of 2001. How many good books got by me three years ago? Eliminate the top layer of entertainment and you discover stratum upon stratum of art buried under the fast-falling sediment of the popular culture. The library's budget can't keep up. The busy videotape room is heavy on the classics, which are not only crowd-pleasers but cheap. I snap up *The Little Foxes.* While I'm at it, why not *Now, Voyager,* with its famous erotic cigarette-lighting motif. I suggest to Paul that we kick off a Bette Davis retrospective.

Before leaving the library, I stop once more at the New Fiction shelf and discover *She Is Me,* by Cathleen Schine. I've read the review, so I know the book is about a young woman caring for her dying mother while trying to write a contemporary film adaptation of *Madame Bovary.* This inspires me to borrow *Madame Bovary* as well, a novel I have not read since high school, and then only because somebody told me it was dirty. Maybe this time I'll find the sexy parts. Or kick off a Flaubert retrospective.

When we get home we eat a quick stir-fry and hurry to Manhattan to attend the one play left from last year's subscription to the New York Theater Workshop. It's Paul Rudnick's *Valhalla.* Funny—how can the lisping fairy king Ludwig of Bavaria not be funny?—but the play has its longeurs. It's another not-so-hot play in a dull season at NYTW. Still, I'm glad I saw it.

Before bed, I peek into *She Is Me.* Flaubert can wait. It's not just because I love Schine's work. I want to read the book for the same reason I wanted to see Rudnick's play. While I don't keep tabs on much of what goes by in the mainstream media parade (I'm ignorant, for instance, of bestselling books and first-run thrillers and weepies), I am avid to read, see, taste—to be alive in—the contemporary culture. I want to read *She Is Me* because it is new.

MARCH 15

I want to read it because it is new. I *need* to read it because it is new. Needing the stimulation of contemporary culture is one reason I tell Paul I could not live in Vermont full time. I don't say I want it. I always say I *need* it. An informed person like me *needs* to see new art, new films. It's not so different from the fashionable person who *needs* to wear this year's skirt length. Or a teenager who *needs* to download this minute's music.

The job of consumer culture (and all culture, in order to see the light of day, must be to some extent commercial culture) is to blur the line between need and want. A poster for Target Stores that is plastered all over the subways this month plays explicitly along this line. The picture is an Exquisite Corpse–like photomontage of a woman's head, the upper half of which is a lampshade of ivory satin, deeply ruched, a bit of twenty-first-century Victorian kitsch. "The lampshade you need," the copy says. The lower half of the montage is the woman's face from bridge of nose to sly smile to slender throat, around which is tied a small scarf in a Fiftiesesque green-and-white circle pattern: "The scarf you want." But because the scarf is a ladylike trifle that wouldn't keep a lady warm in Mississippi in June, and because the shade seems designed to trap dust in its folds and turn gray and want disposal immediately, and because the lady is wearing the lampshade on her head, it's hard to say which is practical and which frivolous, the scarf or the lampshade.

We cannot see the model's eyes, but she is winking at us. For both Target and the consumer know that outside the hard-knocks merchandise in the likes of the *Hardwick Gazette,* almost nothing that is advertised is actually necessary.

MARCH 20

I'm on the street a lot, now that I'm not inside buying, eating, or watching, and I'm delighting in New York's street life even more than usual. I'm also more aware of the peculiarity of the urban relationship and of its basic unit, the glance. "The psychological foundation upon which the metropolitan individuality is erected is the intensification of emotional life due to the swift and continuous shift of external and internal stimuli," writes Georg Simmel in his great essay of 1903, "The Metropolis and Mental Life." Most stimulating of all are the other people in the city: my individuality observes your individuality at the table beside me in the restaurant, rubs up against it in the subway, listens to it across the apartment airshaft in the middle of the night. And my individuality observes yours a thousand times a day, on the street.

To look at others on the city street is to know (or to attempt or assume to know) them. But that communication, like a conversation between foreigners, is aided by interpreters: what the other person is eating, watching, reading, and most important, wearing.

I can date almost exactly the moment I discovered the silent sidewalk chatter of clothing.

In the Fifties and early Sixties, living in Queens, I'd been a baby beatnik in Beethoven sweatshirt; I assumed the look of my red-diaper-baby family friends and the kids at my Quaker summer camp. Then I moved to the suburbs, where junior high school demanded conformity, and attempted to emulate the penny-loafer-and-mohair-sweater-wearing cheerleaders. It was a period of howling sartorial ineptitude, mercifully brief.

At fifteen, I was ready to return to myself. History helped. It was 1967 and a new genre of girl, update of the red-diaper-baby beatnik, emerged on the scene. I could be a hippie peacenik flower child and sexual revolutionary. To realize the last part, I'd need only convince a boy to participate.

I went directly to the Different Drummer on the Upper West Side of Manhattan. The store sold bell-bottoms and Indian shirts, bedspreads, incense, sealing wax, and jingly silver jewelry from India; it smelled of patchouli and mothballs, the scent of Nirvana. There I bought a pair of wide-wale brown corduroy hip-huggers and a translucent embroidered Indian tunic (the kind they're now selling at Macy's for $45). The next week I walked up a narrow flight of stairs to a no-name loft on the Lower East Side, where the clothing lay unironed and unsorted in heaps, as if it had just come from Goodwill with a quick stop at the fumigator on the way. I dragged out an Afghan sheepskin coat with so much of the Afghan sheep left in it that my mother made me hang it outside the door. At a head shop on Astor Place, I selected a pair of rose-colored granny glasses and a jar of tiny colored beads, which I took home and strung. The necklace emphasized my fragile, teenage clavicles and tickled my braless décolletage.

Donning my new clothes, along with a peace-sign button from the Student Peace Union, I walked down Astor Place. It was as if I had donned the tartan of a clan or the headdress of a tribe: my fellows recognized me, and I do mean *fellows.* Suddenly, I could glance at a boy and the boy would glance back, knowingly. I had purchased a costume for the performance of my self, stepped onstage, and was illuminated. Through buying, I became identifiable to others—and visible to myself.

Today you'll find me in my black, oddly shaped Alain Mikli eyeglasses and my Ibex jacket from the Athleta catalogue, which caters to women who want high-performance athletic wear that also looks right in Williamsburg, Brooklyn. The jacket cost $150 (on sale), the glasses more than $350. But the price tags aren't the point. These are not wealth symbols or even status symbols; I wear them with a flea market scarf and scuffed sneakers.

In the city, every one of these nuances speaks. The refinement of individual tastes feeds the urban merchant in pursuit of new customers, says Simmel. In turn, his merchandise feeds that refinement, encouraging increasingly extravagant eccentricity and the competitive sport of "'being different'—of making oneself noticeable." If our identities are socially constructed, then in capitalism they are commercially constructed. My clothes are tropes of the selectively fashionable, rurally urban, wholesomely hip, ironically butchy heterosexual outdoorsy brainiac that I am. (Marketers: note profile.) People call the glasses my "signature" accessory. Alain Mikli signs my name, tells the world who I am.

MARCH 22

In a year without shopping, will I lose my self, and in so doing, my connection to others?

I pass the Video Corner next to the bank on Court Street, where for two weeks there's been a poster in the window for *Lost in Translation:* Bill Murray sitting on the edge of a hotel bed in a kimono, unshaved, unkempt, despondent.

I haven't seen *Lost in Translation* and it's already out in video. Today the brochure came in the mail for next month's Rendezvous with French Cinema at Lincoln Center, which I'll miss along with the New Directors series and who knows what else. The cinema is reeling past me unseen, fashion is reeling past me unworn. The new, the now, it's all getting away.

A girl walks by carrying a cello case. She is wearing cat-shaped glasses, red tights, and Keds. Her hair is cropped shorter on one side. She is cool but geeky, sexy but bookish. I feel I know her. In fact, I feel I *am* her, or was her, or would be her if I were her age. I smile.

The girl looks at me cautiously, returns my smile politely, but without warmth. She doesn't recognize me, doesn't see the girl I was, the girl I think still shines out. But how could she? I am dressed in faded black Gap Easy Fit jeans, a black ski parka, and J. Crew red-and-orange-striped gloves with the left index finger poking through. I look like a Carroll Gardens soccer mom whose husband was laid off from his Wall Street job. Or worse, an ex-hippie soccer mom who thinks she's still hip.

Maybe one of those bright silk pocketbooks from Chinatown

would have helped my fading look. I stare at Bill Murray. He stares back, like me, bereft, bedraggled, and bare. Bill shakes his head in defeated wisdom. *It's not a silk purse you want, Jude,* I hear him say. *It's hope for the sow's ear of your sorry, aging self.*

MARCH 23

I dream I am defining a portion of text on a computer screen and deleting it, over and over.

MARCH 26

Out for my daily walk, I stroll to Fulton Street, the down-market shoppers' mall in downtown Brooklyn, and find myself inside one of the two dozen shoe shops on the strip. The colors draw me in: Bazooka pink, Creamsicle orange, sour-lime-candy green. The shapes of the shoes are cartoonlike, toe boxes balloon-fat or turned up like elfin slippers; some are cloven like the hooves of mythical creatures. The companies have animal names suggesting bounce and bite: KangaRoo, Puma. One brand called Irregular Choice offers pairs in which the two shoes are different.

"Can I help you?" asks the salesman.

I put my hands into my pockets and notice I have left the house without money—a first since returning to New York. "No, thank you," I say. "Just looking."

The historian Rosalind Williams, writing about Paris at the turn of the last century, describes the new "environments of mass consumption"—the department store, the exposition, the movie palace—as "Versailles open to all, at least during business hours." There, consumers could touch and try on clothes, "gaze on luxu-rious goods, travel in style, and otherwise taste pleasures normally reserved for the fortunate few," all "without having to buy." I could eat these lime-green shoes. Not for nothing do the French call window-shopping *la lêche-vitrine*—licking shop windows.

"Perhaps the consumer revolution intensified the pain of envy by bringing within the realm of possibility the acquisition of a degree of wealth that had formerly been considered out of reach," writes Williams. But it "also brought an anodyne in the form of environments . . . where envy is transformed into pleasure by producing a temporary but highly intense satisfaction of the dream of wealth." The young women around me are giggling and cooing, complimenting each other and admiring their own slim ankles. One of them is dancing across the floor in a pair of green spike heels so high that they almost pitch her forward, into an imaginary partner's arms.

Dreams of wealth? Nothing like it. These shoes conjure dreams of dancing and kissing, of hobbling over the curbstones as the dawn comes up.

I find myself debating internally. "Flimsy," scoffs Soccer Mom as she picks up a pair that will be shot after four hours on the dance floor. "Crippling!" Even if the shoes survive, the feet wouldn't.

"That's the point," says Sexual Revolutionary Flower Child. Fashion is about flirtation, not marriage. A pair of lime-green stiletto heels is never meant to be more than a one-night stand.

As I leave the store, I look back through the window. Piles of boxes surround the shoppers. Discards are tossed aside, tangled in their tissue sheets. It's a scene of debauchery. I feel envious, but not of wealth or luxury. What I long for is the cheap thrill of the ephemeral, the instantly consumed and discarded mini-relationship with person or thing, the "quickie" that is urban commerce.

I walk home along Smith Street, pockets empty, licking the shop windows with my eyes.

In/Voluntary Simplicity

Damned if I do shop, damned if I don't. If compulsive acquisition disorder doesn't get me, the deprivation blues will. Same goes for America. Either we keep on shopping until the earth collapses under the weight of our trash, or we stop shopping and the economy collapses under its own stagnation.

Fortunately, for every disease real or invented, America creates a self-help movement. So I go online to seek out the Simple Living Network, a loose conglomeration of recovering compulsive shoppers, anonymous debtors, back-to-the-landers, New Agers, Buddhist meditators, and skinflints. The way of life recommended by the network is called Voluntary Simplicity (VS), a name coined in 1981 in the book of the same name by Duane Elgin. Its tenets, according to Elgin, are "frugal consumption, ecological awareness, and personal growth."

Just as there are levels of medicine from herbal tea to antibiotics to surgery, the anticonsumption lifestyle can be undertaken at various levels of seriousness or, you might say, severity. At one end, there are the people Juliet Schor calls "downshifters." These ordinary middle-class folk get fed up with overwork, stress, debt, and isolation from their families, friends, and communities. So they take it down a notch: they switch from a full-time to a part-time job, sell the house and move into an apartment, or institute minor economies such as twice-monthly instead of twice-weekly dinners out. From 1990 to 1996 Schor put the number of voluntary downshifters at nearly a fifth of American adults.

Somewhat more serious VSers adopt the methodology of Joe Dominguez and Vicki Robin's *Your Money or Your Life,* which at its most elementary is a way to calculate the labor hours required to purchase any given good, service, or experience, then decide if it's worth the personal, financial, or ecological cost. For instance, "Is this Miele Touchtronic dishwasher worth a half a month's toil in the cubicle?" Yeah, sure. "How about another hundred bucks a year for the electricity to run it?" Maybe. "Is it and all its sister dishwashers worth drilling for oil in the Alaskan wilderness— plus an eternity of fighting with my spouse over the correct way to load the thing?" Hmm. Pass me that sponge. You can go as far as you want with this, including eschewal of the sponge for a rag—or your hand.

While much of the VS literature consists of practical methodologies, at heart it is a philosophy, which is linked to a promise. Shopping "saps your energy," it "reduces ingenuity," "harms your health," and generally "makes you unhappy," says Cecile Andrews, author of *The Circle of Simplicity.* Far worse, by supplying a purchasable identity, she claims, consuming makes you false, a traitor to the person you really are. Toss out those old clothes and broken tennis rackets at the back of your closet and you will discover your "authentic self" crushed under the debris. After that, Heaven's the limit: VS, writes Andrews, "is a life that allows the individual's soul to awaken."

In short order I locate a VS organizer I'll call Beryl,* who is forming a new group just blocks from our apartment. By way of

---

* The names of the VSers in the group have been changed.

résumé, Beryl recites an abbreviated life story. Twenty miserable years at a twelve-hour-a-day corporate job, salary of $25,000, "wise investments" (in similarly soul-crushing corporations?), then, starting at forty, with "fully funded retirement accounts," the good life. Today she lives on $12,000 a year, $11,000 of which goes to mortgage, utilities, and health insurance. While I'm tapping these numbers into my mental calculator ($11,000 divided by 12 . . .) she moves on to the sell. Registration for the meetings is just $10, including start-up visit from hers truly and Xeroxed study guide. I set aside my hesitation (is ten bucks for a course on not spending money a necessary expenditure?) and sign up.

But the second I put down the phone I am full of apprehension. What if my soul awakens in a room full of women wearing gingham smocks and men with self-inflicted haircuts and twine for shoelaces? What if I discover my authentic self, and my authentic self is a shopper?

APRIL FOOL'S DAY

Paul and I are seated in a circle of a dozen people in a tidy apartment facing Prospect Park. Our hostess, Elisa, is friendly and welcoming. But appropriate to the abstemious intent of the meeting, no refreshment, even water, is served. One optimistic sign: I see no gingham and no twine, even if the guest of honor, Beryl, has an apparently self-inflicted haircut.

Ensconced in an easy chair, Beryl begins the meeting by retelling the Parable of the Twenty Years, the wise investments, the retirement accounts. Tonight she details her expenses more fully. Basic costs absorb all but $100 a month, of which $80 goes to food ("three nutritious and delicious meals at home for an average cost of $1 a meal"). But Beryl isn't sitting home scrimping. At a length defying the movement's less-is-more philosophy, she describes days chockablock with reading, working out, theater (free as a volunteer usher), even foreign travel. It is during the cheery account of digging people out after the Turkish earthquake (disaster relief as vacation travel!) that I begin to reconsider the leisure of the twelve-hour workday.

Somewhat stunned, the rest of us introduce ourselves.

Sal is putting in six days a week at the office; she feels underappreciated and underpaid. So does Nobuko, a junior architect in a large firm. Marlene's days are fourteen hours long. Dana, a recently widowed mother of two, is stretched not only emotionally but financially: three-quarters of her take-home pay goes to rent, but a cheaper neighborhood would mean inferior public schools, so she stays put. All four women say their workplaces have "downsized" over the last few years.

Jessica, a boyish computer programmer, is not as lucky as these four. She was laid off two years ago and is stringing together the rent with occasional "consulting." Laura, at twenty-five the youngest among us, lost her job in information technology six months ago and has since been searching for "something where I make a difference every day." Gail, out of work for two years, is an experienced VSer, writing down every penny she dispenses; she announces that she has eaten out fewer than ten times in the past six months. Elisa, a corporate librarian, suspects her job is about to be outsourced to India.

Besides Paul there are two men in the group, and they are the only members who can contemplate retirement. Not incidentally, both are union members, both have pensions. Lionel, a city bureaucrat, has retired at forty-eight and is casting around for something to do. Irwin, an unskilled laborer, is about to quit at fifty-five. His has not been a satisfying career: "I've been planning for retirement since I was a teenager." Now he is taking eighty-eight accrued sick days to figure out the next steps.

I mark hatches in my notepad. Of twelve people, at least half say they are underpaid, and even those who don't talk about their salaries lament the difficulty of keeping up with expenses. A fourth of the group have been laid off or fear they are about to be. And the rest are laboring like serfs because half their co-workers have been laid off.

When it's our turn, Paul and I give the basic outline of our lives. I am already feeling smug. We have completed most of what's on Beryl's syllabus: Finding the Work We Love, Managing Our Lives as an Integrated Whole, Setting Priorities for Personal Action, Building Community. We should take the advanced placement exam and test out of the course altogether! I describe our project: "So, essentially, we're not buying anything but plain groceries." Do I hear gasps of admiration?

And while I often feel sorry for myself, a low-paid freelance writer never sure where the next check is coming from, in this room I see how fortunate I am. I recognize one advantage to being self-employed (besides being able to work in your pajamas): you can't get fired. On the roiling sea of the economy, while the rest of the group grasps the handrails of the *Titanic,* Paul and I paddle our agile kayaks, adept at staying afloat.

I probably don't earn as much as most of the others, but I know my simplicity is voluntary. Can the same be said of Jessica's or Laura's? These people are not down*shifting* so much as being down*sized.* As the group moves on to comparing penny-pinching tactics and applauding one another's sacrifices, I wonder: has a movement founded in reaction to the greed-is-good ethos of the Reagan era become a survival strategy for its victims, a tacit capitulation to the greed-is-God ethos of the Bush era? Is Voluntary Simplicity the opiate of the masses?

APRIL 4

Travel is out this year, but we have a months-old obligation (and desire) to fly to Montana in June to celebrate the graduation of my niece, Sarah. We're getting our tickets with frequent-flier miles, so we're not spending money on that. Still, if we were serious about our ecological footprint, we'd keep our feet on the ground. The "footprint factor" of an hour of jet travel—let's say 500 miles—is 5,216, whereas an hour of train travel, 80 to 100 miles, is 17, about half the FF per mile (the FF numbers are abstractions derived from a formula, used to compare expenditures of "nature").

Still, I'm looking forward to the trip. In New York, it's a cinch to think globally simply by walking locally. But if you don't also consume locally, your window on the world shrinks. Chained to my armchair, even my armchair travel is limited. We are seeing and renting no movies, buying no CDs. I am tossing the theater ticket offers when they arrive in the mail. My magazine reading list consists of a staid collection of last year's leftover subscriptions—the *Nation,* the *New Yorker,* and several nonprofit newsletters. I am informed, edified, and sufficiently politically riled at all times. But I'm starved of food for fantasy.

I walk up the street. A stack of *Condé Nast Traveller*s set out for recycling beckons me like a chorus of Sirens. How about a drive along the Caprivi Strip in Namibia, a weekend in Helsinki, or a retreat at a mountaintop monastery in Bulgaria? Now, *Traveller* can make Minneapolis look like Marrakech. But having eliminated cultural gratifications closer to home, all enticements feel equally desirable, and equally exotic. Dinner at Alain Ducasse in

Paris? *Tu rigole.* Dinner at Taco Bell? Who ya kiddin'? In the middle of the greatest city in the world, I feel like I am nowhere.

APRIL 7

I reach into the box for a Kleenex to blow my nose. Empty. I fish a roll of toilet paper from under the bathroom sink to put on my night table. Now that I'm freeing up so much time, perhaps I'll crochet a toilet paper cozy.

APRIL 11

In the city as in the country, Paul and I are finding that free entertainment is about a century behind the stuff you pay for. I'm keeping track of the cherry and daffodil blooms in the botanic gardens the way I used to pore over movie schedules. We're getting intimate with the back stacks of the public library and the Italian Renaissance paintings in the permanent collection of the Metropolitan Museum of Art. (Like most of the museums, it is free one evening per week.) We go to free concerts, open studios, and poetry readings.

Sunday afternoon, Jonathan, a historian, accompanies me to a chamber concert organized by a cellist friend and held at the local Quaker meetinghouse. It's not a perfect space. The acoustics are somewhat dead, and occasionally during fermatas the sound of metal chairs clatters up from the AA meeting below. But the performance—of a rarely played Bach cycle involving tricks like playing the score upside down and backwards—is crisp and witty and far more musical than the pieces' academic game-playing would augur. Afterward, the audience lingers in the foyer drinking apple cider out of paper cups and chatting with the musicians. As I send

Jonathan off to the subway and unlock my bike, I am left feeling as live as the music.

On our lopsided quest for free fun, Paul and I are exposing ourselves to the very surprises that our usually meticulous cultural consumption is supposed to deliver, and often does not. I don't want to wax romantic; some of what we see (open mike at a Lower East Side anarchist bookstore) is godawful. But in dogs per dollar, the money we're expending (zero) is by definition lower than that at any commercial movie house. And if the aesthetic satisfaction of these small-space live performances is not always higher than that of electronic entertainment or more formal (and paid) live theater or music, the social satisfaction almost always is. That's because the vitality emanates not just from the players, but from the bodies moving, moved, intimately, in the audience.

As I pedal down Court Street through the early-spring cold, the numbness in my fingers takes me back to a thousand childhood bike rides home from after-school activities or friends' houses. Those memories awaken others, of returning home late, also on my bike, during the Vietnam War and early feminist movement. I am remembering another kind of live event: the political meeting of the 1960s and '70s. Back then, activism meant sitting in living rooms for many hours with other people planning (and then executing) actions to change things that you wanted ferociously to improve. Commitments were not just to ideas, they were to people. When you took on a task, you made a promise to women and men whom you liked and respected. The "movement" was a network of thousands of such relationships, thousands of living rooms. Community was smaller, and also larger, than an e-mail box.

Culture unites people of like tastes, passions, and politics, and mass culture unites us in an even larger kind of community. This year, I'm acutely aware that not having seen the latest "important" movie or play cuts me out of the contemporary conversation; it isolates me. But the marketplace, where we consume culture, is not the same as the forum, where we create it. It's the distinction that Hannah Arendt drew between the *agora,* which brings people together in work and commerce, and the *polis,* or *oikos,* where speech becomes "deeds." The community of the *agora* is mobilized by "the desire for products, not people," Arendt said. By contrast, the living room *oikos,* hot with strategizing, arguing, laughing, and flirting, was a place of desire for people. There I connected with lovers, collaborated with comrades, and forged many friendships (and—again, not getting overly romantic—enmities) that endure to this day.

These days it is common to refer to the "marketplace of ideas." It's a revealing phrase, implying that rather than becoming deed, speech becomes product.

APRIL 14

As I wade into the world of Voluntary Simplicity, I find that even the Simple Livers can't escape the market economy. "We're not out to get your money!" reassures the Simple Living Network Web site. But linking around, I come upon an emerging sector of anti-consumerist entrepreneurs—coupon-clipping coaches, Simplicity Circle facilitators, hawkers of "essential" primers and newsletters. The registration fee for an online course in the nine-step Your Money or Your Life is $50, plus materials totaling about $50. Maybe, as a step toward frugality, I should join Debtors Anonymous. It's free, and for that I get not nine but twelve steps and all the coffee I can drink.

I receive a catalogue from a mail-order outfit called Northern Sun: Products for Progressives, which offers thousands of posters, bumper stickers, buttons, T-shirts, mugs, and mouse pads that celebrate diversity, Che Guevara, and the polka, and condemn Exxon, malls, and (on one shirt) humans. The environmentalist posters ("Treehugger," "The Last Fish") are printed on heavy-weight (virtually nonbiodegradable) bleached (poisonous) stock and printed in dark blue, green, and brown ink (the colors of the earth, presumably to leach less conspicuously into the water table). Sometimes you have to destroy the forest to save it.

Janice sends me a refrigerator magnet with a comic-book couple embracing on it. "Oh Darling," she's whispering in his ear, "let's go deep into debt!"

The mainstream market has been alert to the peaceful whisper of the Simplicity shopper's cash at least since the founding of *Martha Stewart Living* in 1990. Although the labor-intensive Martha lifestyle was anything but simple, at least not for anyone who held a job, it took a decade before another major publisher went explicitly Simple. Soon Time Warner's *RealSimple*, "the magazine about simplifying your life" by buying new, simple-looking products, spawned a patch of slightly modified offshoots, such as the slightly crunchy *Organic Style* and the slightly crunchier *Organic Living*. A new entry, *MaryJanesFarm*, is *Martha Stewart Living* with dirt under its nails and a clean criminal record. *Plenty* starts from the premise that you can consume as much as you want as long as you throw it away in a biodegradable plastic bag. And then there's *Vegetarian Baby*.

No two ways about it, Simplicity sells. I find a trend report online entitled "The consumer quest for simplicity—How financial services providers can assist customers in their quest for simpler lives." The report, from Datamonitor at $2,795 for a single-user license, instructs businesses on how to "engage mass-market simplicity" by, for instance, setting up a line of "simple and honest" products (quotation marks theirs). It reassures: "Do not be afraid of seemingly anti-business messages."

APRIL 21

E-mail from Ricki:

How's Not Buying It? I do admire you for that; I have become such a consumer, you'd be disgusted.

From Prudence:

I broke down yesterday and bought some Lotus Flower bath gel; sorry. But I'm working another simplicity angle: Doubling my flexibility through yoga as a way of in effect doubling the space in my apartment (assuming I can fold myself into the barking cockroach position before long).

People are confessing. I'm not sure I am worthy of hearing their sins. For one thing, no matter how careful I am, I am spending. A week ago, I withdrew $150 from the ATM, expecting it to last two weeks. Twenty bucks went to an eleven-ride subway card, $42.40 to groceries, $11.95 to drugstore items (toothpaste, floss, shampoo), and $55 for a haircut (necessary?). That's $129.35. What about the remaining $20.65?

I plumb my memory for the image of a hand, my hand, with coins and green paper in it. What is the hand doing? Aha! Reaching over the high counter of the newsstand: a week of newspapers, $9.50. Two quarters here, another quarter there move from pocket to crushed paper cup: beggars. That still leaves $10 and change.

Ann calls it "leakage," this unaccounted-for trickling of bills from wallet to Limbo, not unlike the migration of socks between clothes dryer and dresser drawer. It's also a fact of life in New York, where a friend once estimated it costs five bucks an hour just to be—and that was in the Seventies. This week I also wrote a check for $50 for a parking ticket, a tax exacted from auto owners through the arcane New York system of alternate-side-of-the-street parking regulations. Paul and I use our car in the city only to move it across the street—except, that is, when we forget, at $50 per memory lapse.

Maybe I should add a column to my bookkeeping: "Existence, Misc."

APRIL 22

While attempting to live simply, I collect material on living extravagantly. This is a cinch. From the *Times* I clip articles about the $3,200 medicine chest, the $699 kids' bicycle, the $600 haircut (waiting list: two weeks), the $17,000 gold and diamond flip-flops, the $17 martini. On television, I watch Jessica Simpson justify the purchase of $1,200 bed sheets to her miffed husband ("We sleep on them every night!") and listen to Robin Leach bellow his unquenchable astonishment at a $40,000-a-day Caribbean resort, a $670,000 Ferrari, and a personal-service agency that caters to the life crises of the rich and famous, such as Madonna's craving for an exotic American herbal tea at midnight in London (located and delivered within the hour, fee unspecified).

Like pornography and corruption scandals, these reports trade in both lust and prudery, allowing us to gratify our prurience at the same time as we assuage our guilt. What kind of sicko would buy rubber slippers with diamonds on them for nearly half the average annual household budget! A kids' bike for seven hundred bucks? He'll outgrow it in a year!

Like other unspeakable crimes about which we cannot cease speaking (child abuse, torture), hyperconsumption renders the spectator virtually normal by comparison, even upright. Nothing you want or buy can compare. A desire for the plain-white $3,200 flip-flops, mentioned further down the paragraph after the $17,000 flip-flops, begins to seem temperate. And the shopper who forks over $40 for rubber shoes in Soho is a bargain-hunter. She has saved $16,960!

While getting my voyeuristic kicks, I indulge in my own gratifying comparisons. I am wearing Nike slides, naked even of paste gems, bought on sale two years ago for a piffling fifteen bucks. I'll have them at least a year more; amortized, that comes to $5 a year. Never mind the price of my Nikes was $13 more than the pair in the Kmart bin, and a week's salary for the worker who made them. Next to the vacationer strolling down the $40,000-a-night beach in her diamond flip-flops, I am Gandhi.

APRIL 24

I decline dinner at Bryant Park Café with my classmates at my twenty-fifth journalism school reunion. Paul and I do incur business-related expenses, but we have drawn the line at meals out. Under Debbie's "don't buy, don't tell" policy, I say nothing to the dinner's organizer about why I won't be coming.

The $65 tab, not including tax, tip, and wine, would have been a stretch at any time. But the year of living frugally makes me doubly aware of the choice of this restaurant. The guy who arranged the get-together is one of our better-earning classmates. Does he assume we can all afford a $100 meal? It must also be said that he has volunteered many hours to gather us and treated everyone to a generous spread of drinks and hors d'oeuvres at his office. I should be grateful, or at least gracious, but this project sometimes just makes me surly. I stay for the drinks and when the gang leaves for dinner, say good night, begging an early appointment the next day.

I do have an early appointment. Five A.M. to be exact, for a bus to the Washington, D.C., March for Women's Lives, a massive mobilization for abortion rights. Temma and I have planned to travel together and meet the rest of our contingent at Union Station. Over this three-hour trip, I have agonized for three weeks.

Should I take the bus chartered by the restaurant Florent ($55 round trip, including breakfast, lunch, and pre–return trip cocktails)? Should I opt for the unreserved Amtrak train ($145 with NOW discount), which leaves at 7 and doesn't guarantee a seat? Should I accompany Temma on the Metroliner, which leaves one civilized hour later, arrives at the same time, and has reserved seats—for $100 more? Temma, a professor, has offered to pay the difference.

But it's not that I can't afford the Metroliner. It's that the Metroliner is a luxury, according to "the rules": the price premium is for nothing but convenience. Why then would the NOW train not be a luxury compared to the bus? The rules are fluid. I am making them up as I go along.

So what do I do? What else: I torment Temma with my indecision. After extensive waffling, I accept her offer. She picks up the tickets and pays for them on her credit card. Several e-mails ensue, during which I waffle again, then change my mind decisively. She goes back to Penn Station to return the tickets. On her way there, I change my mind again and call her on her cell phone, but reach her too late.

In the end, Temma and I travel separately. She takes the Metroliner, I take the bus. I rise at 4 A.M. and call a cab to

Manhattan when I realize the subway isn't stopping at my station before 5 A.M. on the weekend. As I pull in at Florent, clubgoers in miniskirts and heels are staggering in for eggs Benedict and Bloody Marys. The bus is an hour late arriving. Half its seats do not recline and its toilet stinks.

The march is a triumph, but I am a wreck. Before getting back on the bus, I down three of Florent's free vodkas, hoping they will make me sleepy. Instead, they make me nervous and nauseated. Rain and traffic delay our return to Manhattan until midnight, but I don't hail a cab to Brooklyn. I trudge four blocks to the subway station only to watch the A train pull out as I descend the stairs. The next one doesn't come for twenty-five minutes, by which time I am in tears of exhaustion.

APRIL 29

The topic for the second Voluntary Simplicity meeting is Transforming Personal Consumption. Along with Beryl's assigned texts (e.g., "The American Dream on a Shoestring") I have been reading a critique of Voluntary Simplicity by Allegheny College political scientist and environmental activist Michael Maniates. Maniates gives the movement its due, but he cautions against the personal focus such groups can adopt. If VS pays no attention to public policy, workplace issues, or political power, he warns, "simplicity becomes a zealous conversation about what one buys and why, to the exclusion of almost everything else."

As it turns out, the group isn't ready to talk about what one buys and why. At the last meeting Beryl issued her own warning. Her previous group, she said, "could never get itself beyond decluttering." Now it looks as if ours too may get stuck permanently in a zealous and exclusive conversation about what one throws away and why.

Marlene reports that she has decluttered two of her apartment's four rooms. Nobuko, whose fastidiousness is evident from her shoe polish to her posture, has decluttered her office. "I filed all past projects," she informs us. "Now I am moving on to current projects." Gail, an experienced Simplifier, is entering the second year of "clutter-cleaning." She lives in a three-room apartment.

Irwin, who always speaks in a tone suggesting long and deep thought, says that he too is "very interested in clutter. I believe a cluttered life is a cluttered mind." Noticing he has at least two of everything, Irwin has removed one of two figurines each of St. Jude and "the BVM" ("Blessed Virgin Mary," Paul, former altar boy, whispers when I shoot him a puzzled look). "So I took one St. Jude to St. Francis of Assisi and one BVM to St. Edmund's." Everyone congratulates him. Maybe he should have kept both Judes, though, as his decluttering appears to be a lost cause. He confesses, "I went to buy a book on clutter and bought three."

Lionel's clutter comes in two principal forms: food and paper. He and his wife buy too much of the former and shove it into the refrigerator, where it gets lost and spoils. They end up eating in restaurants and ordering takeout and paying the financial and caloric consequences. He is also trying to clear the junk from what he has several times referred to as "our eighty-six-inch dining room table." The problem, he avers, is mostly his wife's. An immigrant who adores shopping, she keeps bringing home new things and putting them in the refrigerator and on the table.

But Lionel has a solution: he will buy *a bigger refrigerator!* His wife is resisting, pointing out that a new refrigerator will require a kitchen renovation to make room for it. No one mentions that a bigger refrigerator will also use much more electricity, with graver impact on his budget (not to mention the ozone layer) than lettuce growing slime in the crisper.

Elisa has no need to declutter; her apartment is almost obsessively spare. But she is downsizing. She has let go her cleaning lady and discontinued her premier cable service; she's looking for a stripped-down telephone contract. Another large item has been removed from Elisa's life since we last met, too. As expected, she has lost her job.

A third of the group is now jobless.

As we leave Elisa's apartment building, Irwin holds the door so Paul and I can roll our bikes out. He shakes his head. "People are going to have to start making do with less," he says. Paul and I make "hope-not" and "too-bad" noises. But Irwin's is a different kind of dismay. "They want too much," he declares. "People have been making too much for too long."

This to me is a depressing statement coming from a lifelong union man. But then, Irwin is also a devout Catholic. I'd bet he is banking his salvation on the inheritance of the meek, not the revolution of the proletariat. But like a hellfire-and-damnation preacher, he seems almost to relish the punishments that will come with the next Great Depression—or the Second Coming.

If the renunciative aspects of Voluntary Simplicity appeal to Irwin's religious nature, he is not alone in this group, or in the movement. "The greatest sin is greed," Marlene pronounced at our first meeting, right after telling us her name. "I believe we will all be punished for it." Sal says she is too tired to go to church on Sunday (she works six days, including Saturday), but picks up spiritual wisdom wherever she can. "We have gotten off the track because of our secular lives. Religion always speaks of balance," she tells us, quoting Mel Gibson preaching on David Letterman.

The VS gurus are equally "spiritual." Cecile Andrews begins

her book with "Saving Our Souls" and the spirit hovers over nearly the entire text. Voluntary Simplicity, she claims, keeps a person "in touch with nature and the universal life force." Duane Elgin roots VS in religious traditions from Catholicism to Transcendentalism and speaks often of the mystical, of "reverence" for nature, and the "miracle of creation." He adamantly wants to figure out how to put less trash in the landfill, but his most heartfelt goal is to clear the trash from the path toward truth—and God—within ourselves. Even the ultra-practical Joe Dominguez and Vicki Robin can't help exhorting, "We also need to deepen our identity by reconnecting with our spirituality."

Is all this talk about spirituality simply a New Age metaphor for the good? After all, policy, whether social, economic, or environmental, is the pragmatic codification of values and priorities, and many of the VS gurus are also political activists for environmental conservation and consumer protections. How is the good defined by the Voluntary Simplicity movement?

A fine articulation of its tenets can be found in a 1999 interview of the writer Bill McKibben, one of the preeminent moral philosophers of what might be called spiritual environmentalism (he's also a Methodist Sunday school teacher). "The market forces pushing convenience, individualism, and comfort are still stronger than the attraction of community, fellowship, and connection with the natural world," McKibben told journalist Jay Walljasper. The environmental crisis is also a "spiritual crisis," he says, "a crisis of desire."

Calling the crisis both environmental and spiritual—you might say immanent and transcendent—McKibben reveals what Michael Maniates identifies as a confounded message of anticonsumerism. Writes Maniates, paraphrasing anticonsumerist propaganda, "In the scheme of moral corrupters, advertising is bad, but people are weak in succumbing to it"; SUVs harm the environ-ment, but the people who drive them are selfish. According to this rhetoric, he continues, consumers are "both the victims and the agents of their own moral destruction."

Maniates points out the strategic trouble for a movement that is confused about assigning blame for the problem: it doesn't know where to locate agency for the solution. If environmental decline is the consequence of personal weakness and selfishness, there is no remedy but self-discipline. Irwin indicts advertising and credit cards for creating "a society of instant gratification." But his solution is to gird his desires, not demand regulation of the credit card industry. McKibben, on the other hand, is an indefatigable political activist for energy efficiency and environmental regulation. But in almost all his work, he argues from the position of less-is-more right living, laying out his own life as exemplary of the "alternative desires" he would offer to replace those being created by Disney or GM, from having only one child to killing your television.

I don't want to slice the personal off from the economic or argue that the former is inconsequential while the latter is "real." Integrating these two realms is what all my work (including this project) is about. Yet I wonder whether cutting back my personal consumption will do any more than make me feel better. Is not-buying part of the solution—to anything?

APRIL 30

I've come to the journalism department of New York University, to talk with my friend, editor, and comrade in arms, the cultural critic Ellen Willis. Ellen is one of the country's smartest cartogra-phers of the terrain where the personal meets the political, and for decades she has been writing about the parallels between religious-right and political-left conservatism. Both of these condemn what they see as the excesses of the Sixties and Seventies sexual liberation and cultural freedom movements; each blames these movements for what ails America. Neither has any use for "hedonism," and both preach sacrifice and moderation—chastity on the right, anticonsumerism on the left.

I hope Ellen can help me sort through my own misgivings about the moral agenda of Voluntary Simplicity without entirely undermining my effort to reduce personal consumption. But I know she's not going to reassure me. Ellen has expressed her skepticism about my buy-nothing project. "There are certain ways in which you can regulate consumption. You can take things off the market, like SUVs, for instance," she has told me on the phone. "I'm not saying there shouldn't be any laws. But reducing consumption as a principle is not a basis for political change."

Today, Ellen begins by outlining three historic periods of postwar consumption. In the Fifties, an era of new prosperity following the traumas of the Depression and World War II, "consumption was about security and solidity—houses, appliances, cars, all tied up with an ethos that the most important thing was to have a secure life."

For the Sixties generation, who grew up taking security for granted, "consumption started to be more fun." Rent was cheap, you could work part time and live off the fat, spending your disposable income on motorcycles and records, drugs and travel. Consumption was not antithetical to rebellion. Desiring consumer goods did not preclude desiring other, less tangible, good things—community, freedom, transcendence, orgasms; in a politically optimistic time, both kinds of goods felt near at hand. "The pleasures of consumption could be expanded beyond consuming," says Ellen. For instance, some feminists who criticized the misogyny in advertising and commercial pornography also saw that the sexuality in these media could adumbrate the sexual liberation of women as well as men. "Consumption opened out to help stimulate subversive thoughts," and vice versa, says Ellen.

Ellen's third, current, period began with the rise of the moral Right in the 1980s. Since then, she identifies two contradictory trends. Consumption has been hollowed out of any liberatory content (unless you count Jimi Hendrix as the soundtrack for Pepsi commercials). Getting and spending is everything—more than everything. "There is a feeling that this has gotten out of control," Ellen laments. "Everybody is trying to sell me something at every moment. We better think about buying and selling because if we stop for a minute and think about anything else, we will have a meltdown." At the same time, we are pinched by what she calls a "culture of scarcity," the idea—made real by government and corporate policies favoring the rich and stockholders over everyone else—that there is no money for health care or pensions, no time for leisure, no affordable living space, no room to think about the possibilities beyond private bourgeois comfort. "Utopianism is out of the conversation entirely," notes Ellen.

I agree. "The only utopian movements left are these ecstatic embraces of discipline," I say. "Like chastity pledges."

Or Voluntary Simplicity, she answers, and repeats that VS is not a path toward liberating ourselves from the grip of overconsumption. It is, rather, one more symptom of a culture in the tightening grip of repression: "Anticonsumerism is the Puritanism of the Left."

When I get home, I take out Ellen's 1992 collection, *No More Nice Girls: Countercultural Essays*. "Transcendence through discipline—as in meditation, or macrobiotics, or voluntary poverty, or living off the land—was always the antithesis of the '60s dialectic," she writes in "Coming Down Again," a piece that is as fresh today as it was when it was written in 1990.

> [I]n context it added another flavor to the rich stew of choices and made for some interesting, to say the least, syntheses. But its contemporary variants are the only game in town, emblems of scarcity. Another metaphor: runners by the thousands urging on their bodies until the endorphins kick in. The runners' high, an extra reward for the work-well-done of tuning up one's cardiovascular system. What's scarce in the current scheme of things is not (for the shrinking middle class, anyway) rewards but grace, the unearned, the serendipitous. The space to lie down or wander off the map.

Bill McKibben also wants the space to lie down or wander off the map (though I can't quite imagine him advising anyone to lie down and ingest a chemical that induces wandering temporarily off the planet). He stops short of telling people what they should want, but like other VS proponents suggests that environmentalists break the news gently that what people want is not going to make them happy. "Our task is to demonstrate that to live simply is . . . more satisfying and more pleasurable than consumer society," he told Walljasper. "It doesn't work to just tell people to get out of their cars to save the upper atmosphere. Instead we need to encourage them to ride a bike. It's elegant. It's fun. It makes you feel better. It's important not to say that TV will rot your brain, but that it's satisfying to take a walk in the moonlight instead."

What if I don't fancy elegance and moonlight? What if I relish my nightly fix of *Law and Order* and have not noticed any neuronal deterioration for it? Actually, it *does* work to tell me to get out of my car to save the upper atmosphere. It works a lot better than telling me to get out of my car to save my soul.

So the Left argues (alongside Plato) that a good society is one that provides everyone with his essential bodily needs; spiritual satisfaction will naturally follow material satiation. The religious Right (alongside Descartes and the tree-living extremes of the environmentalist movement) sees spiritual salvation in the mortification of the flesh. But if neurologists teach us that there is no separation of the body from the mind, anthropologists show there is no sundering things from their meanings or from culture and the relationships inside culture. "Take [goods] out of human intercourse and you have dismantled the whole thing," write Douglas and Isherwood. This is as true of Keynes's "second-class wants" as it is of his essentials. "Goods that minister to physical needs—food or drink—are no less carriers of meaning than ballet or poetry," the two continue.

We need bread and water. We also desire freedom and transcendence. Somewhere in between fall the lime-green stiletto-heeled shoes. They are a pleasure: where need meets desire. Listening again to the tape of my conversation with Ellen, it strikes me that freedom and transcendence are also needs, not just desires. And maybe the freedom to desire itself—the font of personal fulfillment, creativity, and democracy, to name just a few good things—is a necessity, too. Will Paul and I have to recognize third, fourth, and fifth categories floating between Necessity and Superfluity?

Unlike Ellen Willis, I'm sympathetic to Bill McKibben's argument. Part of me is disgusted by Americans' sense of entitlement to vast quantities of everything. At the same time, I am loath to ally myself with any movement, right or left, that starts by telling people not to desire. I don't want to tell the girls in the store that it's wrong to want those frivolous shoes, because I don't want to risk suggesting they give up the sexy dream of dancing the night away. That dream is stitched into the soles (and souls) of the shoes.

Scarcity

MAY 1

Things fall apart. The wheel of my shopping cart wobbles off the axle and its pin is lost on the sidewalk. My favorite green-and-black striped shirt is thinning at the elbows, my heels are poking through my socks. The final shard of Body Time rosemary-mint aromatherapy soap slides down the drain. Now we'll make do with Ivory.

Intellectually, as well, a feeling of scarcity is setting in. I skim the newspaper's arts pages daily like a historian surveying the microfiche of an era she did not live through. But I turn my closer attention to the television schedules, scrutinizing them for anything that looks remotely engaging. I rush home by nine every Wednesday for *West Wing* and pencil shows I want to watch into my calendar. On those rare evenings when there is no *Law and Order* episode airing, I feel deprived of the satisfyingly predictable "surprise" endings and go to sleep unsettled. Tonight, Saturday, is such a *Law*-less evening.

What should I do? I don't have a date and Paul is in Vermont. I could take a bike ride, I could read, I could learn to knit or start on ancient Greek. But it's too late to ride and there's nothing I want to read. I'd be irritating company in my present mood, so it's a good thing I haven't any social plans. As for knitting or Greek, the idea of one more homemade, edifying pastime makes me yawn.

"Idleness is fatal only to the mediocre," declared Albert Camus. "Boredom is the threshold to great deeds," wrote Walter Benjamin.

I sit on the couch, noticing how cute the cat is when he folds his little white paws over his little orange face. Sometimes, it seems, boredom is not even the threshold to deeds.

Yes, I am bored—a feeling that is more frequent this year than I'd like to admit. I feel lonely, antsy, and distracted by this prolonged suspension of distraction, like a yogi forced to meditate twenty-four hours a day. The one difference is that my knees don't hurt.

Does this mean I am mediocre? Or am I confronting something I don't usually have to confront?

Adam Phillips calls boredom "the mood of diffuse restlessness which contains that most absurd and paradoxical wish, the wish for a desire." Phillips, a child psychologist, is talking about boredom in children, who, faced with nothing to do, are often powerless to do much about it besides wait around until they think of something. Boredom is "a precarious process," he continues, "in which the child is both waiting for something and looking for something, in which hope is being secretly negotiated." The state he describes is remarkably similar to Benjamin's "threshold."

If the child were an adult, she could skip over the threshold and go shopping.

Shopping defeats, or at least circumvents, boredom, but not only because it fills idle time. Consumption is an exercise in hope—hope for more happiness, more beauty, more status, more fun. This sort of hope requires little negotiation; its fulfillment is relatively simple, even if temporary. But more than this simple, immediate gratification, consumption provides the thing that precedes gratification, the complex something with which Phillips's child is grappling: the marketplace provides infinite names for desire—Ben & Jerry's Chunky Monkey ice cream, *She Is Me*, Chinese silk handbag.

This year, Paul and I have volunteered to be children in a culture that equates adulthood with autonomy and autonomy with the ability to spend your way out of predicaments. Now, the predicament is boredom, the naming of desire. Not once since the year began have I experienced a surfeit of desire; never have I brimmed over with Keynes's "pent-up demand." Rather, pausing at that threshold, I have found myself in this infantile state of excruciating restlessness—waiting to know how to open the door, waiting to know what to want.

MAY 3–4

Monday morning, more purposeful and energetic, I pack a lunch and ride the subway to the Humanities and Social Sciences Library on Forty-second Street for a day of research. It's three days after the photos of Abu Ghraib were released, and I am taking a break from the hideous news by reading a piece from yesterday's Sunday *Times Magazine*. "Fixing Nemo," by Rebecca Skloot, concerns the growth in veterinary medicine for fish. She reports that a common ailment for which pet owners seek such services is the "buoyancy disorder," which may cause Goldie to float belly up or nose down. If the simpler treatment, the administration of a single cooked green pea, does not cure the patient, corrective surgery can be undertaken at a cost of $150 to $1,500. The article makes me feel a little different toward my tuna sandwich.

Before getting off the train, I look through the call numbers

I've printed out from the library's online catalogue. Then I hurry down Forty-second Street to arrive at the heavy wooden doors on the north side of the library at 11 on the dot. The doors are locked, blocked by a sign that says the research libraries are closed on Mondays as well as Sundays, "due to budget cuts." Already, shortened hours have given a user barely enough time to check her coat and sharpen her pencil before the staff takes lunch.

Returning the next day, again with call numbers and sandwich, I wait forty-five minutes for my books to be retrieved from the stacks (last year two hundred New York Public Library staffers were lost to attrition and early retirement). One book just can't be found (the book budget took a 40 percent hit in 2003, translating to 260,000 books). At the end of the day, I'm unable to copy my materials in the usual hour I allot, as three of seven copy machines are out of order (a press release on the cuts refers to "reduced technology, maintenance, and security, leading to equipment and facilities that are deteriorating"). If it's a frustrating day for me, a person who has rendered herself dependent on this public system for a year, I've got nothing on the administrators and librarians whose livelihoods depend on that system and who are its year-in-year-out stewards. The NYPL absorbed cuts of more than $16 million last fiscal year and the system is looking at some $30 million more for 2004.

MAY 5

All right, I'll try the Brooklyn Central Branch. I've adjusted my expectations. This is, after all, a popular library, not a research library. All I want are two texts of anthropology, one by Marcel Mauss, the other by Bronislaw Malinowski. Neither is obscure, and the catalogue says they are both in circulation, on the shelf. In reality, both are missing and unaccounted for.

The librarian initiates a search in Storage, many stories below. A half-hour later, the kid at the main circulation desk looks at the slip and tells me, "Nothin' not found," a confusing but sympathetically delivered message. Back upstairs in History and Social Science, I ask the librarian if there's anything else that can be done. Sorry, he says. Maybe he should indicate the loss in the computer catalogue, I suggest, so that someone else might do something about it. "Oh, yeah, okay," he answers, calling up the entry. But there's no field in which to indicate anything about the book's whereabouts or lack thereof. He starts to delete the entry.

No! I want to shout, but I've made too many demands already. I stand and watch, like a witness to the Stalinist redaction of the record of the destruction of a great public institution. He is committing official indifference; I, complicit silence.

Before I leave, I climb to the top floor, where arts and crafts books are shelved, to borrow a guide to fabric crafts. Since we're not buying gifts, Paul and I are thinking of making two dozen silk roses to give my niece, Sarah, at graduation; I'm looking for a book on silk flowers. But these books, also in the catalogue, are gone, too. "Probably stolen," the librarian tells me, sounding resigned as a widow to absence.

New York's libraries are not alone. Thanks to tax cuts nationwide, the American Library Association's publication reads like the newsletter of a nursing home: everybody is either sick or dying. In Rochester, New York, the public library "may be facing more reductions in hours and staff as a result of the mayor's latest budget proposal . . . State aid to the libraries has remained the same since 1997," says one article. In Brown County, Wisconsin, the library board is fighting the second shutdown (including temporary layoffs of the entire staff) during the last week of the summer. In Rockford, Illinois, school librarians are pleading to forestall the elimination of all the district's professional librarians and thirty-one elementary-school library aides.

Is it any wonder that in many towns Barnes & Noble, with its upholstered armchairs, shiny mahogany tables, and endlessly replenished shelves, has become the new public library? Public except, of course, that you have to buy something to use it, and those endless shelves contain only the books a marketing person considers saleable. On the way home from the library, I stop at Barnes & Noble. After all, the savior of smaller government is supposed to be the marketplace, whose Invisible Hand will distribute those things the state no longer supplies but people still demand. I pass the Chinese calligraphy bookmark display, the Tuscany section, and the For Dummies subsidiary on my way to the Anthropology section in a far corner. I search its two short shelves. The store carries neither Mauss nor Malinowski.

MAY 8

The doughnut maker Krispy Kreme reports a plunge in its share price of 29 percent. It closed yesterday at $22.51, down $9.29 and less than half the stock's peak value of $49.74, reached in August. Market analysts say the company's problem is overexpansion. The company attributes its losses to the popularity of low-carbohydrate diets. Nutritionist and food activist Marian Nestle suggests that both may be right. The food industry creates obesity by pushing more food on us, she argues: "If you eat less, they lose money." On the other hand, Nestle and others in her field consider the low-carb diet another consumer product, falsely advertised and possibly harmful to health. Krispy Kreme is both villain and victim.

More obesity news: earlier this week, the Environmental Protection Agency reported that the average American car or light truck in the 2003 model year weighed 4,021 pounds, breaking the two-ton barrier for the first time since the mid-1970s. Vehicle size is the main reason that gains in fuel economy are at a standstill and crude oil consumption is climbing.

The U.S. economy is getting fat selling fat. Meanwhile, the public libraries are dying of malnutrition.

MAY 9

Jonathan and I are on the phone, arranging this afternoon's date. He suggests we meet for lunch at his favorite cheap trattoria in the Village, then go to a movie.

I can't go out for lunch, I remind him.

Do you want to just meet for the movie?

Nope, no movies. "I'm not buying—remember?"

"You mean you're not allowed to go to the *movies*?" This is the aspect of our project about which my friends are most incredulous.

I'm apologetic. "It's nice out. Can we, like, take a walk?"

"A walk! You want to go for a walk?" He's laughing now (he likes to walk). "Oh, Judy, you're so boring!" When I say nothing in my defense, he laughs more gently, perhaps to soften the grim truth.

Before going out, I settle in with the Sunday *Times*. Images of naked prisoners in humiliating postures at Abu Ghraib are impeding the Bush administration's efforts at convincing the Iraqis that we wish them well. Nevertheless, I learn, Brand America is holding its own. "Even Muslims in the Middle East and Southeast Asia do not seem to translate their anger into a boycott of American products," says the article. A nineteen-year-old Singaporean man emerging from midday prayers at his mosque tells the reporter that "even after seeing the pictures" he has not lost his appetite for McDonald's and KFC.

The *New Yorker* runs a cartoon by Mick Stevens of a dark-skinned man standing in a landscape of rubble, looking stunned. He is wearing a T-shirt with the logo "I ♥ USA" on it, and thought bubbles surround his head: "Am I losing my hair?" "Am I gaining too much weight?" "Is my breath OK?" "Do I need a new car?" "What's on TV?" The caption: LIBERATED IRAQI.

There's hope for Krispy Kreme, in Baghdad.

MAY 14

Paul and I go uptown to the Metropolitan Museum of Art to see the exhibit of art of the Byzantine Empire in its final period, 1261 to 1557. It is an awesome show, in the old sense of that word. Walking among the icons, crucifixes, and cloaks in visceral reds and bottomless blacks, encrusted in gold, gems, enamel, and ivory, I am dazed.

As art institutions go, the Met is as wealthy as Byzantium. This is why over the years I have never paid more than a quarter to get in (read the two-point type: the entrance fee, $12 at this writing, is "suggested"). Maybe I'm paranoid, but I have noticed that the clerks consistently decline to thank patrons like me, who offer less than full fare. It is Friday night, free admission, but we've arrived a little before the cashiers close, so I give a quarter and ask for two buttons. The same thing happens: no thank-you. Suspecting a perverse policy, I ask the young man if the workers are instructed to subtly transmit ingratitude to the less generous public. I'm trying to adopt a tone of scientific disinterest, but it comes out sounding like a rebuke.

"Now you're making me feel pressured," he answers, and due either to pique or performance anxiety, hands over our buttons in silence.

I know, I know. I'm punishing the wrong guy. And even the higher-ups whose orders he might be following are at the mercy of policies even higher up. This fall, when the Museum of Modern Art reopens after its renovation, it will charge a record $20. Facing public outcry, MOMA's president will not back down. Want free arts? he'll say. Me too. I suggest you write your congressman.

He's got a point. America is the only advanced capitalist democracy that does not allocate a substantial portion of its budget to libraries and the arts (we're also the only putative non-theocracy that does not give money to art in which anybody is naked). But many Americans would still rather spend $20 to see the Picassos than entrust Washington with paying for culture. At the moment I share this bias, given Washington's current prejudices, for instance, against nakedness. But I resist my prejudice, since it's a symptom of a pernicious political-economic philosophy: private is good, public bad, business is good, government bad, whether you're showing paintings or building prisons.

Since the New Deal, this bias toward the private sector has ascended from heresy to conventional wisdom to hegemony, gaining the glow of gospel since the Reagan years. It's also been criticized along the way. In 1958, in *The Affluent Society*, John Kenneth Galbraith dissected it with unique elegance. Because history has moved generally from autocracy to democracy, Galbraith wrote, "[n]ot surprisingly, modern economic ideas incorporated a strong suspicion of government . . . Even Marx intended that the state should wither away." Public services "remain under the obloquy of the unreliability, incompetence, cost, and pretentious interference of prices. . . . Alcohol, comic books, and mouth wash all bask under the superior reputation of the market. Schools, judges, and municipal swimming pools lie under the evil reputation of bad kings."

These days, public agencies are compelled to act like businesses. The Motor Vehicles Bureau, Department of Health, and state university systems refer to their service users, formerly known as drivers, patients, or students, as "consumers." Even the most essential functions of government must advertise for business. I recently heard a spot on the radio for a product called "public transportation." Its slogan was something like "So People Can Get Home Faster." I had to laugh; the ad brought to mind Garrison Keillor's Ketchup Advisory Board, promoting its product's domestic-tranquility-enhancing agents. But the joke is on us. America's most ubiquitous condiment obviously doesn't need promoting. Public transportation, arguably more useful than sugary tomato paste, is a disappearing essential commodity.

The preference for private over public is based on at least two fallacies. One is that a dollar circulating through the government's till behaves differently from one moving through Wal-Mart's. Now, there are differences in how these dollars are spent. For one, unlike the Wal-Mart cashier, the worker at the Motor Vehicles Bureau is likely to belong to a union and therefore earn a decent salary and get health insurance and a pension. Antitax pundits would lead us to believe that we taxpayers are bankrolling the fat wage and benefits package of the public-sector worker, while Wal-Mart is carrying its own weight. In fact, by declining to offer its workers insurance or sufficient wages to buy the basics for themselves, Wal-Mart shifts the bill to the state. After all, the cashier gets sick anyway, her children get hungry. When these things happen, she turns to Medicaid or Food Stamps, and the rest of us subsidize not just the cashier but Wal-Mart itself.

Still, if you're looking for growth (and that is about all economists look for as a sign of national health), there's no way to distinguish the Motor Vehicles dollar from the Wal-Mart dollar as they travel through the economy. The gross domestic product is merely the sum of all goods and services exchanged; it does not discriminate between useful and useless, constructive and destructive, public and private expenditure. Uzis and gardening tools, pizza delivery and chemotherapy, football teams and nuclear waste cleanup—it all adds up to the GDP. A fact little publicized by the Bush administration is that in spite of cuts in domestic spending, the majority of new jobs created during its tenure have been government jobs. Is this bad for the economy? People with government jobs pay taxes—that's good for schools and roads and missile shields. And they also shop at Wal-Mart, which is good for business.

The other fallacy is that the axis of evil Waste, Fraud, and Abuse belongs to the public sector, and the private sector never screws up. Amtrak can't turn a profit serving the markets that the private airlines and bus companies have abandoned? A senator stands on the floor of Congress and declares that the government can't do anything right. He doesn't chastise the corporations for leaving travelers stranded. United Water takes over the efficient utility from the city of Atlanta and promptly raises rates and starts pumping out brown liquid? The free marketeers excuse United Water—poor thing, city water delivery turned out to be more complicated than the company had wagered—or, at best, they blame United Water for poor management. But they will never admit that a private monopoly has little incentive to do a good job or that the city was doing a better one.

Under the privatize-everything ideology, no priority trumps market "choice" (like we really want a selection of three electric companies). No strategy can replace business strategies. In the case of troubled public services, that strategy is punish the under-performer. If children aren't learning, cut the school's aid. When trains derail because of inadequate track maintenance, show Amtrak the gallows.

The aim of this strategy is not exactly to improve services. It's to unburden the nation of those pesky, expensive public amenities, amenities for which, under a progressive tax system, the wealthy pay more and the poor and middle-class pay less, even as the rich need and use them less and the rest of us use them more. Diminished budgets also affect the classes unequally. Public services decline. Middle- and upper-class parents opt for private school. Travelers who can afford it take the plane. Now CEOs, not publicly accountable elected officials, make the decisions about how much to pay teachers or where the trains should stop. Shareholders win; children in poor neighborhoods and residents of out-of-the-way towns lose. Tax revolts gain steam, even among those who are their victims—after all, why pay for lousy services? The antigovernment tax resisters have won: "the beast is starved." And the most brilliant part, from their point of view, is that almost everybody is convinced privatization is in the public interest.

So what about art? Without public money, institutions are turning more desperate by the day. At the Atlanta Ballet, I read, the highest bidder at auction wins the honor of owning—er, sponsoring—her favorite dancer. "I had so much fun running up to John [Welker] saying: 'Guess what? I won you!'" bubbled proud patron Lynda Courts after one such auction. Shades of the Paris Opera Ballet circa 1860, when wealthy patrons "subsidized" dancers, in return for favors? Or perhaps of Paris, Kentucky, around the same time. Either way, it brings new meaning to the term *slaves to art.*

"Culture follows money," F. Scott Fitzgerald said. Many of the best things in life are not free. The question is: Where does the money come from and who decides how it is spent? Does each of us have to shop for our own health, education, transportation, and welfare, as well as our own private pleasure and enlightenment? Or might some of these be considered public goods, meriting public funds? The advantages are many, from economies of scale to increased social equality to a more cohesive community. The costs of not having them are many, too. Besides the inverse of the above—inefficiency, social inequity, and a splintered community—the cost, most prominently, is the felt necessity of more private consumption. More and bigger cars, houses, pools, lawns, televisions, and all-terrain vehicles may boost the macroeconomy in the short term, but they eat away at our own personal bank accounts and the finite treasures that make up our earth.

I won't oversimplify the processes by which art gets made and paid for. Arts funding is not just economic, it's political. Back in Byzantium, this Jewish taxpayer might have been no happier with the art her government was buying with her hard-earned bezants than Jesse Helms was with Robert Mapplethorpe's photographs of black penises. Still, as I gaze into the solemn eyes of the black Madonnas at the Met, I think of what a state can do with the public's money if only it has—and we citizens have—the will.

MAY 18

I drop by the home of our neighbors and close friends, Flavio and Ann. Flavio is an Italian journalist; Ann, his American wife, a ceramic artist. Their children, Lucia and Emilio, are at the kitchen table working on an art project that involves gobs of glitter and glue. Both are iridescent. The back door is open to the garden, where the ground is scattered with plum blossoms. Flavio is unpacking groceries from the food co-op. I'm complaining about the privatization of everything.

"You guys should join the co-op," Flavio says, as he frequently does, caressing an organic eggplant and stacking blood oranges in a bowl made by Ann. The organic oranges cost half what conventional ones would at a commercial grocer.

"I know we should," I answer, as I frequently do, then recite my usual complaints about the Park Slope Food Coop, which has a reputation for its many rules and high work requirement of members. "I don't have time for the eight-hour indoctrination," I say.

He laughs. He loves the co-op, and not just for the good, cheap food. After all, low prices aren't everything. The lure of low prices, absent all other considerations, can be insidious, in fact. "I feel when I go into the big store, the big chain, we all become marketing numbers" justifying bad wages, environmental degradation, and unfair treatment of suppliers, he says. "When Wal-Mart tells you they're doing this to give the consumer the lowest price, they are using you as an alibi. Every time you shop there, you have to be conscious of that. It's you that makes this possible. It's not Big Brother watching over you. It's you. And these are big consequences. It's not me buying a fucking egg. It's me buying this egg with all these consequences to everyone else on the fucking planet!"

He pauses to persuade Emilio to put on his shoes before going outside, then continues. "It is redeeming to know you are resisting [by going to the co-op]. But you wonder what kind of alternative is this. You're working at dismantling, but what are you establishing? What kind of global alternative are you creating? You are boycotting, but what is next?" He laughs at what is sounding like a rather a grandiose sales pitch for the Park Slope Food

Coop. The kids run in from the garden, screaming. It's an appropriate punctuation. "I just like to shop in the co-op. I love this little idea that everyone works and everyone benefits," Flavio says. "Maybe it's made up—but I love that idea."

"Okay, sign me up!" I say, practically bursting into the Italian communist anthem "Avanti Populo." But I will rethink my resistance to the work requirement of two and a half hours per person per month. It's not just for the cheap food. I love the idea, too.

MAY 22

Riding my bike to Prospect Park a few days ago, I noticed that a segment of Fifth Avenue has been rechristened Cucina Boulevard, after the restaurant that sparked the avenue's gentrification more than a decade ago. I called the Brooklyn borough president's office, but no one could tell me how this renaming occurred or how long it will last. I didn't ask whether Cucina is required to sweep the streets and empty the trash cans in exchange for the honor (and free advertising) of the street sign, but I suspect the answer is no.

New York has never been a very civic-minded city. It has always belonged to the financiers and real estate moguls. But now its remaining public spaces are also being sold to the highest bidder. Last year, to stem budget shortfalls in the public schools, Mayor Michael Bloomberg extended exclusive beverage vending rights to Snapple, trading textbooks and toilet paper for childhood obesity and cavities. Now he wants to peddle corporate sponsorships, along with naming rights, to subway stations, parks, buses, and bridges.

Paul comes home from Italian class. "I love our library," he calls out as he enters the apartment. His proprietary feeling has grown with our dependence on the institution. I wonder if he would feel it was "our library" if the Central Branch were called, say, Bertelsmann BookCenter or Burger King's Read It Your Way?

MAY 24

Analysis of $350 billion tax cut signed into law one year ago (source: Center on Budget and Policy Priorities):

Average federal tax savings (by household income)
Middle 20 percent $647
Top 1 percent $35,000
Incomes > $1 million (top 0.2 percent) $123,592

Projected federal deficit by 2010
With tax cuts...$675 billion
Without tax cuts........................$100 billion in most years

MAY 25

I have visited four other libraries in Brooklyn and Manhattan looking for the fabric-craft books. All are AWOL: Away Without Loan. "It's tough to keep that kind of book on the shelf," one librarian tells me. "They're expensive, people want to own them, and we can't afford to keep replacing them."

"Don't people get it that the public library is for the public?" I ask her, singing a hymn to the choir. She looks up at me with gentle eyes, as if she has just broken it to a child that people can be mean.

I shake my head and walk away, unable to decide which distresses me more: the rape and pillage of the commons or the idea that a person who makes silk flowers would steal a book from the library.

MAY 27

Tonight, the Voluntary Simplicity group is talking about Finding the Work You Love. Jessica, one of our realists, reports on a conflict between the values of VS and those of the job market. She tells us about a friend who went for an interview at a computer company and took out a pad and pen to take notes. She didn't get the job. Later she heard that the paper and pen had marked her as stodgy and technophobic. The firm wanted to see a Palm Pilot or BlackBerry. Hers was the consumer electronics equivalent of a working-class accent or country manners.

Maybe she couldn't afford a BlackBerry, Dana suggests.

"Too bad," responds Jessica. "You sometimes have to spend money to make money." I flash on my journalism school dinner and the $100 I "wasn't allowed" to spend, according to my "rules." What networking opportunities did I miss? Buying makes you saleable.

Laura has brought an announcement for a "volunteer fair," where visitors can check out good causes as they might do tables at a flea market. Children with AIDS? Cut-rate cosmetics? Hudson River cleanup? Vegetable-shaped refrigerator magnets? Laura, who is intelligent and more outwardly focused than almost anyone in the room, nevertheless seemed to pick her activity without a guiding principle. She spent last weekend working at a stray-cat shelter, even though she is allergic to cats.

The rest of the group is still looking inward. Dana, a therapeutic masseuse and "healer" in her spare time, is adopting a less literal, more spiritual approach to the problem of over-owning. "I think I've made friends with my clutter," she tells us. "I made the decision that it will go in its own time. I can't overstress about things I can't do anything about." Perhaps a Higher Power will take the old clothes to the Salvation Army. In the meantime, Dana is lowering her rent burden by getting a roommate. Jessica is doing the same, and also selling things for other people on eBay. The librarian Elisa, a practical sort like Laura, is discovering things about herself, too. She is surprised that she does not miss *The Sopranos* and not surprised that she misses her cleaning lady.

Gail reports that she is buying only used books. My stomach lurches. When I first talked to my agent about *Not Buying It,* she registered alarm over this one consumer item. "But you have to buy books, Judith," Joy ordered. "You have to support the industry." I often ask myself if a business that hasn't figured out how to sell about 80 percent of what it produces can claim the name "industry." Still, it's my industry, the only industry I've got, so I should stand by it.

This year, though, I am limiting my book-buying to work-related volumes that are unavailable at the library, in the process realizing a savings of about 75 percent. I am also buying used books when possible. (*Mea maxima culpa,* Joy!) Now I hear these proud words from Gail, and the economic impact of lower consumption hits me directly in the royalty statement. Call me a hypocrite, but I resolve right there that I will not market *Not Buying It* with the slogan "Don't Buy This Book."

MAY 28

A. Zito & Sons, which for eighty years has been turning out chewy, crispy-crusted Italian loaves on Bleecker Street in Greenwich Village, announces it is closing. The culprits: a sharp rise in rent due to the gentrification of the neighborhood, and carbopho-bia created by the Atkins diet. If you're a neighborhood, you *can* be too rich or too thin.

MAY 30

Flavio, Ann, the kids, and I visit Emily, an artist who lives in a loft on a dark street in a gentrifying industrial neighborhood next to a vast tract of housing projects. The conditions are ideal for crime. The gentry and the poor are living cheek by jowl. Public services that were never much good in the poor section have not caught up with the residential needs in the gentrifying one, either. There are few working streetlights, and police coverage is spotty at best. This being Sunday night of Memorial Day weekend, it's even spot-tier.

We come out of the house with the dregs of a picnic, climb into the car, and strap the kids in. The car doesn't start. Flavio gets out and looks under the hood. The battery has been stolen. Nothing can be done tonight, so we trudge up the hill to the F train.

No sooner have we settled into our seats than a homeless man enters the car dragging a huge canvas mail cart, most likely filched from the loading docks of the main Brooklyn branch of the post office just a few blocks away. Clownlike, the man starts pulling an incongruous collection of items from the depths of the cart. "Software, software! Got your Windows XP, right here, right now," he barks.

Wanting no software, we look away from him and talk to each other. But he's not giving up. He plants himself directly before us. For two bucks apiece, kids admitted free, we've bought front-row seats for a little piece of New York street theater.

"Get it right here, right now!" He holds up a slightly bent luggage cart, then a Cabbage Patch doll wearing one shoe. "We're here to treat you, not cheat you." The "we" is a nice touch, as if he were the sales rep covering the underground-tunnel territory for a large retailer. "Treat you, not beat you," he sings. On the "beat you" he whips out a spatula and spins it toward me.

"No, thank you," I say. "I have a spatula." I don't tell him I'm conducting an experiment in not buying anything. It seems impolite.

"Do you have a car battery?" Flavio asks. We all laugh.

"Lost your battery?" the man says, concerned.

"Stolen."

The guy shakes his head. "They some damn muh'fuckers, ain't they? You can't have a car in New York, but they goes and takes it." In New York as elsewhere, people who steal your car battery, or your car, are commonly referred to as They. For the moment, this guy is one of Us.

"Dishonor among thieves," I remark to Flavio as our subway salesman's head dips below the rim of the bag.

"Dang, I just *had* a battery, too," he says, emerging with a little fuzz in his hair. "Just had a couple last week. Coulda gotchoo a good price, too." I'm waiting for him to give Flavio a business card and ask him to call next week.

Paul and I have observed the workings of this microeconomy before, when my own car was broken into on our block and the radio stolen. Paul traveled out to Coney Island, where Russian immigrant peddlers just one step up from the pushcart erect plastic-tarp booths beside the boardwalk and sell new and used car parts and accessories. Their suppliers are freelance. As Paul stood haggling with a merchant, a kid of about twelve approached wielding two shopping bags loaded with car radios. The merchant waved him off, mouthing "Not now!" then turned to Paul and pressed on bargaining. The kid melted away, seeking another buyer.

Paul ended up purchasing a previously owned radio very much like mine for $25. I had bought my own radio in a used-parts shop on Canal Street, a few retailing rungs above the Russian booth, for $50. So I was, in effect, getting a formerly owned radio for a total of $75. I was also indirectly profiting off the poor schmuck whose radio ended up in Coney Island courtesy of some underage shopping-bag-carrying middleman.

A few weeks later, perusing the wares laid out by a guy resembling our subway salesman on a blanket on Astor Place in the East Village (size 14 satin pumps, one-handed alarm clock), I spied yet another nearly identical radio. I wondered for a moment if it might be my own used and stolen radio, perhaps resold and reinstalled, re-stolen, and about to be sold again. On this tertiary appropriated-goods market, the price was an irresistible $10.

I met an economist at Harvard who argues that government and corporate corruption is a fundamental part of all economies, along with black markets and other underground commerce. Needless to say, such sectors flourish where necessities, whether material, social, or political, are scarce. So illicit drugs are among the biggest businesses in the world, right up with weapons and oil. Weapons sales are counted in the GDP, as are narcotics agencies and opium defoliants; oil prices are controlled by spectacularly wealthy oligarchs living off the subjugation of their people. Where do beggar salesmen and radio thieves fit into the political economy? Are they saving the taxpayer money? Creating employment, albeit self-employment? Compensating for gaps in the supply chain?

The subway showman now has us all engaged. He's trying to

interest Lucia in a Beanie Baby spider that looks as if it has been worked over by a gang of Beanie Baby flies. Lucia laughs shyly and declines, so he rummages in the bag and pulls out a video game, which he shows Emilio. "Cheat you, son, not beat you!" Emilio, who at four has never played a video game, raises his palms in a "don't ask me" gesture, which makes Ann and me giggle. All this inspires Flavio to fish a dollar from his pocket, payment for the entertainment and perhaps a bribe to end the show (it doesn't work).

Soon we pull into our stop. As we rise, I peek into the cart and notice a pile of ragged hardcover books at the bottom. Too bad I don't have time to look through them. He might have a book on silk-flower crafts in there, or maybe *The Gift,* by Marcel Mauss. I hand him a dollar, too.

"Thank you," he says. "Now y'all get home safe." It's a valediction homeless beggars often extend to their donors. This man is a performance artist, an entrepreneur, a working stiff still on the job at 9 P.M. on the Sunday of Memorial Day weekend. Whatever else you can say about him, he is moving goods and currency through the economy. By all rights, I ought to be able to wish him home safe, too.

True or false: The government can't do anything right. Markets are rational. Art is a luxury. Scarcity is inevitable. We're here to treat you, not beat you.

JUNE

Redistribution of Wealth

JUNE 2

Paul is at the kitchen table, surrounded by doves, storks, hippopotami, dinosaurs, pigs, lilies, and roses. They are all made of recycled typing paper. Defeated by the Great Silk Flower Book Heist, he has moved on to origami for Sarah's present. The library has an abundance of origami books.

Hippo looks a lot like Dinosaur, which resembles Pig. The rose could be mistaken for an artichoke. I'm not thrilled with any of them. "I dunno about origami," I say, as Paul contemplates the pattern for Bull (a cross between Dinosaur and Rose/Artichoke). "It looks"—I search for the word—"*chintzy.*"

Chintzy, aka cheap. Not sufficiently expensive. I'm worried that we won't be able to make anything that is substantial enough. For if it is hard to have fun without consuming or conviviality without consuming or status or a job or even an identity without consuming, it is really hard to give a major gift without consuming. Paper, no matter how lovingly folded, doesn't show enough love because it doesn't cost enough.

It's funny. Our family is pretty nonchalant about gifts. We celebrate few holidays; even birthday cards are exchanged irregularly. I know Sarah will be happy with anything we give her, including our company. And yet I don't think I'm imagining that a bunch of paper artichokes from her fifty-plus-year-old aunt and uncle will seem stingy.

Every exchange, says Simmel, is an "exchanges of sacrifices." How much can we, should we, sacrifice for Sarah? It sure would be easier to pick out a set of luggage at Macy's.

Paul pushes his creased-paper creations to one side of the table to make room for the dinner dishes. I flick a dove from my chair onto the floor.

"Okay, so *you* make a suggestion," he says, fed up.

I'm clueless. "Something . . . bigger?"

Paul pouts, piling the paper animals as in a pyre. I am calling his sacrifice puny.

JUNE 4

Prudence e-mails from work. Two comps to the Mark Morris dance company—orchestra seats—have come across her desk. She can't use them. Can Paul and I? *Can we use them?!* A couple of months ago, Ann's friend couldn't make it to *King Lear* at Lincoln Center. She offered me the ticket. Could I refuse?

Vanalyne, in town from Chicago, buys me three sachets from a shop on Smith Street, infused with some mixture of herbs that makes me want to lie down naked in my underwear drawer. When I protest—no things, please!—she insists. It's been six months since I've had "a luxury," she says. I deserve it.

Jack, a psychoanalyst, suggests we have dinner at a Chinese restaurant near his apartment. I wager he will pick up the tab, and sure enough, when we've finished the meal he offers to. I don't refuse. Then, emboldened by his profession and a beer, I confess my secret. He finds it amusing. When we part at the corner, he says, "Call me any time you need an excuse to cheat." Jack is a sweet, gracious guy, the dinner is inexpensive, and at any other time I wouldn't think twice about his kindness. Now I feel I've conned him.

Paul and I can't stop our friends from being generous. Many of them don't have more money than we do. All of them work as hard as we do. We've taken on this project not out of necessity but as an experiment—you might say, on a lark. Still, they offer and offer, as if we were deprived. And, being polite, we don't refuse.

Being polite, actually, we could refuse. But here's another part of the story. We (or I) don't want to refuse. It is more blessed to give than to receive. But I gotta tell you, when you're not buying anything, an evening with Mark Morris or General Tso is a blessing, too.

It's no wonder we're confused. All our lives, we've been operating in the market system. This year we withdrew to its margins in order to observe its workings. But we remain in the gears of the machine, and our personal transactions are lubricated by the familiarity of its rules.

As time goes by, though, I'm realizing that we have gotten enmeshed in another system: gift exchange. Like all exchanges, gift-giving operates in a social context; it has social codes, rules. The trouble is, in our market culture the rules of gift exchanges are ambiguous and covert, and the values upon which they rest are held in ambivalent esteem. When in doubt, *Homo Economicus*—operating in isolation, in rational self-interest, relating not to a culture but to a marketplace—returns to the marketplace to get his bearings. He values everything and everyone in dollars, "commodifies" even those things that are supposedly invaluable. What is she worth? Fifteen dollars an hour. How important is that country? It has a $300 billion economy. What's the value of Head Start? "Investing" a yearly $20,000 in a preschool child saves $40,000 a year in preventing his imprisonment two decades from now.

And how do you mark a major *rite de passage?* You go to Macy's with a high-limit credit card.

Some cultures have explicit gift economies. In them, giving is also self-interested, gifts have value, too, wrote the French anthropologist Marcel Mauss in 1950, in his signal essay, "The Gift." But the rules that govern those interests and lend value to those things are not material. They are moral. Gifts may be symbolic objects, such as cowrie shells, that have no intrinsic use or monetary value. Yet socially, their value is central. Even in those gift economies that also barter or trade for money or goods, gifts are the currency that glues the society together and establishes or overturns hierarchies of status and power.

How do we give, how do we receive? The questions may be alien to the utilitarian Economic Man, but the social powers and moral obligations that are explicit in gift economies reverberate through our marketplace society. We still honor big occasions with gifts, like ours to Sarah. And we try to follow the rules, ambiguous and covert though they are. We know, for instance, that the wealthier the giver compared with the recipient, the more he is obliged to give. Paul and I can't offer Sarah a pile of paper.

The laws that govern gifts in our society tend to sever giver from gift, underscoring the finality of the transfer. Legally, for example, a testator or philanthropist relinquishes control over his bequest once it is given. If the donor wants a piece of land kept wild and the recipient wants to develop it, a judge will rule in the recipient's—that is, the new *owner's*—favor. Still, giving is not without recompense, nor receiving without loss. Bill Gates distributes a portion of his gold to immunize the world's poorest children. In so doing, he transforms himself from wunderkind-turned-mogul (with a dicey record of labor and corporate practices and a ludicrously big house) into a prince of peace. His largesse makes him *large* in the French sense—generous, far-seeing, a great man.

Giving always establishes a relationship, with its own moral and emotional ties. And whatever the relationship between giver and recipient, whatever the gift, from mother's milk to seashell, college endowment to promise of heavenly redemption, he who gives dominates.

This year Paul and I can give nothing. We are not only stingy but powerless. Yet, self-interested children of the marketplace, we (or I) can't quite give up getting. We are caught between value systems, between roles in our own system.

Sometimes I feel like a mendicant Buddhist among Calvinists. Other times, as a Jew, I know I what I am: a *schnorrer,* the kind of person who always happens to drop by just when supper is being put on the table.

JUNE 6

I meet Debbie (the editor who suggested the "Don't buy, don't tell" policy back in February) for a picnic in Hudson River Park. I've made a lentil salad and crudités and have brought some baba ghanoush that Paul made from scratch. Debbie carries a Zabar's bag of fancy cheeses and crackers, gourmet cookies and chocolate. I suspect she is overdoing it with the delicacies, since, poor me, I don't get out much.

We walk around the Chelsea Piers looking at the yachts. Their prestige, like that of penises, is measured in length and girth.

Debbie tells me that when she and her husband broke up and sold their summer house, they gave their small sailboat to her brother. About a year later, her brother sold the boat and bought a bigger one. She felt uncomfortable about it.

"He was breaking the code of gift exchanges," I say. Gifts are scrutinized and compared for their monetary value (the size of the engagement "rock" indicates the degree of the groom's love for the bride and predicts the richness of the marriage), but the value of the gift is not supposed to be actively transformed into money. "I can send you a bunch of flowers in the hospital, but I can't send you the twenty bucks the flowers would cost," I explain to Debbie. "And you can't sell those flowers to the uncle of the woman in the next bed because he forgot to bring his own."

"Ah-ha!" exclaims Debbie. Her husband thought she was being sentimental about the boat, "but I didn't care about the boat. I just felt queasy about his selling it."

We stroll away from the river and into the streets of the Village. Soon, we find ourselves on Thirteenth Street approaching the Quad movie theater.

"Hey, let's go to a movie," says Debbie. "I'll pay for you."

"No, no. You don't have to do that." It's hard to know which is more wearisome, saying yes or saying no.

"I know I don't have to. I want to," she responds.

Again, I demur. I know Deb is sensitive to the subtleties of the gift exchange, so after a few paces, I say, "Tell me why you want to do this. Do you feel sorry for me?"

"No," she answers.

"Do you think I *should* go to a movie? Like maybe I need one?"

"Of course not." She waves her hand in dismissal. "No big deal," she adds.

But I press on. "Do you want to go to the movie because you're bored with me?"

She feigns a look of exasperation.

"Do you want to give me a present?"

"No!" she exclaims. We both laugh at my persistence. "I just thought it would be nice." She pauses. "I just wanted to go to a movie."

I give her an apologetic look.

"I wanted to go to a movie *with you*," she says with mocking niceness, and a laugh. "But since you're not allowed to, according to your rules, I figured I'd just pay." Ugh, my rules.

So maybe Jonathan is wrong. I'm not boring. I am inconvenient, a costly inconvenience. "My rules" require that if they want to spend time with me doing anything fun, my friends have to buy me. Debbie and I compromise on a coffee, for which I "let" her pay.

Later, on the phone, I recount the exchange to Prudence, who is also a friend of Debbie's. She offers another theory: "When someone isn't shopping, it's as if a vacuum forms," she says. "You feel you have to rush in and fill it."

By not buying, Paul and I have mobilized a small army of surrogate consumers.

JUNE 7

We run out of Q-tips. I try to wash my ears with a washcloth but can't reach the sweet spot. Is impeccable ear hygiene a necessity?

JUNE 10

Paul receives an e-mail from a friend inviting him to join her "gifting circle":

June: Redistribution of Wealth

```
There are 3 gifting opportunities or stages in
the You've Got Friends Circle process—Prosperity,
Generosity and Abundance.

There are 15 individuals in each Circle. There is
1 BLESSED — 2 JOYS — 4 HOPES and 8 FRIENDSHIPS.
The Friendships are the new members coming into our
Circle who gift the person in the Blessed position.
```

Paul is troubled. "These 'gifting circles' are pyramid schemes," he tells me, and explains the marketing and investment con games that promise financial rewards to participants who bring in more recruits (say, each friend brings in six friends). The hitch is, they never inform new members that the odds of recovering their "investments" diminish radically with each concentric circle, since the circle must be complete before they get their money, and each circle grows geometrically larger.

He sends his friend the URL of a Web site that explains the ways people are burned by this specious form of generosity, which cloaks itself in the language of friendship, freedom, wisdom, women's empowerment, and the ever popular "new paradigm." The Web site also reports on the fraud and tax evasion cases being brought against the enterprises by states' attorneys general and the IRS. He feels bad, raining on her hopes, but also is praying she won't be too blessed out to pay attention.

We're leaving for Montana in two weeks. The origami corpses are still taking up most of the kitchen table. We are still agonizing over Sarah's gift. It's a welcome agony, to be sure, the privilege of generosity being ours for once. But we're getting down to the wire.

As I put two bowls of soup on the table, Paul strides into the kitchen, excited. "Hey, I have an idea. Why don't you give Sarah something you own that you love?"

"That's it!" I shout. A gift is a gift by virtue of being given, says the poet and anthropologist Lewis Hyde in his imaginative and generous book entitled, like Mauss's, *The Gift*. Hyde's thesis is not a tautology; rather, it describes what you might call the social physics of giving. The gift, he says, must perish for the giver so that it can it be reborn for the recipient. "A market exchange has an equilibrium or stasis: you pay to balance the scale." I approach the Green Bun Lady. I want a bun, she wants a dollar; we don't want a relationship. I give her the dollar, she gives me the bun. End of story. "But when you give a gift there is momentum, and the weight shifts from body to body."

"Perfect!" I say again. I mentally review my possessions. From body to body: jewelry. I open my Mexican wooden jewelry box (*Recuerdo*—"I remember"—is inlaid on the top, above a picture of a pony) and pull out a silver and turquoise Navaho necklace that my mother bought just after the war. Its design is an unusual cross between folk art and Art Deco, between antique and modern. In my twenties, I noticed Mom never wore the necklace, and asked for it. She gave it to me. Now I rarely wear it. It is tarnished, its clasp broken. It needs a new life.

I call my mother to ask if it's okay to give the necklace to Sarah. She doesn't quite remember it (so much for "lovingly handed down for generations"). Still, the piece is meaningful to me: it feels like an heirloom. Plus, the blue will bring out the color of Sarah's eyes.

In the next days I stitch a pouch out of a remnant of satin brocade and Paul carefully glues opalescent wrapping paper over a small cardboard box that has seen better days. He irons a sheet of wrinkled tissue paper to put inside, as well as a thick piece of grosgrain ribbon for the outside. I make a card. A friend of his fixes the catch and polishes the silver. We wrap the necklace in the paper and load it into the pouch, which we lay in the box. It looks like a small coffin.

JUNE 24

I have paid off my credit card—$7,956.21! I will announce my achievement tonight at Voluntary Simplicity, Paul's and my last meeting before decamping for Vermont. I have to say, I'm proud of myself.

Since the group last gathered, some things have changed, some remain the same. Elisa has a new job in a college library. Lionel's wife has lost her job. One household in fresh crisis; unemployment trends flat. In spite of his wife's plight, Lionel is still lobbying for the big refrigerator. I write in my notebook, *Can this marriage be saved?*

We're not supposed to get to Spirituality until the last meeting, but the theme finds its way constantly into our conversations. For lack of better analysis (or evidence), the group (minus me) has faith that things work out—jobs will be found, budgets will balance, Dana's clutter will go in its own time. Lionel, who says he has been conversing frequently with God, declares that "the universe is bountiful."

Unable to keep my mouth shut, I say, "I don't know if the universe is bountiful or not. But the U.S. government and the multinational corporation sure ain't."

This throws us into a series of doctrinal disputes. Is or is not the universe bountiful? Will the meek inherit the earth (they haven't yet, I mutter). Irwin, always eager to assume blame, hedges our bets by quoting his mother: "God helps those who help themselves."

Another debate: is there anything fundamentally wrong with being rich? Voluntary Simplicity is ambivalent on the matter. The movement may reject the obsessive accumulation of wealth, but it has nothing against the accumulation of wealth (remember Beryl's "wise investments"?). The debate advances: might a camel, under certain circumstances, be capable of passing through the eye of a needle?

JUNE 25

Paul and I take public transportation to the airport. A nervous traveler, I am biting my nails as the bus pushes its way like a balloon catheter through the clogged arteries of Queens, stopping every block to disgorge a fatty clot of schoolchildren. I'm carrying a sack of cold remedies, a product category of which I am a devoted consumer. Before getting on the plane, I take two ginger root capsules, a natural preventive for airsickness. I also appear to have the flu. My head is exploding and I feel nauseated before even stepping onto the aircraft.

Paul has made our supper: mozzarella and homemade pesto with mushroom-onion relish on Italian bread from Caputo's, a local deli, and an apple for each of us. It's bound to be better than the airline "food," if there is any. As soon as we've reached cruising altitude the stewardess offers a snack in a box, and, indeed, it is the typical balanced airline meal of one flat slice of orange cheese and one of beige meat on a roll that is somewhere between the two in color. There's also a bag of multigrain Sun

Chips and a brownie. I guess I'm hungrier than I thought, or hungry for anything commercially produced and served, so I gobble down the sandwich, which is about as tasty as the cardboard box. When Paul takes out our lovely supper, I'm too full and sick to eat.

In the Denver airport, I buy a pack of Dentyne Ice gum to quell my nausea. It costs $1.49 and is the first candy I've bought in five months. It's medicine, I tell myself, but now I feel guilty in addition to ill.

On the next leg of the flight, from Denver to Bozeman, we are seated in front of a mother and son who are discussing the sporting life.

First, fishing. "You pay the guide seventy bucks for the Gallatin, but it's totally worth it. He totally knows the river."

"I think I paid $85."

"Still totally worth it."

"Totally."

. . .

"Corky has the Patagonia waders, right?"

"No, I think he bought the Simms." (These cost $400 a pair.)

"I like the Simms, but the Patagonia fit me better."

"Simms has a new winter kind that are warm but light."

"Yeah, I'm thinking of getting some of those. I heard they're awesome."

Cycling:

"They have a color in the titanium that I really love."

"I like the silver, but I hope it's brushed, not polished."

"I like the polished."

"So, are you going for the custom?"

"It's only about $200 or $300 more, so really, why not?"

"What do they run, all together?"

"A bit under six." Thousand, that is.

They discuss hiking, climbing, skiing . . . gear. They speak of almost nothing else during the two-hour trip.

My brother, Jon, who has come to Bozeman with his girlfriend, Beth, picks us up at the airport and drives us to the Days Inn, about a hundred yards off the interstate.

The receptionist takes Paul's credit card and hands him the keycards. She gives us chits for free breakfasts during our stay. "There you go!" she chirps.

Paul looks at the thin envelope and glances around the small lobby. "So are you going to tell us about the amenities?"

The girl, who apparently had not read the hotel's Web site promising said amenities, remains cheerful. "We don't have any amenities," she says.

"Oh," replies Paul. I look at Jon. We both try not to laugh. Paul and I have decided that the trip is a hiatus in our spending hiatus—after all, we're staying in a hotel, eating in restaurants. But we haven't discussed the rules governing any of these transactions. I didn't rent a car, having counted at least three vehicles in our party of six. But since the project's principal aim was never frugality, I didn't seek out the barest-bones motel in town. This fact becomes obvious when I get a glimpse of the place next door. Its name is something like Little Dogie's Inn, and the rusticated exterior suggests the innkeeper hands you a flea-infested blanket and a tin plate and leaves you to bed down by the glow of the Coke machine.

Still, I've acquired the skinflint's instinct and have unwittingly chosen the second-barest-bones motel in town. "Okay," says Paul, as if to comfort the girl. "Thank you, then."

But our insufficiently disguised disappointment has affected her. In the hopefully interrogative tone of America's young, she offers an amenity: "We have ice?"

June: Redistribution of Wealth

JUNE 26

We are to gather at Sarah's at eleven to go to the campus, and Paul and I have told my brother we will walk the couple of miles there. After a free breakfast of eggs, toast, and coffee (which isn't bad), we take off for a stroll downtown.

It is hard to stroll on a four-lane strip where sidewalks are an afterthought, which makes it hard to stroll in almost any American town west of Philadelphia. *Get your own goddamn car:* that's the message. Here in Bozeman, you get the impression that strolling is considered effete, vaguely European—unpatriotic and maybe illegal. Like pedestrian versions of John Cheever's Swimmer, we navigate from parking lot to parking lot, dodging pickups and SUVs, hopping curbs onto small rectangles of yellowing grass.

After a semi-harrowing half hour, we make it to the edge of downtown Bozeman. Finally, sidewalks—and around them, a beautifully preserved turn-of-the-century Western town. Bozeman's main street is wide, flanked by two- and three-story red brick buildings, which are flourished with the fancywork of nineteenth-century bricklayers and an occasional neon cowboy boot, bronco, or lasso. From the main street, leafy side streets stretch toward snowcapped mountains; on these boulevards, gracious wood-frame houses preside over broad lawns and mature gardens.

Unfortunately, the mall-lined strips also stretch toward those mountains, pouring out in every direction like the rivulets of an oil spill. Along them can be found every fast-food joint and big-box store ever conceived, and nothing else. As I said, it's the typical Western town.

Paul and I pass a Tibetan store in a little gray clapboard house. "Okay if we go in?" I ask.

"Okay with me," he says, and we remove our shoes on the porch. I browse, breathing the incense. I almost try on a pair of cotton pants that look just right, but I refrain. The rugs (on sale today) are thick underfoot; the prayer flags flutter in the half-open windows. It's a meditative space for purchasing. But I only breathe, I do not buy. A little sorry, I say goodbye to those just-right cotton pants.

A few doors down we reach Sack's, a thrift shop that Sarah's mother, Amy, has told us about. She bought the kids clothes here during the years she lived in Bozeman with one or both of them. A sign by the door informs us that profits go to preventing domestic violence and serving its victims. I look hopefully from the sign to Paul, as if to ask permission. For the graduation, I am wearing my green-checked pants, which once looked fashionably odd and fit well and now are baggy at the knees and faded from washing. Maybe I'll find something to change into. He says nothing. We go in.

As I begin to move methodically through the racks, Paul hangs back, fingering an item of clothing here and there. I duck into the dressing room with a sleeveless shirt. The first thing I notice under the fluorescent lights is that my armpits are saggy. When did that happen? (The good thing about not buying clothes is that you don't have to engage in the level of microscopic self-inspection the activity promotes.) I feel disgusted with myself. Out on the floor again, I recover: in no time I am clutching an adobe-colored long-sleeved shirt and a pair of baggy red cargo pants. "I'm going to try these on," I tell Paul, again asking permission, but also defying it.

"Go ahead if you want to," he says in a neutral tone I interpret as disapproval.

I try on both items. They fit well and look good. I can't wear them to the graduation, but I know I'll wear them a lot. "What do you think?" I ask Paul, coming out of the dressing room in my "new" clothes.

"They're fine," he says. "Buy them if you want . . . But, you know"—I brace myself—"the rules haven't changed. We're here for Sarah's graduation. We're not on vacation from not buying."

"No," I say, more emphatically than I mean. "We are. We're on moratorium." Paul and I go back and forth about this. "Anyway, I have nothing to wear."

"That's just the story you're telling yourself," Paul says. "Something else is going on." This always makes me angry, when he informs me I'm telling myself a story. But we're both surprised at how upset I have become, and how quickly.

"Don't tell me something else is going on. What's going on is going on. I have no clothes. It's spring. I have nothing to wear." By now I'm shouting (albeit in whispers). My voice is shaking. He's right. Something else must be going on.

In fact, I have been looking forward to this weekend as a furlough from active duty. And now, having opened myself even gingerly to the small dramas of shopping, the disappointment and triumph, the self-criticism and self-affirmation, I'm like a soldier tasting my first home-cooked meal: I could weep. These feelings may be false consciousness cynically produced by consumer culture. But retail therapy is also therapeutic.

Or maybe I want to break the rules. Shopping is not only socially sanctioned, it is a socially sanctioned "bad" behavior. Ricky catches Lucy with a spree-ful of shopping bags and asks her with a wicked gleam in his eye if she has been bad. The pleasurable tension mounts. She is asking for punishment; he is warming up to give it to her. The scene is almost an S&M assignation. The luxury car ads invite the consumer to wallow in badness. Below the burnished image of a Jaguar XJ8L, a creamy description of its leather seats and teak dashboard climaxes with, "Sin No. 2: GREED. Can you resist?"

The Deadly Sins give the economy life; transgression turns it on. By refraining from shopping I may be transgressing against the consumer economy, but where transgression pays, the consumer economy is one step ahead of me.

As I continue to shop, Paul repairs to an armchair in the front room, in which the cashier is surrounded by crockery and old appliances. I try on a half-dozen more things, put them back, then march into the room and approach the counter with the adobe shirt and the red pants. The bill comes to just under $9. Proceeds after operating expenses go to a good cause. I'm not consuming new resources. It's an efficient, rational market exchange and a gift in motion. If I had to lapse, I've come to the right place: a truly anticonsumerist consumer opportunity, a place to transgress virtuously.

"I did it," I announce to Paul, almost proudly. I notice he's taking notes in his Palm Pilot. "What are you writing about?"

"None of your business."

I try to read the screen. "You're writing about our argument."

"What's it to you?" He shuts the cover, stands, and hugs me as I am stuffing the recycled red plastic bag into my backpack. I don't want anyone to see it. But secretly, I can't wait to put the clothes on.

When we get to Sarah's, I take her aside and give her the gift. As she lifts it from its little coffin, it's as if the necklace is resurrected. The silver casts light on Sarah's face. She smiles, her eyes wide. She reads the card, which tells her it was my mother's and mine and now hers, and maybe (I've written) someday will be her daughter's. "Oh, Judy, that's soooo sweet," she coos. I close the clasp at the back of her neck and she goes into the bathroom to admire herself in the mirror. She comes out beaming, clearly moved. "Now I can have a little of Judy and Grandma with me wherever I go!" Sarah knows how to give back.

JUNE 27

Real Montanans may not walk, but, boy, do they hike. And Amy, who now lives in northern California, is a hiker. She and her Bozeman friends know every trail in the vicinity, and since today is the first day out of the tunnel of my cold, Amy and two of her friends pick Paul and me up to trek one of them. My nephew, Jacob, arrives looking sleepy but game. We've decided on a hike in the Gallatin range, from the Middle Cottonwood Trail to the Foothills Trail to Sipes Canyon, which should take about four hours.

We drive up the canyon to a trailhead at the sparse end of a subdivision. Even as a small boy, Jacob was a mountain goat; now he's long, skinny, and effortlessly swift. He and I move ahead of the group. We climb up a long dry riverbed into the trees. The sun is hot, but there are still patches of snow underfoot, with yellow glacier lilies peeking through them, and blue lupine and larkspur in the warmer spots. We all pause in a grove at the top of the first long rise and share a bar of Belgian chocolate. Paul and I are enraptured by both the view and the refreshments.

Carefully treading a foot-wide path on the edge of a cliff, we wedge ourselves into the mountainside to let pass two men riding their bikes down the trail. When we reach the other side of the ridge, we encounter other cyclists coming up. The grade is steep.

Not easy hiking, this is some tough biking, and the cyclists are sweating hard under the much hotter sun on this side of the ridge. They look miserable.

That is, their faces do. The rest of them looks grand. All are dressed in spanking-new mountain-biking shirts and shorts of cycling-specific wicking fabrics. Their shoes, helmets, and gloves are also made for mountain biking. On their backs they carry close-fitting camel packs, designed to let them sip water without stopping, God forbid, to rest. Their bikes are also brand new, feather light yet fully loaded to absorb all shocks. They and their bicycles are festooned with electronics to monitor speed, calories, heart rate, and distance.

Theirs is a species of consumerism that Douglas B. Holt, a professor of advertising at the University of Illinois, calls postmodern. In the postmodern marketplace "the 'good life' is not a matter of having a well-defined list of status goods," he writes. "Instead, it is an open-ended project of self-creation. The idea is to circulate continually through new experiences, things, and meanings, to play with different identities by consuming the goods and services associated with those identities."

On this mountain track, the identity is extreme athlete, the experience is extreme duress, and the accoutrements are extremely expensive and extremely high tech. Holt describes this self-creation as a kind of play, but it looks like work to me. Nor is there anything playful about the codes that govern it. Just as an unwritten law prohibits travel without a car in the valley below, up here travel on an ordinary old mountain bike (or ordinary old feet) in an ordinary T-shirt is only condescendingly tolerated.

As we drive back down the canyon through the looping lanes of subdivisions that were once thousand-acre ranches, Amy's friend Linda tells us that the people in these houses have been battling the village for years over water. Not only is the area undergoing fast population growth, but each new resident is using up a lot more water than a resident might have done even five years ago. To make matters worse, the region has been plagued by drought on and off for a decade. As I walked with Linda near the peak of one of the mountains we traversed, she pointed out the signs of stress on the needles of a species of evergreen that is nearing extinction. At this lower elevation the natural landscape is mostly brown and yellow. Yet each McMansion stands on a square of brilliant green, sparkling under the sprinklers.

Economists and marketers tend to define consumption narrowly and technically, as the act of exchanging money for things or services. Consumption is what happens at the "point of purchase"—the supermarket, stockyard, or doctor's office. But environmentalists want a more literal definition: the *using up* of valuable and finite things, including the natural resources that go into production: ore, oil, soils.

Another, less often named valuable thing that can be consumed by consumption is social harmony. Proponents of free markets, such as those at the World Bank, stress their democratizing effects. But as consumption increases, so does competition for the resources that support it. This can lead to corruption and violence. Oil is a cause of war. So is water.

Pretechnological societies fought over resources, too. But their cosmologies also recognized the limits of those resources. The animals, fish, plants, and rain were gifts. They demanded stewardship, stint, and sacrificial gifts in return. By contrast, the grand chateaux of Bozeman, with their dishwashers churning, their many bathtubs and thirsty lawns sucking out a parched water table, exemplify the self-interested economic system whose only imperative is to grow.

Are these houses serving utilitarian ends? In 1798 Jeremy Bentham, the philosopher and founder of utilitarianism, defined utility as "that property in any object whereby it tends to produce benefit, advance, pleasure, good, or happiness [or] to prevent the happening of mischief, pain, evil, or unhappiness." Surely, these houses produce benefit, advance, pleasure, and happiness—for a few. But when the moving gifts of beauty and sustenance are hoarded, halted in their progress, their power is perverted.

I watch the vapor rising from the sprinklers and turning to rainbows in the late-day sun. A miasma of mischief, pain, and unhappiness, it is deceptively lovely to look at.

At around seven, Jon and Beth, Amy, her second (now ex-) husband, Jeff, Jacob, Paul, and I meet at Plonk, a tapas and wine bar where Jake's best friend has been hired as temporary executive chef. Waiting for Sarah, we settle into cushy, burgundy velveteen banquettes and easy chairs around a low table. The place is too fussy by half, the art slick, the bathrooms tiled to a fare-thee-well. But having loitered for a half-year outside the precincts of commerce, where taste is constantly and anxiously recalibrated, I find Plonk comfortable, even glamorous.

No one is looking at the prices; we're just ordering a plate of this, a bottle of that. I'm tired from the hike, relaxed after a hot shower and a nap, woozy from the good Cabernet mingling with the antihistamines that are still in my bloodstream. Jake's friend Matt is sending plates up from the kitchen, on the house. I sink into the cushion beside my brother.

Sarah arrives on the arm of a Santa Barbara surfer who is crashing at the house for the weekend. Their flirtation has advanced since yesterday, and she is looking flushed and pretty. On her smooth, tanned chest is the necklace.

We eat, drink, and grow merrier with each bottle of wine. More friends arrive with embraces and congratulations. Gifts move around.

Structural Adjustments

JULY 1

There's a new reality show this month called *Amish in the City*. In it five young members of the ascetic sect are brought to the fleshpots of Los Angeles to test their religious convictions. It's not an altogether artificial test. At sixteen, every Amish kid gets a "rumspringa," a "season of running around" before opting (or not) to be rebaptized into an adult life devoted to God. The show ups the ante by supplying the rumspringers with temptation and idolatry, in the form of everything from bikinis to veganism, and providing them with a team of buff and fluffy Angelenos to aid in their debauchery.

Paul and I have spent our spring as Amish in the City, too, but without the rum. As we've traveled the fast lane at horse-drawn speeds, we've (pretty much) withstood temptation and evaded debauchery. The last week in New York presented one of the year's toughest challenges: I refrained from seeing the politico-pop phenomenon *Fahrenheit 9/11*. More than removed from American culture, I felt I was observing it from Ulan Bator.

So it is with relief that after a six-hour drive from New York to Vermont, I hear the car tires leave the pavement of North Main

Street at the edge of Hardwick village and hit the dirt of Bridgman Hill Road. The first crest of the hill is a threshold from twenty-first-century life to one that looks and feels more like it did fifty or even a hundred fifty years ago. At this boundary, an arched gateway of trees gives way to a vista of pastures that slope from the ridge road to the mountains in the distance. At night, the space closes to a headlight-illuminated tunnel. From the dark periphery the eyes of a fox or a skunk may glint, a frog may leap across the road. There is no sound but the crickets and the rubber on the dirt.

I roll down the car window and breathe in the perfume of cow manure and grass. Now, I think, I can relax. The lures of the marketplace, like the village streetlamps, grow distant in the rearview mirror.

JULY 2

But there is trouble in paradise.

Last week Hardwick's Zoning Board of Adjustment, which oversees land use and building in town, received a permit application from a Barre entrepreneur named Karl Rinker to build a telecommunications tower on Bridgman Hill. The tower's purpose is to enhance the reach of his region-wide pager service, but perhaps foreseeing the imminent obsolescence of pagers, Rinker also promises to improve the town's fire, police, and rescue team communications systems, which now use siren, radio, and telephone. And while no cell phone company has shown interest in our small-fry market, he is also pitching the tower as Hardwick's launching pad to the future. To serve a town of three thousand, his drawings indicate space for six cell phone transmitters.

As proposed, Rinker's tower will rise from the upper pasture of

Wendell and Beverly Shepard's land, the acres that comprise lower Bridgman Hill. The farmer and the builder have already signed a twenty-year lease with an option to renew.

Rinker's application calls for 180 feet of lattice-work aluminum bristling with horizontal and vertical antennae ("like a porcupine!" he will boast at more than one hearing). In addition, a 19-foot, 6-inch antenna extends from the tower's tip. The size of both tower and antenna, claims Rinker, are the minimum required to accomplish adequate transmission and reception. But it's hard not to notice a coincidence: Hardwick's zoning bylaws limit such a structure to 180 feet. Whether auxiliary equipment is included in this maximum allowable height will become a point of contention, but 199½ feet is just six inches shy of the height at which the Federal Aviation Authority requires a red light at the top, and the light is clearly prohibited by Hardwick's bylaws.

To a resident of Tokyo or Boston, 180 feet may not seem tall. But 180 feet dwarfs the highest tree or silo on the hill by about 120 feet. It is more than twice as high as any church steeple in the county. Although electric transmission, radio, and TV (and, increasingly, cell) towers prickle like voodoo pins from mountain ridges throughout the state, they are still rare in the Northeast Kingdom. You would have to travel to Montreal before you arrived at a human-built structure as high as the cell tower Karl Rinker wants to put up in a cow pasture on Bridgman Hill.

Enthusiasm for cell service is high in town. At the first public hearing, in June, Sandy Buck Howard, the owner of a cut-rate furniture business in the next town, Wolcott, rushed to be the first citizen to testify. The board had just completed Step 1 of the process: making sure Rinker has submitted all the necessary parts of the application. After that comes public testimony; review of scientific, economic, or legal documents; and finally, a decision. It will be complicated, and new to the board, which generally considers such matters as whether someone can open a hair parlor over her garage. But Sandy was impatient. "He meets all the requirements," she blurted. "Give him the permit."

Sandy is a champion of "business-friendly development" in Hardwick, which to her means restricting or even abolishing zoning. Wolcott has only recently adopted zoning, and Buck's Furniture is visible testament to an older, more libertarian time— and to her family's feelings about public land-use restrictions. In revenge against some now-forgotten town government offense, Sandy's father painted his formerly white, 40,000-square-foot sprawl of buildings brown with broad yellow and orange horizontal stripes. Wolcott, whose "downtown" is a pass-through on Route 15, is known to many as that village with the ugly brown and yellow buildings.

Not everyone in Hardwick wants the tower. At the first hearing, Karen Shaw, the organic dairy farmer next door to the Shepards, asked that the permit be rejected outright. She has brought the board evidence on the effects of electromagnetic emissions on people and animals. "We are trying to keep farming and have been there for twenty-five years," she said. "Reduced milk production and sick cows would put us out of business." Martha Zweig, a poet, talked rhapsodically about skiing and walking up Bridgman Hill. She noted that preserving the natural and agricultural landscape is one of the goals of the Town Plan, which the board is charged with taking into account.

But the federal Tele-Communications Act of 1996 may exclude Karen's testimony. The law does not permit the consideration of data on the health risks of emissions that are lower than those allowed by the Federal Communications Commission. (U.S.

allowable maxima are higher than those of any other country that has such standards.) In fact, under the TCA, Hardwick's Zoning Board doesn't have much wiggle room at all. It can put limits on the siting, size, and look of a tower, but it can't prohibit the building of a telecommunications facility.

I am sick with worry that the tower will go up. Paul has his own concerns. He is chair of the Zoning Board.

JULY 3

I usually drop about $40 on petunias and pansies, marigolds, lobelia, and nasturtium to fill the flower boxes on our deck. But this year I'm not buying annuals, which I have deemed inessential. Instead, I will plant Sungold cherry tomatoes and herbs—edible only, no ornamentals. Paul has already turned over the soil and put in the rest of the vegetables in the larger plot near my cabin, plus a dozen delicata squash plants in the field beside our raspberry patch. I weed my perennials and, to fill in the bare spots, drive around collecting whatever my friends are separating out of their gardens. It's a nice way to spend an afternoon, but the result can't compare with the immediate, bright-colored gratification of annuals in bloom.

On my way through town, I drop in at the co-op to pick up some milk and eggs. I'm wearing jeans with a split at the knee, a shirt that's now grimy with soil, and my rubber Muck shoes—the raiment of my Hardwick identity. My work clothes are battered but not artificially "distressed" or frayed at the edges like those pink-plaid rags-to-*richesse* Chanel blazers that are fashionable this year. Thorstein Veblen observed bourgeois wives displaying their husbands' wealth and their own indolence on their backs; he called it conspicuous consumption. This liberated unmarried cohabitator wears her labor, not her leisure, on her sleeve. In Hardwick, we esteem conspicuous parsimony.

My last stop is at Surfing Veggies Farm, run by a couple of original back-to-the-landers. The name remains apt: as in their pre-farming days, Louis and Annie still make time to hit the waves. Louis and I chat about the winter, and I tell him about how our project has been going in the city, meeting the challenges of non-consumption while locked into municipal systems of food distribution, energy delivery, and waste disposal—not to mention a social and cultural economy based on purchase. He suggests that I visit some people who are "really off the grid" for a glimpse of what it's like to consume absolutely nothing.

To me, Louis and Annie qualify as really off the grid. They power the farm with solar panels, plant according to the phases of the moon, and wash their clothes with a soapless homeopathic plastic ball, which, as I understand it, cleans the way crystals heal. On the other hand, they do not eschew all the things of this modern world. For instance, they do their faith-cleaning at the Village Laundramat. And as I'm loading a flat of organic Sungolds into the car, Louis asks if I've seen *Fahrenheit 9/11*. When I shake my head sadly, he tells me he and Annie are off to Montpelier to take it in tonight.

Back home, while I pat the mounds of soil up around the tomato seedlings, I reconsider Janice's proposal that documentaries be considered a necessity. I'm still using electric lights from dirty fuel sources. I haven't given up laundry soap. Why not balance my polluting with the soul-cleansing polemics of Michael Moore?

This makes me think again about my vegetable-flower distinction. Vegetables satisfy a primary (physical) need, flowers a "mere" aesthetic desire: that's the rationale. But why draw the line at cultivated vegetables (including eight exotic organic Asian greens, including three different mustards)? Why not forage for dandelions and gooseberries? Thoreau agonized over whether his beans had any more right to life than the weeds he hoed out of the rows. The following year he took the weeds' side. His disapproval of agriculture was echoed in his disdain for all extraneous human-made comforts, and his definition of extraneous was capacious. "A lady once offered me a mat," he sniffs in *Walden*, "but as I had no room to spare within the house, nor time to spare within or without to shake it, I declined it, preferring to wipe my feet on the sod before my door."

Come on, Henry. No room for a mat?

Come on, Judith. No room for pansies?

All art, said Georges Bataille, is luxury. Might beauty be a necessary luxury?

JULY 7

While looking around for an off-the-grid interview subject, I am reading *Radical Simplicity,* by the Vermont author and reformed weapons designer Jim Merkel. Radical Simplicity is one giant step along the simplifying spectrum, beyond downshifting, beyond making do without cable TV or Q-tips. At this end, the remedy for overconsumption starts to taste less like chamomile tea and feel more like do-it-yourself amputation.

The goal of Radical Simplicity is to conserve the earth's resources and do so equitably among its people, starting with one's own personal life. The simplifier starts by measuring her "ecological footprint," the Redefining Progress calculation of the amount of "nature" used to sustain any given life. Merkel pretty much promises his readers that their EFs will be closer to the

American average of 24 acres than the global fair share of 4.7. I take my pocket calculator to the rougher formulas in Chapter 6, entering our frequency of egg-eating and plane-riding, the square footage of our living space and volume of trash we throw out compared with our neighbors. Even with all our interstate travel, I discover that Paul and I subsist on 12 acres of nature apiece. That's half the American average, not too shoddy, but still two and a half times our ration.

To fit your size-24 foot into a more modest resource allocation, Merkel says you've got to cut back—radically—and recommends giving away your excess possessions, walking or cycling, not driving, growing not grocery-shopping, repairing not trashing. I'm sure there are tons, or at least pounds, of waste hiding in our "stocks"—the stuff we own—but I'm dragging my feet before undertaking the more refined formulae at the back of the book. Because to limn Paul's and my true EF, I will have to inventory, price, and weigh everything we own—food, clothing, furniture, and appliances, including the refrigerator.

Like Lionel in the Voluntary Simplicity group, I haven't looked into the back of the refrigerator for a long time. Now I'm supposed to *weigh* it? My reluctance gives me pause. If I'm too lazy to do even this, how will I get anywhere close to a 4.7-acre lifestyle?

JULY 12

Talk at the food co-op is almost unanimously anti-tower. Someone has put a petition on the counter, along with Xeroxed articles about harmful emissions and links between cell phone use and cancer. The page is full of signatures. Whenever Paul walks in the door, someone buttonholes him. He listens, then invites the person to testify at a public hearing. But Paul does not make up his mind before he knows all the facts. At home, the usually high piles of paper are even higher with reams of legal and scientific articles about radiation, wind stress, and FCC rules.

We're struggling. I can't refrain from asking him questions. Factual ones he answers. But he won't disclose his opinion, if he has one, and meets each query with the same answer: he has to use his judgment within the strictures of the law. This only inflames my desire to change his mind (if indeed it needs changing). Neither he nor I owned a cell phone until about six months ago, when both my parents' health worsened and my mother insisted she be able to contact me at any time. Now, we have one cell between us and rarely remember to carry it. I want to appeal to him as a noncellular citizen.

In Hardwick we don't carry the phone for the obvious reason: it wouldn't work. But even if there were service here, I don't know if we would use it. For one thing, no matter where you go in Hardwick or the neighboring towns of Greensboro or Walden, you are never more than ten minutes from home. For another, no tower shorter than about five hundred feet is likely to outwit the ripples of steep and wooded hills spliced by winding river valleys, a geography that defeats cell reception at every dip and turn. You might be five minutes from home but unable to sustain the three-minute conversation necessary to ascertain that yes, we need milk and no, we don't need bread, and okay, I'll pick up milk but not bread and how about the paper, too, yes the paper, too—without losing the signal. Around here smoke signals may be a more appropriate technology than ultrahigh-frequency electromagnetic waves.

"We don't need cell phones," says Angela, as she rings up my milk, bread, raisins, and dried split peas. Angela is one of numerous silken-haired, solstice-worshipping, yoga-practicing vegan earth daughters who work at the co-op, where Annie is the manager and pagan mother superior. "I moved to Hardwick to get away from all that, and I want to keep my daughter away from it, too." When I ask her what she means by "all that," Angela describes a sped-up, consumer goods–choked modernity whose soundtrack is television. When I come to Hardwick, I like to get away from all that, too.

Still there's another "all that" that I, and Angela and Jim Merkel, do want. The aesthetically pleasing recyclable glass half-gallon bottle of Strafford Farms milk and the hand-baked organic multigrain local-bakery bread that I've just packed into my canvas bag satisfy my desire for fresh, unadulterated nourishment, my commitment to supporting the local economy and sustainable agriculture, and my eagerness to stick it to General Foods in any small way I can. Yet each item cost four dollars, more than twice what I would pay for conventionally grown and distributed foods at the Grand Union.

Flavio, who along with Ann is converting a barn in northeastern New York State, has told me he adores walking to his neighbor Jamie's farmstand to buy organic vegetables. But Flavio understands that this politically correct and socially satisfying act depends on his own relative wealth and the flexibility of his life, and that the viability of the family farm next door depends on the growth of a community of urban gentry like himself who have made a weekend destination of this depressed area. Flavio also knows it's a process that is likely, eventually, to displace farmers like Jamie.

"You enjoy the bourgeois privilege of bohemianism," I say to Flavio. Angela and I enjoy it, too. We are all consumers, and like all consumption, bohemian consumption has its costs.

JULY 14

"How much do you think our refrigerator weighs?" I ask Paul. He looks puzzled, so I explain the Merkel system.

A practical man, Paul can't make sense of it. "You mean plastic is good, wood is bad?" He's alluding to one of our favorite ditties, from a skit performed at Bread & Puppet's annual Resurrection Circus. It goes like this:

> *Plastic or wood?*
> *Plastic or wood?*
> *Plastic is bad.*
> *Wood*
> *Is good.*

Paul continues: "According to this system, it would be better to build with plastic than with wood, because it's lighter."

"And better to use pine than hardwood," I add. "Even better, paper."

"Forget the granite countertops."

We move on to furniture. We agree that under the weight system, our iron bedstead in Brooklyn should go: it takes two people to lift in order to store the air conditioner underneath it at the end of the summer (and forget about the AC!). "No waterbeds. Water is very heavy," I contribute. Best, we conclude, to sleep on an air mattress.

What about appliances? Paul asks. New ones are lighter than old ones, though the old ones last longer. Does the system depreciate weight over time? I make a mental note to look this up in the book.

JULY 18

The gurus say you can simplify wherever you are. New York's dense settlement and exemplary public transportation enable us to live without our car, so our EF is about the same there as in Hardwick, where we heat with wood and reduce, repair, and recycle everything. But there are limits. If I were to take Merkel's counsel entirely to heart, I don't know how I'd fit the cucumber plants on the fire escape or explain to the co-op board about the compost heap on the stairway landing.

The problem is not just physical; it's metaphysical. Because at its heart, Radical Simplicity of the spiritual kind is a country thing. Virtually every simplicity primer quotes Thoreau's beautiful passage from *Walden,* "I went to the woods because I wished to live deliberately, to front only the essential facts of life, and see if I could not learn what it had to teach, and not, when I came to die, discover that I had not lived." My own feeling is that, avid naturalist though he was, Thoreau's own emphasis was more on the essential facts than on the woods. He conducted his experiment in rusticity with the intention of returning, vision clarified, to the fog of civilization.

The true role model for Radical Simplifiers is John Muir, the conservationist, nature writer, and cofounder, in 1892, of the Sierra Club. Muir, who is widely seen as the father of American environmentalism, would have had no trouble resisting the nineteenth-century equivalent of lime-green shoes or *Fahrenheit 9/11.* Indeed, it's hard to imagine him losing sleep over missing any movie. Although he maintained a wide circle of friends and political connections as high as the president of the United States, Muir's passionate attachments were to animals, trees, and rocks. The religious principle of human dominion over the earth disgusted him. "Well, I have precious little sympathy for the selfish propriety of civilized man," he once wrote, "and if a war of races should occur between the wild beasts and Lord Man, I would be tempted to sympathize with the bears." To Muir the preservation of human sanity resided in wild, not human, relations. For him and, he implied, for anyone, "Going to the mountains is going home."

The intention, or wish, to return to nature as an antidote to consumer culture is a strong strain in the simplicity movement. Michael Maniates calls it the "pastoral thesis of simplicity," but the notion of the innocence of the "primitive" has a long provenance in Western thought, going back at least as far as Rousseau. In the return-to-Eden narrative, the colonial European sets off into the jungle accompanied by a fleet of porters laden with steamer trunks, only to remove his safari suit in the heat, fall in love with the tribal ways (and maybe a tribal girl), and eventually "go native." The quintessential Simplicity Volunteer packs his Orvis flies, drives his SUV to the Sierras, and, standing alone in the stream with the hawks above and the trout below, confronts the essential facts and determines to sell the SUV, buy a bike, and change his life (he'll probably still need the Orvis flies).

Jim Merkel describes his own rite of passage, which took place on a thirteen-day hike over the Muir Trail in California. On Day 9, at the peak of Mount Whitney, Merkel sees a bear up a tree in pursuit of his hanging bag of food. The man is scared shitless. By Day 11, though, another close encounter of the ursine kind triggers a different reaction: "I felt a primal shiver, hairs on end," writes Merkel. "I was alive!" He reflects on his fear of nature, which he interprets as his fear of death—and confronts it. "Each rotted tree fed new life. I envisioned that I too could nourish life, even after physical death. My place in the big scheme of things was beginning to make more sense."

Today's Sunday *Times* Style section features a new demographic, which it calls Organic Professionals, or "Oppies," who are also looking for their place in the big scheme of things. But their place is not on the craggy edge of a bear-crawling mountain. It is, "ideally in, say, a spiffy new Ford Escape hybrid (nearly $3,500 more than a similarly equipped conventional model), or with a picturesque country house from the reign of George III that has been 'future-proofed,' that is, wired for eco-sensitive climate-control technologies not yet invented," says the article. If the Oppie lifestyle is kind to the earth, that's nice, but its main point is to be kind to the practitioner. Mary Evans, a literary agent quoted in the story, comments, "It doesn't just make me feel better, it makes *me* better." The owner of Rural Gourmet in Livingston, New York, believes "it's more spiritual and natural."

Like those in Hardwick, the longtime residents of exurban New York City are ambivalent about their new neighbors. In Livingston, all that spirituality has raised property values 50 percent, pricing many locals out of the market. In Columbia County, the cell tower's equivalent is a proposed concrete plant. The locals want the jobs. The newcomers are against the plant, as a polluter and a blight on the landscape.

JULY 27

Tonight all the folding chairs on the floor of the wood-paneled second-floor hearing room of the Memorial Building are taken; more people stand at the back and lean against the walls. According to the *Gazette,* thirty-five people are here for this, the second public hearing on the Rinker application, a big turnout for a Zoning Board meeting.

Rumor has it that Sandy Howard has been rallying support. A

few nights ago, driving up the hill after my swim in Nichols Pond, I noticed a half-dozen cars parked at the Shepards' place. All had American flags and yellow Support Our Troops stickers on their bumpers. My muscles, relaxed from my swim, tightened. Which was disturbing me most—my suspicion that there was a pro-tower strategy meeting going on and my fear that they were going to prevail? Or the growing mutual suspicion in town that has me conjuring conspiracies and thinking of my neighbors as They? And what about the stress at home, where I am railing and wailing against the tower, and Paul, impartial judge, is keeping his own counsel?

As the hearing starts, Karl Rinker is in the witness's seat facing the wooden table at which the seven-member board sits. He is a stocky man, his hairy forearms extending from a short-sleeved polo shirt, his dense waist pressing against the belt of his khaki shorts, on which is clipped one of his company's black pagers. His salesman's zeal shoots into the low-key, low-volume atmosphere like high-voltage sparks in a gray sky. Glad-handing and expansive, Rinker addresses all questions at length, referring frequently to the three-ring binder that contains his proposal. Paul listens without interrupting, taking notes. Other members ask for clarification.

Although he has no signed contracts with lessees, Rinker assures the board that if he builds it, they will come. He mentions again interest expressed by the town's emergency services. Again, he fails to name any interested cell company, of which two currently operate in the region. Asked by a board member whether a cell carrier could provide service beyond a two- to three-mile distance from the tower, he replies with confidence that it could go as far as Wolcott, five miles down the road. Except, of course, for the mountains—and, um, trees—that might get in the way.

When Rinker is finished, Paul calls witnesses. Every Bridgman Hill neighbor speaks against the tower. They are worried about their property values, their health, and the health of their live-stock. And they dread looking out the kitchen windows to see a monstrous metal thistle planted where only grasses and wildflow-ers now grow. Joe McCarthy's house is directly across from the proposed site. "I like where I live. It's beautiful up there. It's important that I live there for the rest of my life," he says. Joe has recently survived a near-fatal bout of cancer and has tried to change his life. I see him riding his bike up the hill every after-noon. Yet he seems almost resigned: "I know the service is neces-sary. I just don't want to look at it."

Suzanna Jones, a tall, soft-spoken resident of neighboring Walden, reviews the relevant clauses of the zoning bylaws and Town Plan, explicating how the tower would violate both the let-ter and the spirit of each. She asks that the application be rejected. She hands Paul the co-op petition, with almost two hundred sig-natures on it. When Angela from the co-op, who also lives in Walden, takes the stand, Sandy Howard calls from the audience that she shouldn't be allowed to testify because she's not a Hardwick resident. Paul informs Sandy that the law allows any interested party to testify. A few sentences later, Sandy interrupts again, and Paul calmly tells her she will have to leave if she can-not control herself.

Most of tonight's witnesses want the tower. And from their nods of affirmation whenever Rinker addresses a question, it's almost as if they want Karl Rinker personally. With the exception of Suzanna, Angela, Karen, and a few others, almost everyone feels that Hardwick not only desires cell phones, it needs them, and thus—though he has never promised he will deliver them—it needs Karl Rinker. Displaying a self-esteem deficiency to which struggling towns like Hardwick are susceptible, a number of speak-ers imply that it's a miracle Rinker showed up in this dump at all.

If we don't approve Rinker's application, witness after witness says, we will be left in the dust of history. Charles Sartell, whose family has lived in Hardwick for generations, predicts that his will be the last. "My children want to be part of the twenty-first century and they cannot achieve that here," he says. His kids are moving to another part of the state, where they can enjoy "the benefits" of modern life.

Wendell Shepard's son David testifies that his wife has a "recent disability" and needs a cell phone to contact him in case of emergency. Until such service is available, she will be confined to the house, unable to drive or work.

Susan Cross, who worked on the town ambulance for ten years, says there are dead spots between Hardwick and Morrisville where contact cannot be maintained with the hospital. She does not say if any patient has ever been harmed as a result of these occasional sputterings-out, but "even if only one life is saved by the cell tower," she asserts, "it's worth it."

Cell phones will preserve families, liberate disabled women, and save lives! In the face of these unassailable aims, those who plead for human or animal health or natural beauty are alarmists and Luddites, clinging to primitive illusions. Parroting corporate lobbyists and trickle-down economists, the plumbers, secretaries, and road crewmen of Hardwick extol the civic goodwill of private enterprise and call on their fellow citizens to demonstrate trust and gratitude to the town's would-be benefactor. "Give him the permit," cries Sandy Howard—meaning, all 199 and a half feet of what he wants.

After the hearing I stop on the steps to chat with Angela, who has her sleeping daughter in her arms. Then I drive up the hill. The sky is brilliant with stars. Paul stays with the board to continue the meeting. By the time he gets home, I am asleep.

Memories of Underdevelopment

JULY 30

"The best things in life aren't things," reads the bumper sticker on the red 1986 Toyota pickup truck at the bottom of the orchard. I park my car and walk up the hill, through a sprawl of apple, plum, and pear trees. I have come to the town of Adamant, a tangle of dirt roads and a clutch of buildings including a music school and a food co-op, to visit Richard Czaplinski, a man famous in these parts for occupying an ecological footprint the size of a hare's.

Richard, a tall, sinewy guy who looks fifteen years younger than his sixty-two years, welcomes me into his cabin through a porch hung with tools. He points out the handcrafted flail and the Austrian scythe. "Notice the straight snath," he says, referring to the scythe's long wooden handle. He picks up the implements and carries them outside, showing me how each one swings. The scythe, he says, allows the harvester to stand up straight (better for a man, like him, with a troublesome back). The flail, based on a design by his father, has no metal hinges; it rotates on interlocking rope loops, dropping grain onto a sheet as the chaff drifts off on the breeze. Richard grows his own rye and winnows it. He also buys fifty-pound sacks of wheat flour in addition to wheat berries, which he cracks himself. On the way inside, he points out his "fuel-sipping" porch lamps, recycled Volkswagen license-plate lights.

A tour of Richard's place reveals an abundance of similarly ingenious technologies—except, that is, an oil furnace, washing machine, dryer, television, microwave oven, blender, toaster, or refrigerator. "I'll show you the deep freeze," he says, opening a door in the floor and leading me down the steps to the root cellar, which maintains a constant temperature of 50 degrees. In it, Richard stores canned tomatoes ("Here's my spicy sauce"), ropes of garlic, potatoes, onions. He inventories his food for me: "I'm self-sufficient in potatoes—four kinds—dry corn and beans, greens, sprouts, cabbage, beets, rye, peppermint, basil, dill, thyme, apples, turnips, carrots, apple sauce, cider, jams, and apple butter. I buy oil, rice, eggs, yogurt, rolled oats, millet, soybeans, honey." He hunts deer and catches pickerel and crappie in Sodom Pond, across the road at the foot of the hill.

Fuel to run the small reading lights and computer comes from the sun, collected with photovoltaic panels and stored in four deep-cycle marine batteries. Richard recalls a period when his batteries were running down with inexplicable speed. The culprit turned out to be his pre-owned computer. He was keeping it on when not in use. "You know, by turning your computer off, you can save tens of dollars a year," he tells me, revealing the scale of his economies. Heat is also drawn from the sun: a large south-facing bay window of doubled recycled glass, and the sun photo-synthesized, or wood. Richard burns about two cords a year. Like the lumber for the 600-square-foot house, built in 1978, his firewood is cut on these eleven acres. Wood contributes to the cabin's aesthetic touches, too: the stair rail is a twisted, polished limb.

Nothing is wasted. A circulation system utilizes the wood stove to heat tub water and bring it back as reusable gray water. Soap shards are collected in a sack fashioned from a rag of an old sweatshirt, which hangs from the faucet for dishwashing. The tub is somebody's castoff, as is the piano. Clothes are thrift-store finds. "I bought a pair of leather shoes for a quarter fifteen years ago," says Richard proudly, "and I've been dancing in them ever since."

When it's time to lighten my own load, Richard leads me down a short, steep hill to the composting outhouse. I stick the little bandanna flag in a holder specially made for it, for privacy. The privacy flag, coupled with the open way Richard describes the function of this intimate space, offer a metaphor for the man himself. A reserved, precise person, Richard is also utterly uncensored about the details of his life, which he offers as an example in simple-living classes at the Vermont Earth Institute. From time to time, Richard explains, he removes the catch bucket from the outhouse and carries it to a pile in the woods, where the contents are composted for fertilizer. He informs me that he personally produces a cubic yard of shit a year. I have no way of knowing whether a cubic yard is a lot or little for one man, but I feel shy about asking.

About this time, the person Richard refers to as his "life partner," Kinney, arrives. Kinney comes from "a whole different place," she tells me—a wealthy family, a big house of her own that she shares with her kids, and "all the modern conveniences." The two met when a group of activists from Friends of the Mad River visited Richard's place. It was winter. Everyone went out for a snowshoe, but Kinney just wanted to sit in Richard's sunny window seat. "I loved the silence," she says. They all stayed for dinner, and Richard served venison. "I was stunned by what a good meal he made." To this day, more than a decade later, "everything tastes better here." She lovingly describes the chanterelle omelet Richard whipped up the first time she slept over. They don't live together, though they may when her kids have moved out.

While Kinney and I talk at the table, crafted from a slab of recycled wood flooring, Richard cooks. Ducking into the pantry, he calls out additions to his list of purchased stock: "Yeast, lentils, buckwheat, pasta, coffee, bananas, baking powder." A pause while he reviews the jars and cans of homegrown and homemade foods. "Salt, pepper, vanilla, nuts."

Richard hasn't worked full time since 1987, when he quit his job at the state's Agency of Natural Resources. Now he earns up to $9,000 a year doing a little work for the Earth Institute, a little at the town sewer office, and a little milking for a local farmer. He lives on about $7,000 a year, about $1,000 of which goes to truck insurance, gas, and car parts and the same amount to federal taxes, including Social Security. A published budget in 2001 recorded $512 for "Learning (books, magazines, courses)" and $365 for "Entertainment (movies, one bus trip to Wisconsin to visit family, one bus trip to Nantucket)." There was still enough slush in the fund for "Donations/gifts" of $356. That's $256 more than I gave away in the same year.

Richard pays a dentist for a couple of yearly visits; he practices yoga, and when his back acts up, "it's telling me to slow down," so he rests. "I'm blessed with good health," he tells me. "I've taken a half-dozen aspirins in my life." He carries no health insurance, only a small savings account for a bigger illness. "I don't worry about it," he says. "If I died tomorrow, I will have had a good life. I'll come back up as an apple tree."

Why this radically simple existence? "It's nirvana," is the

first thing Richard says. "I love it." But he lives "low on the hog" for more than personal satisfaction. "It's about justice." If you have a lot, you already have more than your share, he figures. Above a certain amount, moreover, money has to be put somewhere, and if that's not the inside of your mattress, more likely than not your money will be financing some venture that is unfair to people, unfriendly to the earth, or both. In a bank or stocks, Richard says, "money gets up to no good. It's filthy lucre." He laughs, but he's serious. "My goal is to live at the poverty line."

In a way, that means going back to where he started. Before becoming a middle-class adult with a government engineering job, Richard grew up poor on a Wisconsin farm, where his family raised animals and sold eggs at the market square. His only inheritance was an education in frugality and the multiple skills of self-sufficiency. "I have this way of life in my blood and bones and hands," he says.

Dinner is served: whole-wheat spaghetti with fresh tomato sauce made with garden vegetables and herbs, homemade bread, and a huge salad. For dessert there are raspberries and blueberries, also from the garden. At table we talk about politics, mutual friends, Buddhism. From time to time Richard remembers another item he purchases. "Running shoes. Toothpaste."

"Soap," adds Kinney, with a meaningful-looking smile.

"My mom used to make soap. So for twenty years I didn't buy soap," Richard explains. Kinney screws up her face remembering the nasty blocks she was glad to say goodbye to. She's also not a big fan of the slimy sock of shards over the sink.

Kinney has brought wine and coffee and two large containers of water from her house, which she pours into our glasses. Richard's gravity-fed well water "gets a little tasty," he admits. I

notice a stack of magazines on the window seat with Kinney's subscription labels on them. Other than that, there's not much evidence of her in the cozy but spartan house.

When Richard rises to get something from the kitchen, Kinney
confides, "Sometimes I worry a little about wrecking him." She
laughs, adding, "But I did put my foot down about that soap."

JULY 31

Saturday morning, Paul and I gather up the rusty cans that have
been moldering in the shed and cellar and bring them to the haz-
ardous-wastes collection station at the town garage that is set up
twice a year by the state's solid-waste agencies. We pull the car
onto a large plastic sheet, where a team of clean-cut kids empties
the paints and solvents into drums, then places the cans of pesticides and other household poisons into another drum, which
they lower into a still-larger drum with a heavy lid. The liquids
will be blended and recycled as industrial fuel additives, which are
scrubbed when burned. The cans will go to a "containment facility," a kind of super-secure landfill.

The workers are wearing thick yellow rubber aprons and long
rubber gloves, plus sporty short-sleeved polo shirts and dark wrap-
around sunglasses. Their costumes, along with the big metal containers, lend the operation a sinister aura, a cross between a CIA
stakeout and a clandestine dump by renegade nuclear regulatory
commissioners. Indeed, the collection site is a closely guarded
secret. Earlier, we met a friend on the road, driving around unable
to find it.

If the government required manufacturers to pay the expense
of recycling (as in many European countries), they might come up
with some less deadly ways to clean our paintbrushes, Paul notes

as we pull away from the garage. The state, in other words, could make recycling both compulsory and easy.

Instead, it is voluntary, difficult, and expensive. We have had to store our toxic potions for six months, find out about the collection, locate the site, then hand over $23 in hush money to bury the traces of our environmentally illicit addictions.

In America, saving the earth is something of a bourgeois consumer privilege, too.

AUGUST 1

If I haven't been sounding either tempted or penitent lately, it's because Not Buying is becoming a habit. When I'm picking up groceries at the co-op I don't even think about grabbing an egg roll from the cooler; when I'm driving, I have no impulse to stop for coffee. I don't read magazine ads, even for movies, and I peruse the mail-order catalogues casually, like a woman declining the advances of a lover who no longer thrills her. For their parts, J. Crew, J. Jill, L.L. Bean, and my other suitors seem to have sensed my cooling affections and are responding with heightening ardor—more catalogues, more e-mail announcements of special sales, more missives asking where I have been.

Yet I am not beyond seduction.

I am in Burlington with Paul. While he's at his therapy appointment, I've been checking out the used clawfoot tubs at the architectural salvage warehouse, for the upstairs bathroom. With some time to kill before we meet, I walk down the hill toward Lake Champlain. On Battery Street, I encounter Common Threads, a clothing store. The cool, modern window display, decidedly non-Vermontesque, entices me through the door. Inside, the inventory is my aesthetic ideal: simple but not preppy, hip but not trendy, distinctive but not bizarre, with a few bright, frivolous trifles mixed in with grays and blacks like sweets after a classically prepared meal. As it happens (and it doesn't often happen this year), I feel appropriately dressed to walk into an elegant shop like this one. This morning I put on a white sleeveless linen shirt with mother-of-pearl buttons and black Capri pants (touch of Hardwick: they're faded). I'm wearing, not my Nike slides, but a pair of black wedge-heeled sandals.

The saleswoman is about my age, maybe a little younger. Her hair is hennaed red and clipped square at chin length, with short bangs. Her glasses are of a flat-finished pea-soup green in a squarish shape. I compliment her on them; she returns the compliment. We confer on where we bought our glasses. Hers are Danish; she got them in Berlin. Mine are from New York, I say. She knows Mikli. We know each other.

She is wearing a skirt from the store, of gold ripstop nylon with a sewn-in flounce at the back, a joke on the bustle. I take a skirt by the same designer off the sale rack. This one is made of lavender ripstop, sewn flat around the hips with intermittently gathered seams that create billows and an uneven hem. It is a work of art, both silly and sophisticated, gorgeous and humble. I put the skirt on and twirl before the long oval mirror, admiring the garment from all angles. It's a little tight in the waist, I say to the saleswoman, who is admiring it along with me. She tells me hers is tight, too, and lifts her shirt to shows me where it rides up. Not made for ladies *d'un certain âge,* we agree, but still eminently wearable. She suggests that the skirt be paired with a plain T-shirt, like the one she is wearing. "Or dressed up," I add, thinking of a wedding Paul and I are going to next month, to be held at a country inn. She says the skirt looks great on me.

We are flirting. It's a ménage à trois: salesperson, customer, product. But I'm not so smitten as to be out of my head. I reflect: where else will I wear it? Before another opportunity, the skirt will go out of fashion. At $117 on sale, it's a luxury I wouldn't indulge in even if I were buying things. Besides, it's too tight to eat a wedding meal in. I say no, and feel relieved—rescued from myself.

Then I see the pants: a greenish jacquard silk-polyester blend, at only $138 minus 30 percent. They are the right color (the color of the saleswoman's glasses), the right level of dressiness. Woven with a bit of Lycra, they make me look thin and, unlike the skirt, let me breathe.

Those can be worn with a simple T-shirt, too, says the saleswoman.

"Or dressed up," I add. Now we have a history, "our song."

"They look great," she says, smiling at me in the mirror.

I am also flirting with myself. A summer of swimming has made me trim, outdoor chores have made me tan and strong. I look like myself to myself, my best self. I also feel like a woman, doing what women do: preening, flirting in public. Shopping affords a woman this pleasure innocently, like an asexual affair.

"I'm thinking about it," I tell the saleswoman as I dawdle around the racks, still wearing the pants.

"That's allowed," she says, moving to the cash register counter, whose immaculate surface she busies herself tidying. She tells me again how good they look. She is smiling like a cat waiting for the bird to fly into its jaws.

I take out my credit card. Reader, I am fallen.

Paul meets me at Burlington Salvage. We peruse the tubs, but don't buy anything. We will check out the *Green Mountain Trading Post,* a local classifieds sheet in which people sell everything from broiler chicks to used garage doors.

Not until a half-hour has passed and we are walking back to the car do I tell him about the pants.

"Why do you think you did that?" he asks (he has just come from his shrink).

I tell him I lost control; it was an impulse buy. That's a lie. I didn't, it wasn't. I thought it through, right up to the imagined tightness of the skirt's waistband at the third forkful of Nic and Juliet's wedding cake. I premeditated, then meticulously executed my crime.

"An impulse buy," he repeats. "Interesting. I never make impulse buys." He says he's spent ten years in therapy trying to be impulsive.

"So maybe Not Buying It is counterproductive for you," I say. "Let's go to a store and give you five minutes to buy something." I've lapsed twice now, and more times than that if you count the help I've gotten from my friends. I want to deflect the heat from my own transgression. But I'm also getting a little weary of Paul's effortless purity.

AUGUST 4

Linda and Marie are coming to dinner, so Paul pulls a bottle from the last case of wine in the closet. As the stock diminishes, his campaign escalates. "I'm really going to need more wine," he tells me.

I say nothing. After all, I'm not stopping him from buying it.

He repeats, plaintively, "I mean, I need it." Perhaps remembering that comparisons between wine and milk didn't cut it last time, he adds, "I'm Italian. Wine is like water to me."

I shrug. "It's up to you, honey," I say. In Burlington, I wanted him to be bad so that I could look good for a change. Now, I'm feeling a little hope that he will succumb to appetite, like an ordinary fallible human.

Condemn anticonsumerist moralism all I want, it seems impossible to forgo judging consumption—or avoid feeling righteous when abstaining. I chuckled at the spiritual hand-wringers in our Voluntary Simplicity group. But I might have noticed that I was looking down on them from a perch of self-bestowed superiority. They were agonizing over premium cable and Starbucks moccaccinos. *Pfftt!* Paul and I hadn't purchased a cup of prepared coffee since 2003! Now, as he and I wrangle over wedding clothes and wine, the competition is between us. The winner isn't just the person who buys less, it's the one who wants—even *needs*—less. I rejected Irwin's self-abnegation, Sal's denunciation of sinful greed. But here are Paul and I, battling to be the better martyr.

Tonight, Paul will need that wine. The *Hardwick Gazette* is fat with letters to the editor concerning the cell tower. I read out loud from the third (or is it fourth?) submission from Toni May, who has emerged as Sandy Howard's first lieutenant. "The need for people to expand and be a part of the rest of the world is not going to go away," writes Toni. "Our kids are the next generation and are not satisfied with what Hardwick has to offer in the lines of communication. They want more. They've either already moved on to more civilized areas of the state or talk of doing it when they graduate from high school. And who can blame them? If you're happy with the simple quiet life, so be it. But don't expect everyone else to be held back because you choose to stay in the Dark Ages." Toni would no doubt pronounce Paul's and my life medieval, lacking as it does a microwave oven—to say nothing of how she'd judge the Czaplinski homestead in Adamant.

I've been thinking all week about Richard. He inspired me. His house gave me ideas (those VW license-plate porch lights were especially fetching). His tomato sauce was excellent. I learned the word *snath*. The visit was like a refreshing vacation.

But Toni May's letter returns me to the real world, where the bulbs are all halogen and an average family's car-related expenditures come to more than Richard's annual budget. Unlike the stance toward consumption that Richard and Jim Merkel represent, Hardwick's final decision on the telecommunications tower will be neither radical nor simple. Like the laws that inform it, it will be a compromise of legal interpretations, popular priorities, and politics. Nor will the ruling be ideologically pure. Like Paul and me, establishing "rules" for purchasing, the board will have to find a point somewhere between need and desire and call it reasonable.

I've stopped pestering Paul for clues to what he is thinking as he lies on the bed reading the thickening stack of papers in his blue Zoning Board binder (there's no room on his desk). But now, as I read to him from the *Gazette,* he laughs ruefully. "Whatever we decide, Judith, somebody isn't going to like it," he says. In fact, he adds, if the board reaches a decent compromise, there's a good chance it will please nobody.

AUGUST 9

Seven A.M., at my desk listening to the familiar squeal of the modem, I imagine Richard. He is glistening with sweat from work in the field or forest, tucking into a well-earned second breakfast, carting a bucket from the outhouse to the woods. I sigh. Richard doesn't dream of shopping. He doesn't sit at a desk scribbling. He grows things, builds things, fixes things, conserves things. Even Richard's shit does an honest day's work.

"Oh, to go forth and labor with one's hands, to do the poorest, commonest work of which the world has truly need!" laments

Marian Yule in George Gissing's *New Grub Street,* slumping over a scholarly volume at the British Museum. "It was ignoble to sit here and support the paltry presence of intellectual dignity."

Noble: that's what Radical Simplicity is, and Richard Czaplinski is nothing if not noble. He is also gifted in intelligence, ingenuity, health, and strength and possessed of a discipline that in a less amiable person would look like rigidity. Thinking about Richard, his image melts into Thoreau's. Both are polymaths of craft and basic agriculture, knowledgeable about the natural world and careful in all measures. But Richard also appears to share with Thoreau something else, or rather he lacks something else, which is fortunate, maybe necessary, for anyone who wants to live as he does. Thoreau, wrote Emerson, had "no temptations to fight against—no appetites, no passions, no taste for elegant trifles." Do you miss anything? I asked Richard. "Like what?" he asked, seeming unable to come up with something. I projected my own obsession: "What about movies?" He replied: "Most movies are overrated."

This is a common sympathy among Radical Simplifiers. On his road to right living, Merkel rejected the car, the hamburger, and the television, then moved on to the public school and the modern city. In his "wiseacre scenarios" (a series of personal resource-use schema, each closer to an ecologically equitable footprint), he writes, "I excluded paid entertainment, based on the premise that free fun is abundant in the universe." Merkel is channeling John Muir, who wrote: "One day's exposure to mountains is better than cartloads of books."

None of these lives is without comfort, but neither does human-made comfort or human-crafted beauty compel them. Thoreau quotes Cato advising the paterfamilias to keep a well-stocked pantry and wine cellar, "so that it may be pleasant to expect hard times." This the writer contrasts with his own provisions at Walden of "a firkin of potatoes," some peas and rice, a jug of molasses, and a peck each of rye and Indian meal. Hard times are pleasant enough for Henry. His peas have "the weevil in them," which I presume makes eating them more gratifying.

"A fine house, dress, the manners and talk of highly cultivated people were all thrown away" on Thoreau, wrote Emerson. "He much preferred a good Indian."

Kinney doesn't want to "wreck" Richard, but what would she wreck? Even counting his tiny luxuries, Richard lives, emotionally, on the other side of the globe from the mainstream of consumer culture. That's nice for him. But comparing myself to Richard has done little more than make me feel guilty. Can Richard—or Thoreau—be a popular role model? Can noble asceticism ever appeal widely?

Craig J. Thompson, a professor of marketing at the University of Wisconsin, thinks any potentially successful anticonsumption movement shouldn't even try to sell it. "Perhaps a radical politics of consumption should argue for getting more pleasure out of consumption," he writes, "rather than repackaging the age-old admonition that individuals seek 'true' fulfillment by escaping the flesh, or mortifying it." Less can be more, in other words, but the reward is not to be found in the lessening itself, in frugality or abstention. Less, in other words, is not *morally* more.

AUGUST 15

For dinner I make quesadillas with the Mexican *huitlacoche* fungus on them. It looks like sludge and, being mold, tastes like mold. I'm still not sure it's a food.

We are again discussing the sale of my Honda Civic, which would save us about $2,000 a year on insurance and upkeep.

Because of its difficulties with our driveway, in winter the car sits in the snow and rusts. This month, I spent $500 replacing the brakes, which looked positively Paleolithic when they came out. And as good as the Honda's gas mileage is, an online emissions calculator tells me that it and I have burned the equivalent of fifty-nine mature sugar maple trees this month alone.

Still, Paul points out, without the Honda we'd end up driving two less-efficient cars, the all-wheel-drive Subaru and the old truck, and using more gasoline. I'd like a hybrid gas-electric vehicle, but at the moment they start at about $30,000, almost twice what our two cars cost combined. Plus, there's a two-year waiting list, and the all-wheel drive, which won't be out until 2005, is an SUV, which I couldn't bring myself to drive even if it ran on recycled packing peanuts. Now Paul tells me that he heard a woman calling the Car Guys on NPR. She lives in Brattleboro, Vermont and commutes to New York, just like us. Should she buy a Prius, the Toyota hybrid? Tom and Ray said no. She'd need a four-wheel-drive hybrid for the Vermont weather, which wouldn't get the same fifty miles per gallon as the front-wheel-drive models do. Plus, the hybrids have no fuel-efficiency advantage in highway driving. So what should she buy? The guys recommended a Honda Civic.

AUGUST 17

The third public hearing on the cell tower is like the others, only bigger and more unsettling.

Steve Gorelick, Suzanna Jones's husband, presents more petition pages from the co-op with about 130 signatures on them. They are dirty and torn, he says, because someone took them from the co-op and dropped them in the street. Two Bridgman

Hill neighbors bring letters from a local real estate agent attesting that a cell tower would significantly bring down their property values. Toni May has articles to enter into the record that report property values are going up in Chittenden County, which comprises Burlington and its suburbs, the state's most developed county. Toni notes that Chittenden County has a lot of cell towers. Property values are going up in Chittenden County. Ergo, cell towers raise property values.

Rinker weighs in that there's literally a land-office business being done in lots beside a couple of his newer towers. How much do the lots cost? one board member queries. "I'll have to get back to you on that," Rinker says, helpful as always. "But I can say this: they haven't had any trouble selling them."

"Did it ever occur to you they might be a bargain?" the member replies, perhaps tipping her hand.

In their testimony, representatives of both sides speak for the public good and characterize the other side as its enemy. Both accuse the other side of selfishness. Several times Paul has to admonish attendees to be quiet or leave the room.

On lawns in town, meanwhile, Take Back Hardwick signs are springing up. Sandy Howard, their producer, has also made up Take Back Hardwick bumper stickers, covered her car with them, and parked the car on Main Street. She has paid for a series of Take Back Hardwick ads in the *Gazette,* accusing the Zoning Board (without substantiation) of bias and foot-dragging.

Her slogan echoes Take Back Vermont, the quasi-organized rumble that spread across the state after the gay and lesbian civil unions law passed. That law coincided with another law prohibiting clear-cutting of trees on large land parcels. People who tacked the signs to their barns and homes were disturbed not just by these two pieces of legislation but by what they viewed as a takeover by liberal "flatlanders," trying to run the lives of "real Vermonters" like themselves. To some extent they were right.

Sandy has announced that as part of the effort to Take Back Hardwick, she will run in March for the Select Board, which appoints the Zoning Board, and assemble a conservative slate to run with her. Her campaign will be "pro-business" and anti-zoning, changes that she believes will entice people to spend money in Hardwick. This in turn will raise property values and improve the quality of life in town. Her ideal commercial residents, she tells the *Gazette,* would be a Wal-Mart and a prison.

Ask people if they want their property values to go up, and almost everyone will say yes. But unless they want to move to a slower-developing community, a rise in property values does no more for the working inhabitants of Hardwick than it does for the working-class homeowners in my gentrifying neighborhood in Brooklyn. Low property values have long kept Hardwick stable, allowing generation after generation to buy homes and take up their fathers' and mothers' trades, plant a garden, volunteer at church, and drop the kids after school at Grandma's, a few houses away. Now, for the first time, many young adults who grew up here cannot afford to settle in town.

Ask people if they want economic development, and they will also say yes. But the truth is, it's Vermont's *un*developed beauty that has saved the state's economy: tourism is the Number 1 industry. Much of Vermont's unspoiled character can be attributed to a decades-old body of stringent land-use law and aggressive private conservation programs. But what has also kept Vermont, and the Northeast Kingdom, beautiful is poverty. Despite its growing popularity as a hip place to be, Hardwick is still remote, good local jobs are few, and Main Street's landlords can never manage to fill all the storefronts at the same time. Land prices are climbing, but on Bridgman Hill you can't build a spec house for less than the price of its potential sale, and that has kept development to a pace of one owner-built home at a time.

This frustrates realtors, and the town's small size and relative poverty might also be the reason that no cell service company has yet deemed Hardwick a wise investment. But these conditions have also preserved the local family farm. Pressures to sell open land mount yearly, but around here working farms whose out-buildings are caving in and yards are littered with derelict tractors outnumber trophy estates with newly painted red barns and a few sheep picturesquely nibbling on grassy hillocks. Organic farming, the one agricultural segment offering potential for value-added pricing that translates to livable income, is outpacing conventional farming around Hardwick.

Will growth bring cell service? Will cell service bring growth? Will more consumption bring happiness to the people in town?

Sandy Howard may be right that if Rinker puts up his cell tower, Hardwick will see more development. The stockbroker from Boston may move here, buy ten acres, and build a half-million-dollar house with a home office in it. He'll be able to take calls from clients while weeding his garden or on his bike training for the triathlon.

In one sense, this homeowner is Sandy's ally: he is fiscally conservative and antitax. In another, he's not. He may belong to the GOP, but also be a member of the GMC, the Green Mountain Club (or Trout Unlimited, the gentleman's conservationists); he may even eat organic foods and feels spiritually good about it. Once he's got his house and acreage, furthermore, he'll be clamoring to increase the zoned lot size to 25 acres to keep more people like himself out of town. Before you know it, he'll start lobbying the Zoning Board to prohibit Main Street shopkeepers from painting their facades brown with yellow and orange stripes.

Sandy Howard wants economic development and a better quality of life for Hardwick. She believes the only way to get these is to rescue the town from marauding Luddites and erect an aluminum monument to modern consumption on Bridgman Hill. But the irony is, if she manages to Take Back Hardwick, she may lose the Hardwick she wants to save.

AUGUST 20

I go for a bike ride with Alison. She tells me she was hiking on Mount Washington and heard a cell phone ring.

AUGUST 27

Our friends Kim and Alec arrive for a visit from Washington. Fall is already in the air. A few nights this month I have covered the tomatoes to protect them from predicted frost.

Kim and I walk up Bridgman Hill. We pass the few houses that have small satellite dishes on their roofs; no longer necessary are the ones that looked like UFO landing pads. Up here you can get hundreds of channels, just like anyplace else. My neighbors' windows on the world are not as small as I often assume.

When we arrive home, I excuse myself to go online and download a document I have to look at before the end of the day. If we had DSL (which I have since learned needs no extra infrastructure except phone wires), I could do this fast and return right away to Kim and Alec. If we had one of those satellite dishes, I could see the movies I live in New York to have access to. I would miss terribly the polyglot pleasures of street life, but with the right gizmos I could purchase much of the convenience and cultural enrichment of a globalized world in the twenty-first century—at least the electronic media's simulacra thereof—while continuing to live in "unspoiled" nature. I might start wanting a cell phone.

In a few weeks, Hewlett-Packard will launch a gorgeous advertising campaign for its Photosmart R707 digital camera and 375 printer. The photographs in the ad, in deep shades of jungle green and ocean blue with accents of tropical red, show a small, simple cabin on a tropical isle, the back of a white woman with a sarong wrapped low on her slender hips, a black cat sleeping on a wooden deck.

"YOU have no razor, tension, fork, watch, plan, mail, ice, comb, road, electricity," the text reads. "But you have beautiful prints. Find your soul. Print it anywhere."

The ad turns upside down a myth of preindustrial societies, that the image of a person or creature steals its soul. Here in Paradise, where the native's soul has been stolen by the photograph and his land has been stolen by a golf course developer, the digital photograph infuses the experience of the Organic Professional gone native with another, newly aestheticized incarnation of soul.

More important, the ad reverses a fantasy held by civilization's discontents, the "pastoral thesis" that a rejection of technology can return you to a prelapsarian state of virtue. Instead, HP's is the same story told by the advertisements of the SUV parked at the top of a butte or snowcapped mountain. In both narratives, the retreat from the industrialized world is accomplished, and enriched, by the use of technology. So what, no actual 4.7-acre-footprint island resident would consecrate precious sampan space to a digital printer. You can arrive by motorboat with the equipment, then switch to sampan travel once you've unloaded it. So what, global warming will melt that snowcap right off. Until then, drive your ozone-searing SUV to freedom.

If less is more, you need more of some things in order to experience the fullness of less.

But even if you went without the HP printer or the SUV, these days it would be nearly impossible to front Thoreau's essential facts without buying anything. Want to walk in the forest? You need walking shoes and may have to pay to enter the park. Want quiet? You'll have to post your land against snowmobiles and hunters—which means owning land to post. Want that pure organic milk? Presuming you don't own a cow, you will have to go to the store, which is two or three or, if you're really off the grid, fifteen miles away. In the summer you might bicycle, but that won't be doable when it's ten below zero. And if you want to recycle the glass, you'll make two trips, one to buy the milk and one to return the bottle.

Richard Czaplinski has Kinney, who brings him magazines and purified water; he stores his fish and venison in a friend's freezer. Thoreau dropped by regularly at the Emersons' and the Alcotts' for port and conversation. "Some Concordians claimed that 'he would have starved, if it had not been that his sisters and mother cooked up pies and doughnuts and sent them to him in a basket,'" wrote one of his biographers.

None of us can go nobly to the woods, for the simple reason that there are no woods. The pastoral thesis is a pastoral reverie. The woods are a mind-set, an imaginary place where you can be "more natural and spiritual" between stock trades from your WiFi-equipped computer. And Paradise is a picture made with an HP Photosmart R707 digital camera and 375 printer.

I would not write off that photograph as superfluous, though. The future needs it—to evoke the memory of the fantasy of under-development.

Security Fraud

SUNDAY, LABOR DAY WEEKEND

In Central Park's Sheep Meadow, Phil T. Rich, Alan Greenspend, Lu Tenpillage, and other Billionaires for Bush are playing croquet to welcome the Republican National Convention to New York City.

They're additionally gleeful that the city has won a months-long battle against United for Peace and Justice, the anti-RNC coalition that sought a permit to rally on the meadow. The permit was denied: the grass, said the city, couldn't take it. Lawyers for the protesters appealed, pointing out that about 100,000 fans of the Dave Matthews Band had convened here just this summer. But in a contest between free speech and the downtrodden lawn, the lawn won the day, and now the Billionaires are raising glasses to Mayor Bloomberg for his support of their own Keep Off the Grass campaign to privatize the park as a playground for the rich.

Their highest praise, though, is reserved for the man in the Big House, who will arrive triumphant at the end of the convention. Oh, yes, we are grateful to President Bush, crows Mr. Rich to a clutch of reporters. "Never before has one man done so much for so few at the expense of so many!"

A few New Yorkers are genuinely celebrating the novel presence of so many Republicans in their midst. More than sixty-five corporations and a dozen wealthy party members are throwing fund-raisers around town, adding the take to more than $245 million already in the chest, including $64 million to be spent on the convention (some of this fund-raising, according to *Business Standard*, was outsourced to call centers in Noida and Gurgaon, India). Four percent of the convention funds, a reported $7 billion, was raised by New York's own billionaire mayor, who last night joined the governor and the CEO of Pfizer Inc. in hosting an event at the Rainbow Room.

No donor to either party pretends to attend these soirées for the gravlax. The corporate guests this week will use them "as relationship-building vehicles with committee chairs and others who have oversight over their business," says one lobbyist. "It's a very practical view of the political world."

Or, as the faux oligarchs of Billionaires for Bush put it, "Buy your own president."

SEPTEMBER 1

With a half-million converging on the city for a week of protests, Mayor Bloomberg is hoping to distract them from angry thoughts or attention-getting acts with—what else?—shopping. His administration is distributing lapel buttons printed with a picture of a cute Statue of Liberty and the words "Peaceful Political Activist." The button entitles the wearer to discounts at museums, restaurants, and other businesses (including such local mom-and-pop operations as Applebee's).

Showing neither fear nor favor (besides that seven mil), the mayor is offering discounts to the 4,000-plus RNC delegates and alternates, as well. Differences of taste and income have been considered. The protesters get $5 off admission to the Museum of Sex and may purchase cards and toys at the Pokémon Center store with a 10 percent discount. The delegates may enjoy the family-friendly American Museum of Natural History's space show at $3 off; Tourneau, the jeweler, is offering them discounts on $100 gift certificates. For reasons unexplained, the conventioneers are not required to wear buttons.

Inside Madison Square Garden, convention organizers are also doing their best to assuage crankiness and, perhaps, negative coverage. The RNC is offering free facials and massages to overworked members of the press corps.

SEPTEMBER 2

The Democrats have so far gathered $153 million, far less than the Republicans, but they are hardly finished amassing the fortune needed to market their own presidential product. To show voters what a regular guy he is, they've distributed a photo of John Kerry in what look like his boxer shorts, windsurfing off Nantucket Island.

SEPTEMBER 4

For taxpayers uneasy about the $65 million the feds and the city have spent to keep the barbarians from the Garden gates, it may be a comfort to note the high productivity of the police in making arrests. Rather than inefficiently waiting around for an individual to break the law before taking him or her into custody, new tactics call for several officers to unfurl a spool of orange plastic snow fence, trot around a large group of people—for instance, some 300 pacifists from the War Resisters League, most of them very senior citizens—then preemptively corral protesters, reporters, and unlucky passersby in one swoop.

The move is more than quick and elegant; it is also inexpensive. The "crowd control fence" sells for less than $50 for a hundred-foot roll and forestalls the use of billy clubs, tear gas, or hand-to-hand combat, saving the city potential millions in police brutality claims. Rather than old-fashioned steel handcuffs, the department also uses plastic disposable cuffs, which resemble the cinch strap you'd use to tie up a garbage bag. These "flex cuffs" can be easily carried, dangling in multiples from the belt or pant leg of an officer. And a package of ten costs $11 from NEXGEN Tactical & Law Enforcement Supply Inc., half the price of just one pair of conventional steel cuffs.

New York's local economy stands to turn a profit this week of as much as $250 million, city officials predict. *New York* magazine reports that similar optimism preceding the Democrats' gathering in Boston last month was not rewarded, however. There, predictions put the convention windfall at $154 million. The actual take was $14.8 million.

The official tally will show a net gain of about $163 million to New York, but it's hard to say whose pockets that money will end up in. Besides the delegates, who stayed safely inside Madison Square Garden, and the protesters outside, who were on the whole not big spenders, there is no one around to buy anything. Commuter transit officials are reporting ridership down 40 percent. Shopkeepers complain that closed streets and subway stations and a general siege atmosphere are cutting into business. Lap dancers have never seen a slower week.

SEPTEMBER 5

Today's Peanuts Classics comic: Linus hands in a composition entitled "On Returning to School After Summer Vacation." "The true joy lies in returning to our halls of learning," he writes, and wins a compliment from the teacher. He leans back suavely on the desk of Charlie Brown, who is seated behind him, and comments, "As the years go by, you learn what sells."

Terror sells. The Democratic Convention projected John Kerry as a macho warrior. That gave the candidate a bump in the polls. The Republican gathering—where September 11 was evoked by every speaker, and the opponent was portrayed as a terrorist-placating wimp—has pushed Bush's numbers up beside and, some polls say, ahead of Kerry's.

SEPTEMBER 11

As if to commemorate this otherwise quiet third anniversary, the week's biggest-opening film is *Resident Evil 2: Apocalypse*.

Here in Hardwick, apocalyptic visions are being put to their own political uses. Wendell Shepard, would-be cell-tower land-lord, writes the *Gazette* about getting caught in a hurricane while visiting his daughter in Florida. He describes a terrible scene—doors, roofs, small trees flying—and then gets to the point. "Unfortunately, many people died, but it's amazing under these conditions that the numbers were not worse. Until I had this experience, I was not really appreciative of the need or value of the 'cell' phone link in communications." Wendell prays that Hardwick will never see such a disaster, but hopes the Zoning Board will "look at the 'whole picture' and allow this tower to be built and serve the common good of this area!"

The police chief also weighs in with a letter. "Due to the concern of inadequate dispatch communication as an 'officer safety' and 'public safety' issue within the Hardwick-Greensboro Police Department patrol area," the department has procured money from the Department of Homeland Security to hook into the state's public-safety communications system. This can't be done without "tower space currently not available within the police department's patrol area," he writes.

Steve Gorelick has written in response to these letters. "To hear some people talk," he says, "you'd think children in Hardwick were bleeding to death, houses are being reduced to ashes, and police cruisers are being lost in the wilds of Greensboro," all for the lack of a tall enough antenna. He wonders why no one has ever complained about our emergency services before.

This is an excellent point. Because believe me, they would have complained. The *Gazette,* a large tabloid-format weekly, routinely runs three or more pages of letters. Usually, at least half of these communiqués voice complaints: bicycle-riding juvenile delinquents on Main Street, bovine growth hormone, excessive property taxes. Letters in the following issues rebut the complaints or complain about the complainers. Among the things people have complained about for years are the police, who have committed every sin from costing too much to running off with teenage girls. But one problem never before heard about the police, or the volunteer firefighters or ambulance team, is that they could not be reached due to inadequate communications technology.

Before Karl Rinker showed up, the lack of cell phones (which is general in the Northeast Kingdom) was an inconvenience of living in an otherwise fine community that had a few things wrong with it. Then Rinker arrived, brandishing his three-ring binder like a prophet with the banner of the new Christ aloft. His tower was the quintessential late-capitalist product: the solution to a problem people only vaguely knew they had (not unlike the weather-related foot comfort problems my SmartWool socks addressed). Fantasies of the tower turned an inconvenience into a dissatisfaction, a dissatisfaction into a desire, a desire into a need, and a need into a matter of life and death.

In the event of a hurricane or terrorist attack, Hardwick's survival balances on the tip of Karl Rinker's tower.

And in the event of another terrorist attack . . . well, let us just say that since September 11, 2001, disaster has been a boon not only to the Bush administration but also to the economy on which its popularity depends. *TechNews* has been transmitting elated bulletins since the planes hit the towers. "The entrepreneurs are coming out of the woodwork," Richard Veleta, director of loss-control services at Dolle Risk Management Inc. of Cincinnati, crowed in the trade journal in 2002. By now, these capitalists have spawned products from advanced biometric iris identification technology to anti-shattering window film ($8 a square foot), part of a fast-growing merchandise segment that its maker, 3M Corp., refers to as "bomb-blast mitigation."

Insurance companies have sold about $10 million of antiterrorism liability and property policies this year. Private-sector antiterrorism and other security measures may amount to as much as $40 billion to $50 billion, three times the annual outlay before 9/11, according to *CQ Homeland Security,* an online newsletter put out by *Congressional Quarterly.* A grant of $100 million will help Northrop Grumman and BAE Systems develop an electronic shield to be mounted on commercial airplanes to "defend them against shoulder-fired missiles." And $12 million for the data-mining tool Matrix is only a fraction of what the Justice and

Homeland Security departments will disperse to private companies for computer-aided surveillance of ordinary citizens.

I clip an ad screaming, "ARE YOU READY FOR THE NEXT EMERGENCY?" I'm not sure I am. Might I need an Etón plug-in or crank radio with built-in flashlight and blackout alert ($29.99 and $39.99, respectively)? Or perhaps something stronger? I find my way to the Web merchant Terrorbusters Inc., which purveys a substance called EasyDECON 200, from Envirofoam Technologies, a "nanoemulsive decontaminator" that, "used as directed . . . has proven to neutralize all known chemical and biological warfare agents, while at the same time is non-corrosive and adds no environmental load to the appropriate clean-up operation." If I had kids I might consider a new line of "night vision" bedding and bedroom accessories from JC Penney, including World War II–era jet- and tank-shaped pillows complete with "sound chip[s] for special effects." Everything comes in camouflage pattern, including window coverings, which I assume can double as blackout curtains.

The brilliant thing about all this terrorism mitigation is that it does nothing to assuage anxiety or its close cousin depression. In fact, the marketing of terror mitigation may actually exacerbate those feelings, which are themselves excellent promoters of commerce.

SEPTEMBER 12

Identify lemons, sell lemonade. The financial services company AIG is also reaping the fruits of personal insecurity, sown not by jihadists but by the Bush administration's own domestic social policies. The company's ad shows a handsome elderly black couple embracing. "Social Security is in question," it reads. "Personal security doesn't have to be." Should Social Security be privatized, AIG stands to make out like a one-armed bandit.

I keep thinking of an interview I saw, in which a Cantor Fitzgerald trader who survived the Twin Towers attacks admits to a journalist that the instant the first plane hit, he thought, *What's this going to do to the price of gold?* In fact, gold went up. Notes the trader, "In devastation, there is opportunity."

SEPTEMBER 14

Identifying our own household lemon, Paul is making something like lemonade. Optimizing the upside of our private Prohibition, which he finds as misguided as the last, federal one, he has begun to brew beer at home. It's relatively quick and extremely cheap: ingredients come to as little as $1.40 a six-pack and fancier brews cost only twice that (we allow all manner of food ingredients on our Necessities list). Paul has borrowed equipment from Charlie and his son, Nic, and collected used bottles; now the first batch, an amber ale, is burbling in a carboy in the pantry. Paul spends countless happy hours checking the vapor lock and reading a book on the "joys" of home brewing written in the Sixties. The buzz of beermaking is contagious. I'm reading the book, too, skipping the technical parts and turning straight to the hippie bacchanalian philosophy and photos of bosomy chicks giving head of the foamy variety.

SEPTEMBER 16

Incorrigibly, Ann sends Paul and me a CARE package of videotapes and DVDs. We immediately break out *Touching the Void*, about a climber who falls down a crevasse in the Andes and over the next six days—crippled, frostbitten, starving, parched, hallucinating, and given up for dead—crawls down the mountain to safety. The film puts our own deprivation in perspective.

Still, I can't help thinking, if only the mountaineer had had a cell phone! If only the mountain had had a cell tower! Of course, then he would have either had to seek out a more perilous feat (fighting terrorists?) or miss this opportunity to face death and change his life. And we'd be out a good movie.

SEPTEMBER 20

My birthday. I can't buy myself a gift, but to be around my favorite consumer item I stop in at the Galaxy Bookshop to visit with Linda, the bookseller. I mention the news that Hardwick has received $9,500 from Homeland Security to build a six-foot-high cyclone fence around the town reservoir, with three rows of barbed wire on top. In 2003, the feds granted our police department $995 for bulletproof vests and $600 for "explosives mitigation." Violent crimes in Hardwick that year numbered seven, mostly domestic disputes. The number of homicides was zero. As far as I know, there were no arson attacks, anthrax deliveries, or suicide bombings.

Linda tells me a customer has suggested a way to get a piece of the disaster dividend. The Galaxy could sell those Support Our Troops yellow ribbon car magnets that are such a sensation in town. "We can put them on our cars. Then liberals," said the customer, apparently assuming that "liberals" constitute Linda's entire clientele, "can take back patriotism."

Linda and I ponder the problem of how to distinguish liberal, antiwar support for our troops from the conservative, war-positive kind. The yellow ribbons already have undergone several rounds of repurposing. They were originally created to raise money for military families, but the idea was appropriated by a company that started manufacturing them in Taiwan—a kind of war profiteering that, incidentally, drove the original makers out of business. Now, the branding of the yellow ribbon is pretty much complete. It doesn't just mean Support Our Troops, it means Support Our President's War in Iraq.

To telegraph troop support minus war support, "you'd definitely have to put the ribbon on a Volvo," I venture.

An auxiliary sticker might also help—perhaps from Northern Sun: Products for Progressives, promoting random acts of kindness.

SEPTEMBER 21

I clean out the third and last jar of hoisin sauce. If we had a bigger refrigerator we could have stocked up and made it through the year.

SEPTEMBER 23

We do have a bigger closet now, and will soon have many bigger closets, which we hope will give order to our many possessions. Paul brings home $500 worth of Mill's Pride coated particle board closet drawers, shelves, dividers, and poles from Home Depot. It's a "permissible" purchase, since it's part of the new construction.

The closet "system" is one element of "household storage," a manufacturing and retailing industry that is large enough to pack away everything everyone has accumulated since the Middle Jomon Dynasty. On Google, the entry "household storage" yields over 2,350,000 hits, including enterprises like the Container Store, StacksandStacks.com, and Hold Everything, all of which sell nothing but things to put things in. In addition to household storage, there's out-of-household storage, or "self-storage," the windowless boxes dotting the outskirts of American cities that contain, at this writing, 37,000 facilities, averaging 80 to 90 percent occupancy.

Everyone wants someplace to put her things, whether she owns one cup and saucer or half the Russel Wright dishware in America. But household storage is not just a space, it is an attitude. Things-to-put-things-in create a pleasant paradox. They allow a person to enjoy the comfort of owning many things and also, since they place those things out of sight, the illusion that she does not own them. She may have her cake and throw it away, too.

Bolstering this sense of owning little, household storage containers are often made of materials evoking the lives of people who actually own nothing. Last season, Hold Everything featured Bamboo Fence, a "crushed, laminated bamboo rattan" (a word of Malaysian origin). This year it's Hapao wicker, named for a terraced rice-field district in the Philippines, woven up in side table/boxes (two sizes, $150 and $300), a desk set for paper and pens ($38 per basket), a "media box" for CDs ($84), laundry hampers, and so on. These fibers speak of grit and flintiness and thrift (hasn't that CD box been in the family since Great Grandma homesteaded the Great Plains?). They look light and sturdy, as if you could strap the side table to your back and take up the nomadic life.

In case you do (or even if you don't), you can deposit whatever you're not taking with you in a self-storage unit. These facilities preserve not only the things, but also the fantasies that inspired their purchase (say, that the owner will start hooking rugs or train for the Tour de France), as well as the fantasy that she will soon exhume the thing and pursue the fantasized activity. Generally, neither happens. As a National Public Radio reporter delicately mentioned to the renter of one such unit, "Uh, I notice you have an ab cruncher over there."

Modern consumer culture cannot be blamed for this hoarding. It's old, really old. The Egyptians, believing you *could* take it with you, gathered up a person's jewelry and cutlery and her mummified cat and packed them into the pyramid, along with a chicken picnic, for the voyage to the next world.

And then there was the nineteenth-century version, which, true to form, Thoreau condemned:

> Not long since I was present at the auction of a deacon's effects [he writes in *Walden*]. As usual, a great proportion was trumpery which had begun to accumulate in his father's day. Among the rest was a dried tapeworm. And now, after lying half a century in his garret and other dust holes, these things were not burned; instead of a bonfire, or purifying destruction of them, there was an auction, or increasing of them. The neighbors eagerly collected to view them, bought them all, and carefully transported them to their garrets and dust holes, to lie there till their estates are settled, when they will start again. When a man dies he kicks the dust.

I go upstairs to find Paul reading the instructions of the Home Depot closet parts and measuring the inside of the closet. A man who has trouble acquiring new things, he nonetheless grieves to part with old ones (it's a mystery how he got so many in the first place). Maybe his disposaphobia can be traced to his mother's death, when he was nine. Maybe I—and Jim Merkel and, retrospectively, Thoreau—should be more tolerant. Maybe Dana, in the Voluntary Simplicity group, was right when she undertook to "make friends" with her clutter. Mortals adrift in this terrifying world, we need our things to weigh us down. When Paul is feeling insecure he says, "I want to go home and touch my stuff."

SEPTEMBER 26

When an ab cruncher dies, it ends up in the *Green Mountain Trading Post*, whose function is to facilitate the migration of things from body to body, one person's garret to another's dust hole. Perusing the publication, I have located a promising clawfoot tub in East Northfield, so Paul and I drive the Chevy down to take a look.

The tub is not in a garret, but it is in a dust hole, lying rusty and filthy under the falling timbers of a 150-year-old barn belonging to a couple of fourth-generation Vermonters. They want $300 for the tub and a hideous sink and toilet. Paul drives the truck through a thicket of alders and he and the man heft the tub out of the barn onto a plank, over which the three of us slide the tub into the truck bed. Paul and I can't persuade the couple to let us leave the toilet and sink behind, so we throw them into the truck, too. On the way home, we figure we should have offered them $250 with the toilet and sink and $300 without them.

The tub is another allowable house purchase, and recycled to boot. But the shopping is not fun. Paul and I have a spat driving back. I'm not sure I like the tub, which is narrow and has stumps instead of feet with toes and toenails. It's an amputee clawfoot. Paul says he felt we had to buy it, having committed a three-hour round trip to viewing it. This is the rationale of someone who can stand to shop only once for any item, but now he is suggesting that we put the tub in the cellar and keep looking for another tub, at which point we can sell this one. Consumption, it is rarely noted, is a full-time job.

We stop in Woodbury to pick up two Adirondack chairs from a filmmaker friend named Abby, which she's left at her ex-girlfriend's house. The chairs are rotting and their screws are falling out, but they are pretty and surprisingly comfortable, with wide flat armrests just right for holding gin-and-tonics. We load them in beside the tub.

Back at the house, we leave the disputed tub in the truck, set up the chairs beside the pond, break out the gin (last year's; we're not buying tonic), and watch a pair of ducks feeding. We are gaining skills as gift receivers and losing them as shoppers.

SEPTEMBER 27

Now that I've got my tub, I can begin thinking about what color to paint the unenameled outside. This leads me to thinking about the color of the wood floor beneath it, which leads to thinking about the color of the bathroom walls and door and from there, the color of the walls outside the bathroom, and so on.

After dinner, I take out the paint chips I have been collecting and spread them across the kitchen table. Engrossed in the pure, flat colors, grouping them in twos and threes, placing them in light and in shadow beside fabric swatches and blocks of wood, I forget global warming, the war in Iraq, George W. Bush and John Kerry. As I make a note to bring home several cooler grays from the hardware store—Benjamin Moore alone must have a hundred—it occurs to me that I have better choices in paint than I do in presidents.

But organizing our things in the new closets, buying a tub, and envisioning the colors of the walls are more than distractions from other anxieties, more than creative outlets or excuses to shop. They make the world manageably small, personally controllable. Hodley Red, Garrison Red, Yellow Marigold, Pale Smoke— each square of color suggests a mood, a possibility, narrates its own little story of tranquility or surprise, stability or adventure. But like charmed tarot cards, all my paint chips foretell a future that is bright, warm, and safe.

Back in April, Ellen Willis talked with me about the consumers of the Atomic Age, fortifying their suburban garrisons with Buicks and Kelvinators against memories of devastation past and fears of devastation future. Now we are entering another age of security consumption, its salesmen in the White House and the housewares department goading on our purchases with visions of terror real and manufactured. If only we buy the right things and arrange them in the right ways, we will be immune to uncertainty and disorder. We will be ensured against loss.

The ease with which I cozy up to the idea of security through stuff tells me I am as susceptible as the next person to its lures. But not shopping has also had a paradoxical effect. As our stockpiles of socks and sauces dwindle and the buffers between ourselves and extremity fall, I can see that Paul and I have everything we need. This makes me feel less, not more, afraid. Add to the picture of the future the kindness of our friends, so solidly demonstrated these nine months, subtract the acquisition of most new things from the budget, and the requisite thickness of the garrison shrinks considerably. Having less, I feel financially more secure this year than I have in decades.

Meanwhile, outside the window the clarion of terror blasts, the amber alert flashes. When the terrorists come, will I be able to withdraw to my perfectly painted room, spray the perimeter with my personal canister of nanoemulsive decontaminator, and hope my AIG account is still full when the air clears?

The president's first post–September 11 speech sought to persuade us that a united front of shoppers would buy the safety of our homes and homeland. But in my year of loitering on the margins of the *agora*—the market square where people go desiring products, not other people—I am coming to know that the opposite is true. There is nothing wrong with painting my walls; in these fearful times we will all want and need the prettiest of homes. But security, or the hope thereof, can be found only by walking out the door into the roiling *oikos*—the forum of human conflict and human exchange, of deeds, not things, and of politics, not purchases.

Brand America

OCTOBER 2

Buy Your Own President! I'm doing my best. But contributing money through the ether of the Internet—the point of purchase of presidents these days—is not as rewarding as spending money the old-fashioned way, whether that means dropping a buck in the papier-mâché hat, or sliding a five across the counter for a tube of mascara. Beyond a momentary flush of virtue, all you get when you type in your credit card number and click Submit is the most attenuated sense of belonging.

Still, if participating in the election by joining MoveOn or Concerned Women for America is not as satisfying as shopping, it feels a little like using an Apple computer or wearing Nike shoes—what Merkley + Partners brand manager Douglas Atkins calls "joining a brand." The twenty-first-century political group is not a group in the human sense. It has no voice, no flesh. There is no room to meet in, no one to meet. You send your money (or not), you get your e-mails (just like your software updates and porn-site come-ons), you "buy in" to the organization's politics. Shopping may be "in lieu of," as Ann says. But this kind of joining is in lieu of, too. You might say it's in lieu of political engagement.

What do I expect? The transformation of the American from citizen to consumer has been a long, slow process, nearly imperceptible until virtually complete. The candidate with the better commercial almost always wins, but no matter how loud, insulting, or fictive the TV spot, political advertisers have the same problem as laundry soap hawkers: getting the consumer to pay attention for thirty seconds—not to mention for a significant enough portion of the campaign season to decide which candidate to vote for, then actually vote.

In this election, Karl Rove and GWB Inc. are not leaving brand loyalty to chance, or even to advertising. Rather, they have engineered an unprecedented strategy for indentifying potential Republican voters, "mining" consumer data and dividing the electorate into demographic "buckets" (also known as market niches) by the beer they drink, the cars they drive, or the guns they shoot. Looking at the election this way, I see that John Kerry has the same problem as the Volvo with the yellow-ribbon bumper sticker. Windsurfing gunboat captain, Ivy League union supporter, pro-choice Catholic, the man's not a flip-flopper, he's not even a moderate consensus-builder. He's a brand drowning in a bucket of confounded consumer demographics.

OCTOBER 4

I stop to chat with Karen, a South African émigrée, at Mai-Mai, her shop on Smith Street. Mai-Mai traffics in elegant serving plates woven from reused telephone wire, pull toys made of recycled tin cans, hand-painted hair-parlor placards, and other crafts bought directly from native South African artisans and their co-ops. I adore almost everything Karen sells. Two of my favorite possessions, a beaded doll with a high African derrière and a paper-cloisonné bowl made of red and yellow sardine can labels, come from Mai-Mai.

As usual this year, I apologize for not buying anything. Karen knows about my project, and far from disappointed, she is enthusiastically supportive. If she didn't own a boutique, she says, laughing at the contradiction, she'd stop buying, too. "Sometimes I can't believe I am in retail," Karen tells me today. "I feel so guilty."

No, no, no, I reassure her. Your store does good. You're supporting the livelihoods of black South Africans, helping the struggling post-apartheid economy. Plus, you introduce Americans to South African culture—you're an ambassador! I blather on like this, sounding like a World Banker.

"No, there's no excuse for it," she says firmly. "I'm in retail." It's as if she has said, "There's no excuse for it. I killed him." We laugh.

Karen and I have often talked about "socially responsible business," some of whose boosters believe that the Body Shop and Working Assets will save the world. Most businesspeople who try to act responsibly, like Karen, are humbler about their effect. But today I'm a little worried she is feeling personally responsible for the world *not* having been saved yet. If she decides to do something more meaningful with her life, I will miss those sardine bowls.

Karen used to be an art historian studying the indigenous art of South Africa. Now she sells it. But her choices are historically shaped, not just personal. I tell her today about Robert, an artist and revolutionary turned entrepreneur of my acquaintance, who has set up shop as a custom housepainter serving the gentry who displaced him and his friends from their lofts in Soho. Robert doesn't make art (or, needless to say, revolution) any more. What he makes is a mint transforming the former artists' garrets into small versions of

Versailles. His clients like to think they are living in an artists' neighborhood, and the housepainter does not disabuse them. Appropriately, he specializes in *tromp l'oeil*. Robert is philosophical about the last decades' cultural-political changes. "What's left of the counterculture," he likes to say, "is the counter."

OCTOBER 5

Prudence is taking off to Prague for a week on a previously delayed trip, but she tells me she'd rather not leave the country right now. "I feel I can affect the election more by staying home and obsessively reading about it," she explains.

You can buy Obsession in perfume form, but the most obsessive things in life—love, religion, dieting—are free. I'm trying Prudence's tactic, but reading more than a few paragraphs at a time requires concentration beyond what I can muster. So instead, I've been devoting six to eight hours a day—preferably in ten- to fifteen-minute periods separated by ten- to fifteen-minute intervals of nonspecific woolgathering and carbohydrate loading—to toggling among the polling sites that track the vacillating sentiments of those sixteen undecided voters who will determine the outcome of the election. As the weeks progress, my own data become more reliable than the off-the-cuff prognostications of the TV pundits. At this point, I am about 95 percent certain that Kerry will prevail, so long as he pulls down Ohio, the Ukraine, and Uranus.

OCTOBER 7

Intoxicants, including vodka, Oreos, and OxyContin, are off-limits. I wanna be sedated!

Thankfully, Paul's cottage industry in alcoholic beverages is showing healthy signs of expansion. The first batch of homebrew has turned out well. It's rich tasting with a fine head, almost as good as Sam Adams. Paul has already mixed up another, trying out a slightly different formula for a lighter ale. And this morning, he joined Flavio and his friend Oratio, experienced backyard vintners, in crushing 1,200 pounds of Cabernet and Merlot grapes, the first step in a half-year process of making wine. After a pleasant several hours of work, Oratio put out a lunch of homemade pasta, bread, salad, and, of course, last year's wine. When I arrive at three to see how they're doing, espresso is being poured.

Oratio invites me to sit at the long wooden table and brings out a little cup. I sip the bittersweet coffee and look around at his frescoed walls, listening to the men talk. Flavio recounts stopping into Smith & Vine, the new wine boutique on Smith Street: "The guy in there says, 'Oh yes, I have heard of your wine. Bring it here, I'll sell it. Label it—you can get a very high price for that.'" Flavio laughs loudly. "Here I am because I don't want to go out and spend money for this grape juice I can't live without. I know how much it costs me—$2.20, $2.30 a bottle. Now I learn I'm drinking a $50 bottle of wine!"

For my own minor intoxication, I ride my bike to Fulton Street to the shoe store whose pink and green Popsicle toes had me salivating last spring. Needless to say, the neon-colored cloven and curly-tipped cuties are now shopworn, marked down, and available only in sizes 2 and 14. Predictably, they have ceded pride of place to the new round-toed pumps in brown and oxblood, along with a fair number of boots in black, which (since nine-tenths of my shoes are this color) I am hoping is the new black.

Fashion depends as much on repulsion as attraction. By the fifteenth and sixteenth centuries in England, France, and Italy, notes the historian Chandra Mukerji, "the fashion-conscious . . . were beginning to be ashamed of wearing outdated clothing." At the turn of the twentieth century, Veblen described the way in which "the best of our fashions strike us as grotesque" a few months past their prime. He called the phenomenon "aesthetic nausea."

So, surely as summer follows spring and autumn follows summer, the lusciousness of last spring's shoes has turned to a dusty aftertaste and a gummy feel in my mouth. After five months of fasting, though, something else has happened: I have lost my appetite for the fresh new offerings. I look down at my red Giraudon shoes, bought for a trip to Paris last year, where wearing flats on the street can get a woman deported. My Giraudons turned out to be wrong, wrong, wrong: too sensible, too thick, still too American (no Giraudon store in Paris carried them), and of course, flat. Also, no one was wearing red shoes that spring. I decided I had two choices: buy a pair of skinny French or Italian high heels and hobble over the cobblestones, or wear my red shoes as badges of *résistance* in fashion-fascist Paris. I did the latter and felt good for it.

Surveying my clothes from the feet up, I note that the right pant leg of my black jeans is still folded into my sock to keep it out of the bike chain. The sock is striped in an off-kilter variety of off-center colors, which refer to but do not match the faded stripe of the boat-neck shirt with no elbows (though you can't see this) that I've got on beneath a black fleece vest flecked with orange cat hair. Over the vest I'm wearing a short green leather jacket that I bought in a flea market. Its pewter buttons are dangling and its skin is so distressed it should be on Prozac.

Let's face it, Month 10 of the Year Without Shopping and my wardrobe is worse for the constant wear. I rarely bother with makeup any more; my mascara is nearly dried out and my eye pencil sharpened down to a stub.

But my dishabille is not altogether unintentional. "It's a look," Paul says when he can't understand one of my outfits. Yes, it's a look, my look, the look that has stayed with me, varying slightly from year to year, since I was old enough to select my own clothes. Having dug out my favorite things and worn them every day this year, almost unwittingly I have reassembled the fashion identity of the girl in the Beethoven sweatshirt, the flower child in the stinky coat gazing at the Lower East Side through rose-colored granny glasses. I am reclaiming my bohemian identity, in its latest incarnation: counterculturalist to the culture of the counter.

OCTOBER 9

Speaking of countercultures, I get an e-mail from the Simple Living Network, informing me that October 24 is Take Back Your Time Day. I go to TBYT's Web site and learn that, unlike Voluntary Simplicity, which is a cluster of persons each making a personal change, TBYT advances numerous collective political demands, including universal paid vacations, family leave, sick leave, higher minimum wages, affordable child care, and guaranteed adequate retirement income. Still, perhaps realizing that any political movement worth its salt sets realistic goals and knowing that in America at the moment its demands are utopian, the group hopes at least to change the culture one harried American at a time.

I call Peter Fraenkel, a psychologist and director of the Center for Time, Work, and the Family at the Ackerman Institute for the Family, and New York City's premier take-back activist. Among other things, Peter studies the effects of time strain on family life. I ask him if we might spend TBYT Day together.

Peter offers his regrets. Alas, he won't be in New York that weekend; he is giving a talk at an out-of-town conference. But he will pass my name along to his colleague Mary Kim Brewster, who will be running an event at her house in Brooklyn Heights.

So how about another time to talk? I ask.

Peter consults his calendar, mumbling to himself, "Next week, no. Not the next . . . Next . . . doesn't . . . look . . ." Finally, he tells me he has a couple of hours to meet with me the week before Thanksgiving. He's a little sheepish, neither of us mentioning the obvious. He apologizes: he's just, well, so damn busy.

I commiserate, but disingenuously. I don't tell him that these days I have plenty of time on my hands, having given up movies, theater, restaurants, and recently, nearly every other activity except worrying about the elections. When I have a little extra free time, I use it productively, doing research that inspires me to worry more.

"Industry and utility are the angels of death who, with fiery swords, prevent man's return to Paradise, and in all parts of the world it is the right to idleness that distinguishes the superior from the inferior classes," wrote Friedrich Schlegel, a German Romantic ironist. Schlegel condemned the predominant lifestyle of his time (circa 1800) as one of "empty, restless striving," which he dismissed as "nothing but a Nordic bad habit [that] produces nothing but boredom."

By mid-century, Marx had turned the Romantic yearning for idleness into political manifesto. "A nation is really rich if the work day is six hours rather than twelve," he wrote. Legend has it that as its first order of business, the workers' government of the Paris Commune of 1870–71 (of which Marx wrote admiringly) burned the money and smashed the clocks. Now *that's* taking back your time.

Today, idleness belongs not to the superior classes but to the "underclass," who, being underemployed, undereducated (and, conservatives charge, undermotivated), have nothing better to do than hang out. The "superior" classes—the executives, surgeons, and frequent-flyer inspirational speakers—are paid well enough to while away half the year at the beach, but they do not. Their status depends in part on being busy. They don't even while away the hours between 4 and 6 A.M., when, speaking of Nordic bad habits, they are all on their Nordic Tracks, making cell phone calls and watching CNN. To be superior, you have to be industrious, even if what you do (say, manipulate your company's earnings reports to artificially raise stock values) is not useful.

Peter asks if I would like to make an appointment to get together in November. If I don't shoehorn myself into his schedule now, I know I'll lose him for another two months. But I demur; I'll call him soon, I say. The fact is, I feel embarrassed. Here I am, rich in what this man is devoting his life's work to gaining, and do I feel superior? Ha. I feel like a dust bunny swept away in the tempest of his busy-ness.

OCTOBER 10

Mary Kim Brewster calls to invite me to her house on Take Back Your Time Day. She's asking a dozen guests to "talk about two of your biggest time-management problems and also some solutions." Although I had hoped for something more subversive— say, a Paris Commune memorial alarm-clock sacrifice—I accept.

The good news is that TBYT Day falls on a Sunday this year, so sympathizers are more likely to observe it. The bad news is that since it's on a Sunday, no one else is likely to notice. And I'm not sure how many people will give up their one day of leisure to talk about making more time for what they want to do.

OCTOBER 12

On NPR's *Morning Edition* I hear that one quarter of America's working families are living in poverty. In another story, it is reported that since 2000 the use of food pantries has increased 67 percent. My list of "necessities," I realize for the thousandth time, is rarified to say the least, containing as it does Internet access and insulin for a diabetic cat. One skeptic suggests that harboring a diabetic pet might itself be considered a luxury. What can I say? Love must surely be counted as a necessity.

OCTOBER 17

Well, I'm finally doing more than clicking the Submit button at the bottom of the petitions and promiscuously handing over my credit card to any half-decent candidate I meet on the Internet. I've been making voter phone calls, and today I take a bus chartered by America Coming Together to canvass for Kerry in the Philadelphia suburbs. Joining me is my friend Leonore, a therapist and indefatigable activist, and on the bus we run into Eunice, an American writer who lives most of the time in Paris but has returned to the States to spend two months working on the election. Eunice is also the consummate shopper, a connoisseur of things culinary and sartorial (who else would choose Paris as her home? There's a reason the words *connoisseur* and *bourgeois* are French). At the moment, though, Eunice isn't buying either— she's a writer and her husband is an artist, and they are in a broke phase. She tells me that oranges are so expensive on the Upper West Side that she slices one in half to share with him for breakfast. I suggest she not buy oranges. From her laugh I can tell she considers that going to absurd lengths.

We are en route to well-educated, well-heeled Bryn Mawr, a

swing county in a swing state, and a bellwether in past elections. The bus drives along quaint maple- and chestnut-shaded streets lined with gourmet food and designer clothing shops.

Leonore and I are assigned to a subdivision of immense new houses, in whose driveways stand immense new vehicles, several per home. Landscaping is going on at a torrid pace. Every blade of grass appears to have been trimmed with a nail clipper to match the one beside it. No plant is allowed to touch another plant. The mulch between them is black, another fashion trend I must have missed this year.

Our goal is to recruit volunteers, so we are canvassing Democrats. One of the categories on the walk sheets is Lazy Dem—people who lean Democratic but don't always vote. None of these people looks lazy to me (all that landscaping! Such clean cars!), but I am spectacularly unsuccessful in persuading any of them to donate even an hour of their time. They are "crushingly busy," "unbelievably busy," they plead. The superior classes.

"Okay, then," I say to one woman whom I have caught climbing out of a late-model Lexus. I glance at her car, perhaps too meaningfully. "I hope you send money."

Her smile is tight; her gaze tells me she is slightly appalled. The fate of the world may depend on campaign contributions, but, she communicates with this look, what she buys is her own private affair.

OCTOBER 20

I get an e-mail from Mary Brewster. In it is a list of depressing statistics: Of 168 countries in a recent international study, 163 guarantee paid leave for mothers in connection with childbirth; 45 offer it to fathers, too. Paid sick leave is guaranteed by 139 countries, and 37 guarantee paid time off for parents caring for sick children. Ninety-six guarantee paid annual vacations; 84 legally limit the workweek. The U.S. does none of the above. Almost a third of American women workers get no paid vacation at all.

The main message of the e-mail is this: "Our planned event for TAKE BACK YOUR TIME has been canceled so that you can Take Back Your Time." When I call Mary, she explains that no one except me could come.

OCTOBER 25

Paul fixes the sink. Dried, flaky gaskets in the handles are preventing them from shutting off entirely, so they leak. He goes to Mazzone, the local hardware store, where the guy puts the part together for him, comes back home, and installs it in about ten minutes. A $100 plumbing job accomplished for $4.60 in parts plus about an hour of time. My watch band breaks. Instead of going to Canal Street to buy another one, Paul fixes it with some rubber cement. I get a little thrill from each of these repairs, like a runner wringing fifty more meters from her exhausted body.

OCTOBER 30

In Philly for the weekend, the last push before the election; anxiety at an implacable pitch. Sleeping in my friends' third-floor guest room, I descend into a terrifying and endless dream. In it I am with Janice and Paul. Bad things are happening. We walk down a high stoop and suddenly a flood is rising around us. Paul and I jump to the side, but Janice falls into the water and starts to go under. We drag her out and push her, soaking wet, into a car. Paul takes the wheel and starts to drive fast through

Brooklyn. When we're almost home we career into a wall, which crumbles like chalk. Paul screams and disappears into the wall. Janice and I are alone in the car and now I'm driving, but there are no landmarks. We might even be in another city. I am frantic about Paul's disappearance. The brakes cease to work. The car is screaming through intersections, mowing down pedestrians.

Then Janice leans over and looks into the backseat. Crumpled but fluffy, as if they'd just come from the dryer, are my bed sheets, the white and red all-cotton cherry pattern I bought last summer. She reaches back to touch them. "These are really nice," she says. "Where did you get them?"

The colors of the dream brighten. "Oh, yeah," I say. "The Company Store. They were on sale. I got them for $19 each." I glance into the rearview mirror and smile maternally. "They *are* nice, aren't they?" I forget Paul, swallowed by the wall, forget the bodies littering the intersections. I love my cherry sheets. My panic cools like a face against a fresh pillowcase.

OCTOBER 31

Alec Dubro, editor of the satiric Web site *Washington Pox*, comes to dinner. He and Paul have been tossing around an idea for a public service campaign about campaign finance—but not campaign finance reform. While in the Vermont legislature, Paul concluded that limiting donations from large organizations cannot be achieved without violating the First Amendment or leaving gaping loopholes through which billionaire candidates can drive their Hummers. Alec agrees.

So we are thinking up slogans for a campaign to start creating a culture in which people consider donations to candidates as part of their civic obligation. I take a stab: "How about 'It's not money in politics that's the problem. It's whose money.'"

Pretty good, the guys say. Paul writes it down.

Consumption is political, sometimes in the most literal of ways. On the radio, I hear the Israeli writer Amos Oz talking about the perennial debate in his family's home about cheese. The Israeli cheese was the cheese of the Jewish People, the cheese of the great Zionist project. The Arab cheese was the cheese of the enemy. "On the other hand," says Oz, his voice warming with Jewish wryness, "the Arab cheese was a little bit cheaper . . . and much tastier."

Consumption is political, and politics is a form of consumption. Getting a candidate elected takes more than time, imagination, and bodies in the street. The person running for office has to talk to at least several thousand and as many as several hundred million people. That means advertising, travel, staff—money. MoveOn calls during supper and I give them another $25. Back at the table, I find Alec verbally sketching the image of a candidate kissing a baby, with the caption, "He's bought and paid for. By you."

Like wine and shoes, democracy must be bought. But a political party is not a brand, a candidate is not a cheese, and politics is the antithesis of the stagnant exchange of the marketplace, dollar for product. The price of democracy is eternal haggling; its value must be negotiated again and again. And all the while, it must be owned and used by everyone.

The Ownership
Society

NOVEMBER 4

"Let me put it to you this way," an ebullient president-elect tells the press this morning. "I earned capital in the campaign, political capital, and now I intend to spend it."

George W. Bush has won 51 percent of electoral market share and now, he says, he's got "the will of the people at my back" (he invokes this democratic mandate jocularly in refusing to take follow-up questions from reporters).

And what is he going to do with our windy will?

Transform America into the Ownership Society: make tax cuts to the rich permanent, starve just about all government functions to the skeleton, then hand what's left to a snarling pack of private corporations hungry to own or run them. The policies of the Ownership Society will accelerate a twenty-five-year trend that has more than doubled the share of the wealth held by the top one-thousandth of America's taxpayers and shrunk the portion owned by the bottom 90 percent. That means not just the increasing poverty of the poorest people, but also the impoverishment of everything Americans own collectively: public schools, housing, transportation, hospitals, parks, museums, courts, colleges, environmental protection, scientific research, and veterans' benefits, to name a few. Homeland Security will scrimp on guarding the nuclear power plants; the Pentagon will forgo bulletproof vests for the frontline troops. You might call it the Owners' Society—the Lear Jet Owners' Society.

But today, two days after the divisive elections, Americans seem eager to get back to the business and pleasure of America, and as far as American business is concerned, it's not a moment too soon. In a story about the auto industry, the *Times* quotes a Chrysler sales analyst named Gary Dilts as saying: "The guys on the showroom floor think this"—that is, the election of the most powerful man on earth—"has been a negative distraction."

In a similar piece in today's *New York Post,* economist Steve Spiwak predicts a merry Christmas for New York retailers: "With the voting over, the negative impact of the election on consumers' moods should dissipate, paving the way for a solid holiday shopping season."

I take the garbage out and run into my neighbor Jack, getting out of his car in front of his brownstone. Although the car has a Kerry-Edwards sticker on it, the negative impact on his family's mood has already begun to dissipate.

"How're you doing?" Jack asks me. He rests a large package on the sidewalk.

"I've been better," I say.

"I know what you mean," he says. We exchange glum looks. "But," he adds, "life goes on!" His wife, Melanie, is balancing several more bags while corralling their two children, who are, as usual, gorgeously dressed and, just now, manifestly unhappy.

Suddenly, I am enraged at Jack and Melanie, who are as lovely a pair of neighbors as anyone could wish for. Yes, life goes on, and if you have kids it must go on. But how will it go on if everyone just goes on shopping? I think of those suburban Philadelphians in their big houses, at this moment unloading bulbs and fertilizer from their SUVs: "Well, honey, I guess we can expect World War III in a few months . . . What do you think—some narcissus over by the hyacinth?"

My life is going on, too. If I were not not-shopping I might also be nursing my wounds with a three-Mimosa restaurant brunch and a trip to Ikea. Instead, I'm biting my neighbors' necks. Are Jack and Melanie the enemy? I'm casting around for something or someone to blame.

NOVEMBER 7

The privateers are swarming over the Ownership Society as if it were a done deal. In his financial advice column, Ben Stein warns Baby Boomers that to be old and poor is miserable—"terrifying." Thanks for the news, Ben. A third of Boomers have less than $50,000 in savings, he notes, and a family now earning $50,000 a year (roughly the New York average) will need $1.25 million in principal at a 4 percent rate of return to yield the same after retirement.

But don't count on "miracle cures from the federal government," says Stein. In less than a week, Social Security has gone from an entitlement to the act of a merciful god. "It's up to us, and the time to start is right now . . . even if it takes sacrifice."

I just happen to be that hypothetical fifty-year-old, give or take a couple of years. It just happens I've put away that hypothetical $50,000 nest egg, give or take a few dollars. I don't quite earn

$50,000, but for the moment let's assume I do. Bring on the sacrifice. I'm a pro.

I Google "Retirement Savings Calculator," find one that looks simple enough for a person who barely made it through ninth-grade algebra and doesn't make me sign up for a $29.99 credit check in order to use it "free." I enter my age, current savings, desired monthly income at retirement, and hit Calculate. Okay, here it is. To reach $1.25 million by sixty-five on my $50,000-a-year salary, I need to save only . . . $58,000 a year!

NOVEMBER 9

"I Shop, Therefore I Am," a 1983 serigraph on vinyl by the feminist artist Barbara Kruger, sells at the Chelsea auctioneer Phillips, de Pury & Company for $601,600. When the gavel falls, the packed salesroom erupts in applause.

NOVEMBER 11

More good news about my golden years. In the science section of the *Times,* I read that some robotics experts at Carnegie Mellon have designed a soft, heat-radiating pillow that will use sensing and wireless phone technologies to provide a physical touch from a distant friend or relative, "because their research found that what older people often needed most was emotional support." Emotional support and a million and a quarter a year. But one thing at a time.

The pillow is called the Hug. Each conversant has one. To get started, they squeeze the paw and speak the other's name into the belly of the Hug. A wireless connection is established, and after that, each squeeze or pat of one Hug is converted by sensors into a data stream that travels to the other Hug, where a small motor vibrates inside the device, sending out a gentle vibration. It's exactly like embracing a living person, except that instead of a person, it's a vibrating pillow.

NOVEMBER 13

E-mail to Alison:

Subject: The Empire Strikes Back

Here's a plot for a novel: Europe invades the U.S. to halt its imperial aggressions. Too bad I don't know how to write a war novel or want to. Know anyone who needs a plot? Later, J

Reply from Alison:

Subject: RE: The Empire Strikes Back

Sell it on eBay.
Yr pal, Alison

NOVEMBER 15

In the mail, a promo on heavy, glossy, red stock: "What's Hot! A Profession with Respect! Cardiovascular Monitoring Technician is in big demand. Earn $1000 a week plus!" It goes on: "The demand for CMTs is endless because the leading cause of death for men and women is heart disease. . . . Starting salaries are great ($1,000 per week)!"

Another disaster dividend.

NOVEMBER 16

Paul and I are sitting on the stoop in the sun, assessing our collective net worth. He's got his Vermont acres, I've got my ever-more-valuable fourth-floor walkup in Brooklyn. "If we cash it all in ten years from now," Paul says, "we'll have nearly a million dollars."

"But we'd be living in the cars," I say.

"If we sell those, we'll be worth about a million two thousand," he adds.

"We'll be millionaires, but we'll be homeless. Homeless millionaires."

NOVEMBER 17

E-mail from Common Cause's ActForChange, in response to some (no doubt urgent) suggestion I sent them a few weeks ago.

Dear Judith,

Thank you for taking the time to offer your suggestion
for a future ActForChange action. Your feedback is
vital to us and we are taking care to read each and
every incoming e-mail. Please know that your active
participation in ActForChange is greatly valued and
that your suggestion will be considered for inclusion
on the site.

Mandeep goes on, touting the high quality of the product ActForChange. Then she thanks me several more times:

Thank you again for your support. If you have any fur-

ther questions or concerns, please feel free to let us
know. Thanks for helping to build a better world!

Sincerely,

Mandeep K.
Customer Relations

Mandeep. I wonder if Common Cause, like Microsoft and the
New York State Unemployment Department, is outsourcing its
"Customer Relations" to Bangalore.

Dear Mandeep,

Thank you for taking the time to send me a form e-mail.
One thing, though. I'm not a customer, I'm a citizen.

NOVEMBER 18

"People are good," reads a two-page magazine ad for eBay. The
photograph shows the backs of a few thick-torsoed moms and
dads on bleachers, watching a small-town car race, and a buck-
toothed kid kneeling before the bench in the foreground,
engrossed in his NASCAR Hot Wheels. "There are thousands who
love the things you love. How will you find them?" The eBay logo
picks up the colors of the toy cars. Beneath it, the slogan, "The
power of all of us."

Mandeep's e-mail reminds me that I can't blame the corporations or the Republicans for eroding the line between communities and markets, citizenship and consuming. People are
disenfranchising themselves. Voter turnout in this election was
higher than usual, but at 60 percent of eligible voters it still
ranked 139th out of 172 countries. At the same time, Americans

are becoming a full-time volunteer army for the marketers. In the hours when they are not buying, they are selling to others.

It may have begun in the Eighties, when everybody's handbag, chest, and butt became a billboard for Yves Saint-Laurent or the Gap. Now, PR agencies are taking advantage of the public's desire to be of use to the corporation by hiring ordinary people to sell products to their friends and co-workers. *Hiring* may be the wrong word, as these "social marketing agents" are not paid. So might *selling*, as the friends and co-workers are not generally informed that their interlocutors are praising a particular perfume or sausage on behalf of the product's makers.

Why do people do it? The firm BzzAgent at first offered free products, but most neglected to pick them up. The work is apparently rewarding enough in itself. Some participants say they like being on the cutting edge. But rather than *in front of* the crowd, many seem to want to feel *of* it, to belong to . . . something. "For me, it's being part of something big," buzz agent "JonO" told *New York Times Magazine* reporter Rob Walker. "I think it's such a big thing that's going to shape marketing. To actually be one of the people involved in shaping that is, to me, big."

At a party, Ellen Willis says to me, "There's a thin line between consumption for pleasure and consumption that is a substitute for the other pleasures you are not having." Replace the word *pleasure* with *agency* and the same is true. Forty percent of the American electorate didn't bother casting a ballot this year. On a survey question *"I feel I have more effect on (a) the U.S. government or (b) the sausage market,"* how many would answer (b)?

NOVEMBER 20

Paul and I have to go shopping. I mean, we really have to. My father is moving into a nursing home and he needs clothes. Because he's occasionally incontinent and laundry isn't done frequently at the home, he needs lots of them. We're not looking forward to a fun spree.

We don't want absolute crap, but we also don't want to pay a lot. (A year ago, I would have said, "We also *can't* pay." Now I know that to a large extent I'm choosing.) So we've come to Fulton Street, where one thing counts and one thing only. The words on the wall of the strip's busiest store say it all: "Conway's is Cheaper."

We start out swift and methodical as Marines. In short order, we've picked up slippers at Payless and socks, sweat pants, sweatshirts, and a jacket at Modell's. Then, with only shirts, undershirts, and pajamas, we stall.

We enter the doorway of any merchant whose display, or even whose name, does not imply Fashion: Price Mart, ABC Stores, Conway's. We skip places like Extasy, which, we reason, is unlikely to cater to eighty-five-year-old Jewish nursing home residents. We are at first overwhelmed by volume. We wade past acres of pastel-colored polyester children's clothes, risk live burial under the racks of down parkas. The merchants are getting every penny out of every square inch of Brooklyn's valuable real estate. It's hard to breathe.

With all this merch, though, we keep hitting what Paul calls the Home Depot Effect: we browse rows and rows of a given consumer category, but find not a single thing we want to purchase. On Fulton Street as in Home Depot, the store buyers have selected products to please everyone, so they please no one who does not want what "everyone" wants. Not only are the selections limited, they are all limited in the same ways. One store might trend a little gangsta and another a little preppie, but at all of them this year's jackets are puffy and black; a few are puffy and red. If you want yellow, you're out of luck. Blue jeans are acid-washed to suggest prolonged frottage around the buttocks and thighs. Never mind the president's abstinence campaign, chaste blue jeans are not on offer.

And if each store's stock is the same, so are its deficits. We're seeking a humble grail: three packages of white, size-large cotton undershirts with V-necks (to ease dressing). Each underwear section carries a full size range of Hanes crewneck T's, but no V-necks. We find Fruit of the Loom V-necks in small, medium, and extra-large, but no larges. Giving up on the cheaper stores, we stop at Macy's, where we locate a stack of large V-neck T-shirts. But, made by Calvin Klein, they sell for about twice the price, which I can't bear to spend. I'm sure the deltoid-bearing cap sleeve and hint of spandex across the pecs make a difference in fit and sex appeal. But with his advanced dementia and all, I'm figuring Dad won't appreciate these touches.

So much for the brilliant efficiency of the U.S. marketplace.

Yet how can I complain? At Modell's our bill for twelve pairs of socks, four Russell brand sweat pants, and a down jacket comes to $112.92. At Payless, the slippers are $7.99. Six pairs of pajamas at Price Mart come in under $60. Aren't we getting more for less?

Yes and no. Or rather, I'll rephrase the question: more of what?

"Boy," I say to Paul as the cashier rings up Dad's new down jacket, $29.99, reduced from $39.99. "How much could the person who sews this possibly be making?" Like almost every other item on the racks, this one is produced in China. On the street, I tell him the joke about the recent Harvard Law School graduate who is paid a visit by a suave Devil in a well-cut Italian suit. Mephisto offers Harvard a brilliant career at a prestigious Wall

Street firm, a million dollars a year, a beautiful wife, a house in the Hamptons, and a new BMW annually. He asks for only one thing in return: the lawyer's immortal soul. Scanning the contract, Harvard takes up his Montblanc pen to sign on the dotted line. "Wow," he says to his future business partner, "this all looks great. I have just one question: *What's the catch?*"

In the past I have relished shopping for bargains, unearthing my own little token of this moment's street fashion from the ho-hum heap. But now the rewards of shopping have stepped to the wings, and "the catch" is front and center. Not to put too fine a point on it, the immiseration of the workers of the world and the destruction of the environment make it harder to enjoy my beautiful house and my beautiful wife. Of course, shopping at a posher venue would not change the picture. I tend to doubt that the extra dollars for those Calvin Klein designer undershirts are ending up in the pockets of the seamstresses and salesclerks.

Speaking of immiseration, there's another way you get what you pay for on Fulton Street. By ten in the morning, seven out of ten people wearing store uniforms have reached an intermediate stage of either narcolepsy or rage, which they are expressing in the form of malign neglect of the customers.

Paul and I stop for toothpaste at Duane Reade. On the shelf, a Special card advertises Tom's Natural at $3.15. The girl at the counter pushes her copy of *Us* an inch to the left and rings up the toothpaste at $4.75.

"Over there it says $3.15," I protest.

"It's $4.27 plus tax," she answers, her eyes moving back to the magazine.

"But it says $3.15."

Now she gazes sideways and speaks into the air. "Do you have a Duane Reade Customer Card?"

"No."

"Okay, it's $4.75."

"Can I have a customer card?"

"I don't have any cards."

On the street, I read the sales slip. It taunts: "YOU COULD HAVE SAVED $1.18 TODAY."

At Conway's, with only a high counter between her and the restive hordes, one checkout clerk has scrawled her defense across her red smock in black marker, like a crucifix on a warrior's breast-plate: "I DON'T DO CUSTOMER SERVICE."

We customers respond in kind. We growl at the workers and at each other. When a teenager steps in front of me carrying a bushel of sweaters, I ask her, not terribly politely, to go to the end of the line. "Bitch!" she spits. "You probably voted for Bush." I guess we blue-staters are all feeling a bit touchy.

By the time we get home, I feel frustrated, exhausted, and, though I've managed to amass three enormous shopping bags full of most of what Dad needs, ineffectual. Nothing we bought is beautiful. Everyone on Fulton Street was nasty to us and I was nasty to them. If, as Georg Simmel observed, we assign value to those things that resist our possessing them, then why did I feel, increasingly throughout the day, that I would not spend more than $5 on a three-pack of large-size V-neck undershirts unless, well, unless they paid me five bucks to buy it?

Shopping as pleasure and agency? Gimme a break.

NOVEMBER 26

The tough go shopping, they say. We weaklings can't take it. But if last week's trip enervated me, the exercise limbered up my store-crawling muscles. I'll need them today, the Friday after

Thanksgiving, biggest shopping day of the year, called "Black Friday" for its anticipated role in pushing the bottom line into the profit column. Today is also Buy Nothing Day, sponsored by Adbusters, who are trying to make it the smallest shopping day of the year.

I'm up at six and emerging from the subway at the Atlantic Mall and Terminal Market by seven to catch the first wave of shoppers. Good thing I don't live in Kansas, where the malls unlatched their doors at four-thirty. In civilized New York, Target opened at six.

Climbing the subway stairs, I spot Jackie, a well-dressed white woman with sleek auburn hair, a friendly take-charge mien, and a well-thought-out shopping list. She buys gifts for about fifteen people, she says. "I'm really good at getting the right present. I put a lot of time and thought into it." This season she plans to spend about $1,000, not counting wrapping, decorations, and holiday entertaining. She will charge it all on her American Express card, which must be paid in full when the bill comes. "I love Christmas," Jackie tells me. "I'm a giver." She also mentions that she buys wrapping paper right after the holidays at half-price and has an eye out for the "right present at the right price" all year round. I'm impressed. Is Jackie typical of the cohort that sets its alarm clock for 6 A.M. after a daylong marathon of eating and drinking, just to save a few bucks on a George Foreman grill?

Inside the mall, I take the escalators up three floors, on the way passing a half-dozen stores. Their staffs are pottering around the piles of sweaters and scarves; the rooms are empty of customers. Only McDonald's is doing any business, as shoppers stoke up on fats and carbohydrates for the rigors of the day. When I reach Target at the top of the last escalator, I finally encounter human beings picking up products and putting them into carts, which are plastic and red and the size of shipping containers.

The mall is a microcosm of the U.S. retailing industry: all commerce is being sucked upward. A couple of years ago Ames succumbed to Wal-Mart, Kmart, and Sears. Last spring, Wal-Mart crushed Toys 'R' Us. Last week, Kmart paid $11 billion to acquire Sears, which two and a half years ago ate Land's End. Now Sears/Kmart is the third-biggest retail box after Wal-Mart and Home Depot, kicking Target down a notch. In New York, though, with Wal-Mart still trying to muscle its way past resistant communities and small business owners and Kmart a pale presence on a dull corner of the garish Lower East Side, Target opened with a celebrity bash and immediately became the "It" store. In this mall, the red giant sits atop its competitors like a lion on a heap of smaller, recently slain prey. We customers step over the carcasses as we ascend to pay homage to the victor.

The 6 A.M. shoppers are indeed motivated and organized. Lakeesha, a twenty-one-year-old mother out for the day with her cousin Sharone, is already on line at the cashier. She has completed all her shopping for her son, Antwon, and her two nieces. Lakeesha considers herself a prudent shopper. "I'm not goin' in the hole," she swears. Sharone has made the same pledge.

These good intentions may be no more grounded in reality than those of the retailers who call this Black Friday. Lakeesha has budgeted $700 for the holidays. Her purchases on this first day—before 8 A.M., a full month before Christmas—total more than $250 and she's told me she's got "a big family, a bih-ih-ihg family." She's not buying gifts for others only, either. Along with the Disney brand Winnie the Pooh and two My Baby Princess Cinderellas, there's a three-CD music system and a Black & Decker grill in her cart, both for herself. Sharone has purchased a

DVD player, also for herself. "I already got one," she says, "but it was $19.99, so I couldn't afford *not* to buy it." The act of spending in order to save, whether you need the thing or not, is called "spaving."

As I watch the cashiers tapping on the keys and swiping the plastic, I think of the reports last week by *Frontline* and the *New York Times* on the predatory practices of the credit card companies, which draw in high-risk borrowers with offers of no- or low-rate cards, then swoop in and raise the rates (to as high as 30 percent) after one late payment or the discovery of delinquent payments on other credit, such as a car loan or mortgage. Similar schemes plague low-income homebuyers. These practices are one reason that last year 1.5 million Americans declared personal bankruptcy, twice as many as a decade ago.

If Lakeesha or Sharone find themselves in the hole after all, consumption critics Cecile Andrews and Robert Frank will be proven correct, in one way. In another, though, they are dead wrong. Introduce these two women to Cecile Andrews and she would not recognize them as shoppers. "Shopping makes you unhappy," says Andrews. It might have made me unhappy last Saturday. It might make Cecile Andrews unhappy. But Lakeesha and Sharone are having a grand time.

The same is true for almost every other person I speak to in the store today. Not only are they having fun, they feel they are doing good. Friends and family recruited as scouts and stevedores say that they too are here to serve. "She's my best friend, so I help her," says one young woman along "to carry." She's launching her own expedition Sunday. A tall young man in dreadlocks says he buys presents throughout the year for a list that is "constantly growing, with all the new arrivals." Does he do it out of obligation? On the contrary, "it's a sense of self-satisfaction," he says.

I find the Cruz family, a mother and two adult daughters, Martha and Elizabeth, considering a camouflage T-shirt with the legend YOU CAN'T SEE ME across the chest. "For Jessica!" Martha is exclaiming. "Is this *adorable?!*"

Approaching the women when they have moved to the boys' pajama table, I ask if they know it's Buy Nothing Day. Elizabeth thinks she's heard of it, and adds, "I respect that opinion. I mean, I appreciate the message, that the holiday is not about materialism." For the Cruzes, she says, it isn't anyway.

"Sometimes we have, sometimes we don't," explains Martha. "When we don't, I bake cookies and wrap them up beautiful . . . It's not about price or value."

"Remember the year I gave everyone a lint remover?" asks Elizabeth, and they all laugh. "For us, it's just, 'I wanna say an extra I love you.' We thank God that we are together even if we didn't have food on the table." I walk away feeling fuzzy and a little sheepish, wishing I had one of those T-shirts under which to camouflage my nonbuying self.

Not everyone is as skilled as Jackie, as jovial as Lakeesha, or as warmhearted as the Cruzes. In housewares, I trail two thick, bewigged Russian-speaking Orthodox Jews. Unlike my Czech tenant, she of the air fresheners and toilet bowl cleaning system, these women have obviously not yet mastered the art of the deal. They stand for a long time before an armory of electric openers—the squat, cylindrical Black & Decker Jar Opener ($29.99), the B&D Cordless Can Opener ($19.89) and Extra-Tall can opener ($12.99), the Hamilton Beach Classic Chrome Smooth-Edge Can Opener ($19.99). They pick an item off the shelf, exchange a few gloomy sentences and pessimistic head shakes, then put the item back on the shelf. Then they pick up another item. Finding all the openers unsatisfactory, they move on to the coffee grinders. After a while, one of the women disappears and returns with a Diet Coke. They stand mid-aisle, gulping greedily.

Leaving the Russians to fortify themselves for their next salvo at the free market, I drift through the aisles examining the merchandise, pricing a hundred-pound bag of dog food and an econopak of Scotch Magic tape, handling a pink silk teddy and an Italian ceramic mixing bowl. Things look good here; unlike Wal-Mart, Target offers a mix of bottom feed, hip kitsch, and higher-quality goods.

I search the tags for the provenance of the products. Tiny Hot Wheels cars (49 cents each, reduced from 87) are from China; DVD players, toys, and swimsuits are from China. A pair of Cherokee plush infant overalls, at less than $8, though, are made in the U.S.A. I calculate the cost of the babywear in my head. The fabric is a good, soft cotton; that can't be cheap. The design is sophisticated; they've got to pay for that. I conclude that the price comes out of the paychecks of the women at the sewing machines, who must work in Chinatown in New York or Los Angeles, not China.

On Fulton Street I perceived a general level of misery. At Target today, I note that spirits are high. Is it just me? Was I projecting my sadness about my father and my frustration over the stores' selection and quality onto everyone else? Am I doing the opposite today, just because it's a beautiful day and I'm in a better mood? Should I pronounce shopping a good thing, or anyway, not so bad . . . as long as it's practiced in moderation . . . without overcharging the credit card . . . in a spirit of giving . . . responding to true need . . . with social and environmental consciousness . . . and the stuff looks good?

Having read the paeans to shopping and the screeds against it, the analyses of consumption as fundamental to culture and the polemics against consumerism as a machine creating insatiable desire, I can identify with my fellow shoppers or condescend to them from the heights of my superior taste, as I choose. I can paint them as harried or happy, as spavers or savers, dupes to advertising or sophisticated agents of postmodern identity formation. I can indict them as collaborators in the exploitation of their global sisters and brothers or forgive them as uneducated and underpaid victims of the same system.

I can make judgments about their needs and their desires. Does Lakeesha really need that Black & Decker grill? Does the teenager on Fulton Street who accused me of voting for Bush need all the sweaters she was purchasing? Do Jack and Melanie need . . . whatever they had in all those bags? And while we're at it, does my father really need a half-dozen pairs of pajamas?

Would the sweater girl decide not to buy the garments if she knew the connections between them and the worker and the manufacturer and the stockholder and the lobbyist and the World Bank and the president she loathes? I know those connections and I'm still buying a half-dozen pajamas, made in India, for a total of $59.99.

As I ramble through the aisles, a young salesman asks if I need help. He seems genuinely concerned, as if offering spiritual counsel or a hot meal. But I don't need help. In fact, I am feeling almost lightheaded with the absence of need or desire.

And just as I realize I am free of the desire to shop, I also feel free of the desire to judge others who desire to shop. I can condemn overconsumption and the systems that support it and it supports, but I don't have to condemn the shopper.

Here in front of the rack of ergonomically correct kitchen gadgets, I fall into a reverie. It's not the reverie of a shopping-free heaven with the Brian Eno soundtrack, not Richard Czaplinski's cabin with the homemade snath hanging from the wall. Rather, it's one in which the Chinese worker and the Chinatown worker both join a union, so they're not stealing each other's paychecks from the same thin envelope. The factories that make the sweaters are governed by international antipollution laws. The sweaters cost more, but the price differential between the China-made sweater and the Chinatown-made sweater isn't so great that it shuts down the Chinatown shop or encourages the sweater company to ship the product from halfway around the globe, adding barrels of oil to the environmental costs of the sweater. In my little heaven, the banks don't hawk credit cards with the cynical expectation that the borrower will fail to pay them off, and if the companies do prey on weak debtors, a strong government regulator whacks them good. Without the credit card, the girl at Conway's is paying in cash, and higher wages make the sweater a little more expensive. So she is buying one sweater instead of seven, but not going into debt for it.

In this heaven, law and policy prevent some destruction of the worker and the earth and discourage some consumer self-destruction. People will still want sweaters; desire for the new won't melt altogether away. But buying a sweater will not have to be a moral decision—nor refraining from buying it constitute a moral judgment.

I leave the celebrants of Buy Everything Day and catch the train to Times Square. There I will join Reverend Billy and the Church of Stop Shopping in commemorating Buy Nothing Day. The staging area is on the median at Forty-fifth Street, midway between Macy's and McDonald's, Starbucks and Virgin Megastore, a half-block north of the Naked Cowboy strumming a guitar in his underpants and a half-block south of the World's Largest Snow Globe, a transparent Bubble Boy–like chamber in which Santa and Mrs. Claus are receiving (and disinfecting?) children in ones and twos.

The Buy Nothing Day warm-up act is a street theater troupe called Green Dragon, reenacting The American Revolution ("Take 2"). "My stars haven't spangled since Election Day," proclaims Johnny Washington, a skinny twenty-something with a sparse red goatee, as he leaps from among the actors. In their ratty three-cornered hats, brass-buttoned castoffs, and kicked-down boots, these young women and men resemble America's original ragtag revolutionaries, except for the pierced lips. "But today we celebrate the people we love and not the crap we buy! Happy Buy Nothing Day!" Cheers rise from the spectators. A few bemused tourists slink in closer, clutching their shopping bags.

Johnny Washington is recounting the heroic battle against Mad King George W: "We flanked him on the West Coast, we flanked him on the East." A battalion of punk Santas bearing pink "Thank You for Not Shopping" signs filters into the growing crowd. A plastic-bucket drum starts to beat, and the syncopated chant increases in volume: "Today is a good day . . . Not to Buy! Today is a good day . . . Not to Buy!" Visions of Target are fading from my mind.

The performance meanders through something like a tale of the 2004 elections, until word passes to the players that the Main Act has arrived. Johnny Washington motions to the drummer for a bucket-roll. "I give you the man," he announces, "who put the *odd* back in *God!*" And with this, a tall, broad-shouldered man, almost opalescent in a white suit and pastor's collar, struts to the center of the crowd. His chest is thrust high, lifting to the heavens in hope and bombast, his bleach-blond pompadour is brushed back as if windblown; his gaze is level, yet focused in the distance. The whole posture suggests he has just now been dealt a blow, or a revelation. This is the Reverend Billy (aka performance artist Bill Talen), come to exorcise the demon of consumerism and cast the money-lenders, money-spenders, and money-makers from the temple of American democracy. In the name of the worker, the artist, the tenant, and the citizen, Billy speaks in tongues, only partly in cheek.

"Hallelujah!" "Praise Be!" Four female Dopplebillies in white suits and collars surround the Reverend and repeat his ecstatic calls. The audience is getting into the spirit. "Amen!" "Preach it, Brother!" we reply. At least two video cameras are trained on Reverend Billy. In hundreds of actions around the world, he has gained the irreverently reverent regard of activists and artists and a discredit verging on hatred from his corporate nemeses, plus a rap sheet of nonviolent civil disobedience arrests that would impress Martin Luther King, Jr.

Reverend Billy presses his large teeth and fleshy lips to the cardboard megaphone and addresses the neon canyon. His eyes close in concentration, his free hand opens to the angels of God and Mammon—Billy Crystal to his right, a wrinkled beauty advertising Dove soap to his left—and to the cold clouds above. "My chil-dren-ah!" he cries. "PEACE-elujah!"

"Peace-elujah!" "Tell it!"

As if asking us to turn to a page in the hymnal, Billy directs his "children" to the fliers Green Dragon has distributed, on which is printed the First Amendment. We recite it together, solemn as a prayer.

"We are here in this cathedral of logos, this STONE-henge of logos!" preaches the Reverend. "You!" he directs his megaphone at Crystal's friendly face. "Especially you, Billy! Listen up!" For an instant I imagine the brilliant billboards and screens broadcasting children's art, artists' videos, recipes, and safe-sex comics.

Reverend Billy spins on, half sermon, half soapbox speech, poem crossed with polemic. From time to time, he is convulsed in a limb-flinging dance ("Phew! The spirit seized me there for a moment"). The effect is indeed odd and godly, silly and strangely moving.

"Praise be!" call the Dopplebillies.

Billy steps back to rest his voice while the Dopplebillies unfurl a huge sheet of paper: the "Nine Theses Against Corporate Rule," symbolically posting it in this cathedral door to global capitalism. The theses start with "Stop Buying Our Government" and "Stop Fetishizing Growth," proceed though "Stop Selling Our Thoughts ("You capture our unguarded remarks and ship them overnight to a fluorescing big box where they're sold as frozen mottos. Know this: we are actual citizens; we will take back our language"). The last is "Say Hello," a plea for person-to-person communication that ends, "Leave the logo behind. Find the old gift."

"Bill of Rights-elujah!" cries Billy.

"Bill of Rights-elujah!"

"Freedom!"

"Freedom!"

In a raucous line, we follow the Reverend off the median, past the Snow Globe and the queue of slightly frightened children, and across the street to McDonald's, where Billy performs an outdoor "cash-register exorcism" beneath the golden arches. At the Virgin Megastore, he riffs on a poster of billionaire Richard Branson in free fall from a plane, along with a half-dozen other adventurers. "This man is not Jesus!" Billy declaims, "yet look at these an-gels-ah, about him!" Two kids elbow into the space beside Billy, pull out a stack of their own CDs, and start to rap. "Preach it, brothers!" shouts Billy, upstaged by the street-level capitalists.

By now, the tourists are warming up, sensing they've stumbled on the Real New York. Which is exactly what this fake minister is after: something like authenticity.

When the exorcism of the Virgin Megastore breaks up, about two dozen of the remaining crowd make our way to the northeast corner of the square, to a sleek new building with a large Starbucks at its base. I hear Bill, stepping out of character for a moment, turn to one of his compatriots and say, "I can't get arrested today." (Later I see on the Web site that he is slated to participate in a demonstration in London tomorrow.) For more than four years Reverend Billy has targeted Starbucks for its refusal to buy beans from Latin American coffee farmers at prices supporting a living wage, but more symbolically for the way it has turned the small, personal institution of the café into a homogenized retail monopoly. The coffeehouse company has had so many run-ins with the Reverend in California that it has procured a protection order to forbid him from entering its premises. In 2000, Starbucks circulated a memo entitled, "What Should I Do If Reverend Billy Comes Into My Store?" As we approach the store, I watch its security guards mass near the door, eyeing us as we stack our hands on top of Billy's in a "joke prayer" for the children of the farmers.

Then Billy steps inside, followed by about ten demonstrators. I slip into another door at the side, from which I can observe the action. Within seconds, two guards are pressing in on the Reverend and the demonstrators, ushering them out the door. At the same time, from the east side of the street, a dozen police are converging on the corner. A paddy wagon pulls into Forty-seventh Street.

Three cops muscle through the group to the Starbucks door and order Reverend Billy to leave. He complies without protest, motioning the flock to follow. As he crosses the threshold, he is arrested (for resisting arrest, I read later), cuffed, and rustled to a waiting white cop car. An officer presses his hand into the crisp pompadour, ducking Billy into the back seat.

"Shame, shame, shame," chants the crowd. "Let him go! Let him go!"

"Get that bitch," I hear a woman cop say to a male officer, nodding toward a Dopplebilly who has climbed onto a concrete planter to get a better view. She is pulled down and cuffed, as is Billy's wife. Both are pushed into the paddy wagon. A cop thuds the metal door shut and padlocks it with a clanking jerk.

The tourists are excited. "Mommy, Mommy, look!" cries a small boy. "They're arresting that lady!" A German woman beside me is shouting at the cops: "Heil King George! Heil! Remember, they elected Hitler, too!" One of the Dopplebillies is crying.

Mingling with the police as if they were another city squad, the Starbucks security guards are grabbing protesters and ordering them away from the corner: "Move off this sidewalk. You may not remain on this sidewalk!" This is a sidewalk in the middle of Times Square on the day after Thanksgiving. You couldn't move off it if you wanted to.

Anger rises to my throat and tears to my eyes. I am trying to hold on to the sweetness, strength, and silliness of the event, but they are being pulled from my grasp like a newspaper in a hard wind, scattering my high spirits in the chaos of the crowd. As the paddy wagon pulls away down Forty-seventh Street, I gaze up to the billboards above it.

The signs serve as a Greek chorus echoing the drama below. A forty-foot-tall Sean John assumes the iconic pose of the two African-American sprinters on the medal stand at the 1968 Mexico City Olympic Games, head bowed, fists raised in a Black Power salute. (Pointing out "the brilliance of contemporary capitalism . . . to steal [emotion-laden oppositional] images and rebrand them," journalist Jonah Engle notes that Sean John apparel "is manufactured at the Southeast Textiles factory in the San Miguel Free Trade Zone by Honduran workers who make 15 cents per $40 sweatshirt and whose deplorable working conditions were the subject of a campaign by the National Labor Committee for Labor and Human Rights last year.") At John's feet, a ticker mounted by the Center for American Progress ceaselessly counts the rising cost of the war in Iraq; the number on November 27, 2004, surpasses $146 billion. A vertical neon sign beside the hip-hop salesman and the Iraq War bill summarizes the theme: Argent. One door west, atop the marquee of a sleek new hotel, a simple, solid, sans-serif red letter stands like a sentry: W.

NOVEMBER 28

In Hardwick, Sandy Howard is bombarding the *Gazette* with letters accusing the Zoning Board of favoritism to "lobbyists and special interests." Around the country, property rights groups are drafting copycat bills to Oregon's Ballot Measure 37, which forces the government to compensate property owners for conservation, planning, and zoning rules, rendering community control of development almost impossible.

Closer to home, in Brooklyn, developer Bruce Ratner is pushing to get several blocks of homes declared "urban blight," in order to raze them from the site of his proposed Jets stadium. And on Bergen Street, a half-block from the communal house I lived in when I moved to Brooklyn in 1973, a guy named Pietro Costa is building a three-story, twenty-one-foot-deep extension into his forty-foot backyard, breaking up one of the quadrangles of green that have lain unobstructed behind every block of brownstones in the community since the 1860s. His neighbors are distraught, but the addition is legal and Costa is unmoved. "Life leads us down different paths, and people should be allowed to use their properties in a suitable way according to their needs," he tells a reporter.

On Friday, at the Battle of Starbucks, I shouted at a chunky young cop with a clutch of flex-cuffs on his belt, "Thank you very much for defending the right of Starbucks to sell coffee, instead of the rights of New Yorkers to exercise their freedom of speech!"

"Move on," the cop replied coolly. "You may not remain on this sidewalk."

At his post-election press conference, the president spoke of the "security and independence that comes from owning something, from ownership." It was a pitch to privatize Social Security, rendering it neither social nor secure.

"Private property has made us so stupid and inert that an object is ours only when we *have* it," wrote Marx. "The physical and intellectual senses . . . have been replaced by the simple alienation of all these senses, the sense of having."

Another way of putting this: capitalism gives us everything except what is free.

Prosperity

DECEMBER 4

Not Buying It has given Paul and me a holiday gift whose value we could not have anticipated: nothing special. Free of the obligation to buy or to be merry, life is gloriously ordinary.

On a Saturday morning just twenty-one days before Christmas, Paul is online pricing materials to insulate the steam pipes in our Brooklyn building's cellar, a chore for the co-op.

I glance over his shoulder at the Web site he has up. "Insulation At Its Best," I read the slogan aloud.

"Insulation doesn't get much better than this," answers Paul.

I go into the bedroom to put on my shoes. Jonathan is arriving soon to give me a walking tour of Walt Whitman's haunts in Brooklyn Heights.

Paul concentrates on insulation; I follow the historian following the poet through his old neighborhood. While the rest of the city schleps parcels, I am fleet of step and light of encumbrance. My backpack is so empty that there's room in it to carry around the 600-page library book in which I am engrossed, Andrew Solomon's *Noonday Demon: An Atlas of Depression.* Glad tidings!

DECEMBER 5

Our holiday cheer may not be generally shared. The sales figures from the day after Thanksgiving are coming in, and for many retailers Black Friday was black in the customary sense. Like last year, stores at the top end are giddy with business, while at the bottom prices are being slashed to subterranean levels.

The one profit center that seems to be thriving comprises the seasonal products and services I'd call shopping alleviators. "'Tis the season to be stressing," AOL's opening screen announces. The article links to lists of day spas and sites selling relaxing lotions and potions. Personal shoppers are rushing to the scene like combat nurses. Pharmacists are stocking up on Celexa, as diagnosed compulsive shoppers steel themselves for thirty days of authorized bingeing. My friend Vera tells me her sister Sandy, age sixty-seven, has been arrested (again) for shoplifting from a mall in Sacramento. Her lawyer is planning to tell the judge that his client ran out of her prescription and, due to other Christmas obligations, had no time to refill it. She was temporarily insane.

Even for the symptoms of shopping overload, there is retail therapy. Anecdotal evidence points to an upswing in "self-gifting," which, from Target to Tiffany's, may be outpacing other-gifting. "When we do our holiday gift guide," the editor of *Lucky* tells a reporter, "it's two for me, one for you." In case the self-indulger experiences a scintilla of guilt, a purchasable pick-me-up assuages that, too. Every boutique counter this year offers a garland of silicone bracelets, each in a different color signifying a different endangered species or incurable disease. For only a dollar, the shopper gets to do good, broadcast her generosity, and—not to be underestimated—acquire an accessory in the season's must-have material, rubber.

DECEMBER 10

This morning on public radio, the host Brian Lehrer is devoting a portion of his show to the commercialization of Christmas. A British woman calls in to say she is gobsmacked by the volume of holiday decoration here in the States. "If you ask me, the whole thing is a waste of electricity," she snorts.

And if you ask me, the Sistine Chapel ceiling is a waste of paint.

In Carroll Gardens, each homeowner is a Leonardo of holiday decoration. Every front yard boasts a fully loaded crèche: the Holy Family, attended by the shepherds and their reindeer, a phalanx of Tin Soldiers of the Cross, and the Three Wise Men, Melchior, Balthazar, and Frosty. A bit apart from the mangers are stationed the inflated Elves, like massive, menacing bouncers. Tape loops alternate religious and secular fare—for example, "Silent Night" and "Here Comes Santa Claus." They sound like angel choirs translated into cell phone ring tones.

I love these displays not for their religious fervor, but for another kind of devotion that they show: the devotion to something from which absolutely no profit is gained. Yes, there is in them an element of what Juliet Schor calls competitive consumption, whose prize is social status. One year, everyone on my block had to have a string of white lights resembling icicles, the next it was webs of evenly spaced lights that fit over the shrubs like hairnets, the next, the magna-inflatables (each of these innovations shows up a year or two later in Hardwick). But this is friendly competition, Frisbee football as compared to the Super Bowl, and the decorating is a labor, most of all, of love. "Labor divorced from purpose appeals to me," says a character in Ben Katchor's musical theater piece "The Slug Bearers of Kayrol Island." Is this not the definition of art?

DECEMBER 12

We are not entirely avoiding holiday purchases, though the ones we are making are consistent with the rules—food only. There's a tradition to uphold. Today is our Fourth Annual Chanukah Latke Bash. Paul and I shop and clean for two days, rise at six and fry eighteen dozen potato latkes, toss a huge salad, and pour jars of homemade applesauce and a pint of sour cream into blue bowls. In butterfat alone, the sour cream exceeds our yearly ration of utter non-necessity. Paul breaks out a few six-packs of his October batch of homebrew, and we've bought a case of seltzer, in this instance a necessity, to cut the latke grease. When the table is set and we're dressed for the party, I send Paul out for an extra pint of sour cream. This last-minute precaution, including my anxiety and Paul's easygoing compliance, is part of the yearly ritual.

Because we're not buying it, we've asked friends to bring wine. Under the circumstances, adherence to this rule is somewhat academic. Case in point: on a huge oval platter, I lay out two smoked whitefish from Russ & Daughters, about four pounds of smoky flesh and skinny bones, for $60. Necessary? Are you kidding? Everything purveyed by this venerated Lower East Side establishment ("the Louvre of Lox," the *Times of London* called it), two doors down Houston Street from Bronfeld Myron Foam Rubber Cut to Order, is the most superfluous of superfluities. The spotless stainless-steel case that runs along one side of the shop is a shah's jewel case, displaying watered-silk lox, gilt-skinned trout, silver-plated herring, caviar pearls at $100 an ounce. Beside the humbler fare on our table—potato, onion, apple—the fish fulfills that gift-economy code that requires magnanimity be answered with magnanimity. Our year of receiving is coming to an end.

The feast is like other gifting rituals, such as the potlatch: by definition an orgy of extravagance. Animal or human captive is sacrificed, gifts too numerous to count are spread before the guests; sometimes, to demonstrate the profligacy of the giver, they are smashed or burnt or thrown into the sea. By the time it's all over, food, table, house, or village may lie in ruins.

To the philosopher Georges Bataille, this devastation is not the unfortunate consequence of a celebration gone overboard, à la frat party. Devastation is the point. "It is not necessity but its contrary, 'luxury,' that presents living matter and mankind with their fundamental problems," Bataille writes in his meditation on consumption, *The Accursed Share*. Classical economists are wrong, he argues, in assuming that humans act on an innate drive toward gain and that consumption is therefore "productive expenditure" in service of accumulation. No, consumption— Bataille uses the word literally, like an environmentalist economist—is *destructive* expenditure, compelled by the need to diminish, to annihilate the excess energy that is around and in us, from the sun to sexuality. No matter how materially poor a society, it is driven to "squander," he says, through gifts and feasts, sex, art, and war.

Our Latke Bash aspires to such grand-scale squandering. It is a single-minded event. People greet and meet, but they are here to eat. Today, as every year, the guests arrive around four, throw off their coats, move straight to the table, load their plates, and gorge until a fatted stupor descends on the room.

December: Prosperity

By the time they finally trickle out, it is late and dark. Paul and I survey the remains of the day: scattered paper plates and cups, empty wine and beer bottles, pools of latke grease, stray leaves of arugula, two clean fish skeletons, a dollop or two of applesauce and sour cream in the blue bowls. I open the refrigerator to put away some leftovers. Inside, like every year, the second pint of sour cream rests unopened.

"You never know what is enough unless you know what is more than enough," wrote Blake. The year has taught Paul and me that where getting and having are concerned, enough is significantly less than we, and Americans generally, think it is. But giving is another matter. Today, there was more than we needed, more than anyone desired. That is, precisely enough.

DECEMBER 14

E-mail from Jim, a former co-worker at *BusinessWeek*, writing from the office to remind me of the bounty I'm missing:

```
Christmas specials at the card shop downstairs:
The Year in Kittens calendar, Julius and Ethel
Rosenberg salt and pepper shakers.
```

Another popular 2004 holiday special, I see on the eleven o'clock news, is the plastic-surgery gift certificate. Giving is self-interested, said the anthropologist Marcel Mauss; I find it hard to know whose interests are being served when a husband gives his wife a boob job for Christmas. Apparently, the plastic surgeons have also pondered this question (though not enough to interfere with marketing). It's entertaining to watch the (all male) shrink-wrapped faces of the doctors on TV, playing down the relational hazards that face such a gift-giver.

DECEMBER 15

The Hardwick Zoning Board of Adjustments issues its decision on the Rinker's Communications application to build a cell tower on Bridgman Hill. Going through the relevant bylaws one by one, the Board finds that the tower will not create new demands on community facilities, services, roads, or renewable energy resources. However, sited in an open hayfield amid farms and single-family houses, 120 feet taller than the highest tree, the structure would be "significantly out of scale," "imposing," and "industrial in appearance," in short, "inconsistent with the appearance and character of the area." Recognizing both the potential benefits to the town's private phone users and emergency services and also the board's own responsibility to preserve and protect the rural qualities of Bridgman Hill, in a four-to-three decision it compromises. The board gives Karl Rinker a permit to build a tower on the Shepards' land, but limits the height to 100 feet and attaches conditions to its use.

I'm sad that our beautiful hill will be marred by the structure, but I'm also proud of Paul for wrestling with the debate in town and wresting a majority decision from a divided board. It seems to me that Hardwick will gain and lose in more or less equal measure. If I've learned anything this year, it's that this ratio—a wash—is about the best you can hope for when consuming anything.

I may, however, be the only satisfied person in town. One side wanted nothing, the other wanted everything. Both feel they have lost, and both intend to appeal.

DECEMBER 17

As he does every Christmas, Paul has been baking for a week. Most of the thirty dozen biscotti will be divided into recycled boxes, labeled "I Famosi Biscotti di Paulo," and mailed to our families in the provinces. The rest will be carried to parties and served at home. This year, Paul is also making twenty-four dozen raisin and nut rugalach. The recipe was chosen for its maximal use of sour cream.

We pack a box for our neighbors Howard and Nanette, and they drop by a bottle of wine in return. They've also been leaving their empties in the hall for Paul, contributions to the March bottling of the 2004 Côte de Gowanus (after the putrid canal up the block). Paul brings one of the bottles into my office, where I am at the computer. He clears his throat dramatically and points to a quote printed on the label: *Good wine is a necessity to me,* allegedly from no less an authority on the aesthetic life than Thomas Jefferson. Paul lifts his chin. "I rest my case," he says.

DECEMBER 23

UNICEF announces that over half the children in the world—more than a billion kids—suffer extreme deprivation due to war, HIV/AIDS, or poverty. The report notes that global military spending totaled $956 billion this year, while the cost of effectively combating poverty would be $40–$70 billion. The U.S. spent $450 billion on the military and $15 billion for development help to poor countries, a 30-to-1 ratio.

Here in the U.S., self-gifting escalates. A Texan woman clones her deceased cat, Nicky, at a cost of $50,000. Rupert Murdoch buys a co-op on Fifth Avenue for $44 million.

DECEMBER 24

Emily has invited us for a late Christmas Eve dinner, so we decide to take a walk in the early evening, then return home, dress, and pick up some biscotti to bring with us. Strolling through Brooklyn Heights, we find ourselves at five-thirty in front of the Plymouth Church of the Pilgrims, the historic Congregationalist pulpit of the abolitionist Henry Ward Beecher and the first place Lincoln spoke when he came to New York. The doors are open and the ushers are welcoming in gay little groups for music and candle-lighting. Though we feel schleppy in our sweatshirts and jeans, Paul and I slip into the last pew.

The sanctuary is small and simple, though not severe. Painted white throughout, its pews are trimmed with curved mahogany armrests, which echo the curves of the organ loft above the altar and the graceful staircases that ascend to it from either side of the chancel. Against the white, the mahogany seems to float.

There is no vaulted ceiling, no raised pulpit—the room pulls attention to the congregation here on earth. You can practically smell the gladness in the evergreen bows that deck the hall, hear it in the voices of children, dressed in red velveteen, and in the gallop of their party shoes over the stone floors. Across the aisle from us, a tiny boy is squealing in uncontainable glee.

The service is as earthbound as the architecture. "Come friends, and gather together on this long night in the year," begins the minister in the Call to Worship, to which the people reply, "We come, seeking light." "Come in from the cold and the approaching winter." "We come, needing warmth." It is a pagan prayer—asking refuge from the elements—and in this spirit, the collection will go to a neighborhood homeless shelter.

As the singing starts, I am suffused with both happiness and longing. As usual when I hear music in churches, I am immedi-ately brought to tears, which dribble through the ceremony. I never quite know what this is about. Tonight, it's not the music that so moves me. The selection is conventional and the soloists are mostly amateur. Maybe it's the fact that (as the minister says) "the news from the world is bleak," and (the congregants answer) "we come listening for the glad tidings of peace." Tidings of peace have been sparse this year. Or perhaps I weep in envy of faith, the comfort of knowing *anything* without skepticism. An atheist never really comes in from the cold.

This year, happiness wins out. When the choir rises to sing "Oh Come, All Ye Faithful," I join lustily in the lyrics that no American Jain, Jew, or nonbeliever can avoid knowing by heart. "I really feel the holiday spirit," I whisper to Paul. He looks at me as if I'd just announced I was moving to Colorado Springs to join a mega-church.

"What's this *holiday spirit* stuff?" he asks as we stand in the foyer putting on our hats and gloves for the walk home.

I'm hardly less surprised than he. "I don't know. I feel peaceful. It's all . . . easy."

At home, I shower, spritz on some basil and red-currant perfume by Fresh (purchased last December and applied judiciously during the year, so as not to run out), and don the black Eileen Fisher pants and sweater I've worn for every festive occasion in 2004. Then I dig out of my jewelry box a necklace made of shiny, bright-colored wrapping papers that have been rolled and saturated with resin into large, irregular cylindrical beads. I wear the necklace only at Christmas, since it makes me look a little like a decorated tree.

Tying its satin string, I think about the diamond advertisements that are as ubiquitous this holiday season as every other. The actors in the ads look as if they have achieved a certain station in life. They are handsome and fit, but old enough and wealthy enough to go to Rome and bestow a major jewel on the wife (it's always a husband giving to the wife). The ads tell us that love is a good investment, accruing material returns; in return for those returns, love accrues. The rich get richer.

My necklace, made literally of paste, is a parody of the gem and of the very idea of the increasing value of things. Like the cowry shell that is worthless except as a ceremonial gift—and can be crushed into sand at any time—this bauble is worth only as much as it is cherished. The necklace is a package wrapped in itself. All scintillating surface, unable to be opened yet perpetually open, it holds nothing but the potential to please, the essence of the gift.

DECEMBER 25

Christmas Day dawns mild and cloudy. Waking, I feel a pang. Usually Paul and I make coffee, then unwrap the few presents we've bought for each other. He almost never expresses a desire for a particular thing, but I like figuring out what he'd like. Last year I bought him a Scalex MapWheel for measuring how far we've skied or walked, and two martini glasses. He got me martini glasses too, and my brother sent us a MapWheel. So either we're good at expressing our wishes, or not good enough.

I make shiitake mushroom omelets and we read the Saturday paper. My niece calls from San Francisco, where she has moved after graduation and is sharing an apartment not far from my brother's house. Sarah reports that she's working in a clothing store. She says she may be "interested in retail" and likes the clothes the shop sells. But the job pays minimum wage, so she's looking for a second job, as a waitress. Sarah seems happy—she always does—but also is vague about what she might do with her life.

The phone rings again and it's Jon, calling to thank us for the cookies. We talk about his kids, and I tell him I wish I could help Sarah find something that really excites her. I feel lucky that my own ambitions were so passionate when I was her age. Lucky, too, that dreams were in the air and rents were cheap enough to allow their pursuit. I try to be philosophical. Sarah is not yet twenty-five. But I so want her to want something badly, whatever it is.

I make a second pot of coffee and (talk about excess) bring out the biscotti. We settle in to do the difficult Saturday crossword puzzle and by the time we've given up it is afternoon. I take a shower and wash my hair with yet another of the hundreds of tiny plastic bottles of shampoo Paul amassed during his years of traveling for business (conclusion of our unscientific but massive study of shampoo brands: they're all the same). We put on our sneakers and head out for a walk in the neighborhood. Within a few blocks, we run into some friends, Ron and Jill. They are having a "traditional Jewish Christmas," they tell us, dim sum in Chinatown and a movie. What are we doing? they ask.

Paul and I exchange glances and amiable shrugs. We're having a traditional atheist Jewish/lapsed Catholic/nonconsumer's Christmas. "Nothing special," I answer.

Did we get any good presents? Jill wants to know.

Paul explains to them about the project that is just coming to an end.

"You must have saved a lot of money," comments Ron. It's what most people say first when we tell them about Not Buying It.

I respond that saving money wasn't the goal, but in the end, we couldn't help it. In fact, I've been going through my accounts and comparing 2004's expenditures with those in 2003. My basic nut, including mortgage, utilities, health insurance, and the like, consumes about three-quarters of my gross income, which usually comes in between $40,000 and $45,000. But the remaining one-quarter, discretionary expenditures, have seen a noticeable drop. On my 2003 tax return, I claimed $2,701 for "professional books," which include most of what I read; this year, thanks to increased library use, borrowing from friends, and second-hand purchases, that item will be $610. Last year, $719 went to "professional viewing tickets" and $1,494 to "meals and entertainment"; this year, I will enter a zero on both lines. Among other expenses, last year I dispensed $1,664 on clothing. This year the total dispensed during my two lapses, at Sack's in Bozeman and Common Threads in Burlington, came to $105. "Walking-around money"—the cash I withdraw from the ATM for groceries, gas, subway fare, and sundries—totaled $5,500 in 2003. In 2004, the little door has so far dispensed $3,180, and I've got all the cash I need until New Year's Day. Plus, I paid off a credit card balance of $7,956.21 in the first half of the year and did not run it up again. In all, I have spent about $8,000 less in 2004 than I did in 2003.

Paul and I have learned to think thrice before handing over the cash, and I believe this lesson will last. For instance, in 2003, I spent $249 for a half-year gym membership that I used maybe six times, a fee of approximately $40 per hour-long workout. I hope not to do that again. On the other hand, a three-day weekend in Paris with my French teacher in the spring of that year was worth every sou of its $645 bill. I intend to begin squandering cash in equivalent fashion starting in 2005. But only now and then. When I describe this to an Alexander Technique practitioner, she says, "It's mindfulness."

This kind of mindfulness is emotional as well as financial. By not assuaging transient needs, say, with a pack of whole-wheat fig bars from the Korean deli or a stick of blue ski wax, we've made ourselves available to a wider range of small experiences, including hunger and vulnerability. These feelings are not always comfortable. But they have their own unexpected rewards, such as the loss of a few pounds and the discovery that people like to help you.

Paul and I have bickered about what is necessary and what is not—and learned that the line cannot easily be drawn. We've bickered about other things largely because I have been, not infrequently, in a cranky mood. But for the first time in our lives together, we have passed an entire year without a single worried discussion (okay, fight) about money.

DECEMBER 27

There's another way of looking at what we have netted, aside from financial soundness or domestic tranquility: time. In twelve months, I have "banked" at least three months, for uses yet unspecified.

Who does not work shall not eat. The complementary proposition to Paul's much-quoted admonition to the Thessalonians is rarely invoked: *Who does not eat shall not work.* Paul and I are "eating" less this year, and if we continue to do so, could continue to work less, too. This is a comfort, since, barring a full-body stem-cell transplant, as we age we probably will have to slow down.

Yet here I am, on the holiday Monday of a holiday week, in my office. In this sense, I am pretty typically American: we work, as I've mentioned, more than almost anyone else in the industrialized world, an average of nine weeks more per year than Europeans. Juliet Schor blames the "upward creep of desire," Robert Frank, "luxury fever." As well, as I witnessed so chillingly in the Voluntary Simplicity Group, there's plenty of blame to be placed on the upward creep of employers' productivity demands and the downward creep of real wages and benefits.

But there is more to it than all the above, if my own behavior is any clue. I mean, with three temptingly free months socked away, what am I doing buckling down on a holiday? To shed more light on the question—or maybe to cure myself of a case of this pandemic workaholism—I am buckling down in search of defenses of loafing. Not surprisingly, these are hard to find.

Throughout *Walden,* Thoreau contemplates the work-eat equation. A chapter called "Brute Neighbors," for instance, begins with an exchange between two personages, the Hermit (who, according to *Cliff's Notes,* represents Thoreau himself) and the Poet (who, according to *Levine's Notes,* probably represents Thoreau, too). The Poet stops by the Hermit's cabin, hungry and ready to fish; he wants company. The Hermit is absorbed in thought, loath to lose the train. "Shall I go to heaven or a-fishing?" he muses. While the Hermit tarries, pursuing his meditation and *almost* grasping the "essence of things," the Poet goes out and digs the worms, coming back with thirteen big ones and a mess of pieces for "smaller fry." Having done enough thinking for the day, the Hermit picks up his pole and joins him.

Thoreau had time for both, fishing and heaven: he earned enough for a year's subsistence with six weeks' labor, leaving the rest "free and clear for study." Was that possible only in 1845? A hundred and sixty years later, Richard Czaplinski gets by on $5,000, living "low on the hog." Still, you'd hardly call either of these guys loafers. And remember Peter Fraenkel, determined to Take Back Your Time and mine—but not his own?

Even the labor unions, to whom we owe such modern labor-saving conveniences as the weekend, have never accepted a week of Sundays as a seemly goal. Nineteenth-century socialists demanded "the right to work" (ironically, the term has been appropriated by pro-business legislation that guarantees the right to work "free" of unions). Today the Left continues to struggle for "full employment." The Right is bigger on the obligation to work, even when there are no paying jobs, whether that means doing laundry in trade for the workhouse gruel in the nineteenth century or picking up trash in the park to earn a welfare check in the twenty-first. The Protestant ethic reigns: in America, you get to heaven by digging more worms.

If you make your way past the pro-work ideology, however, you can uncover another school of what might be called anti-labor labor theory. In 1883, for instance, Marx's son-in-law, the French labor activist Paul Lafargue, published a pamphlet called "The Right to Be Lazy." Lafargue quoted the Greeks and Jesus on the virtues of idleness and declared that Jehovah himself toiled six days, then lay on the couch watching football for the rest of time. He indicted the capitalist as a slave driver, but was equally distressed by what he saw as the worker's masochistic lust for labor, even when technology might have eased his lot. "The blind, perverse and murderous passion for work transforms the liberating machine into an instrument for the enslavement of free men," he wrote. "Its productiveness enslaves them." And this was before e-mail.

Lafargue called for a three-hour workday. In the 1970s, Zero Work, an anarchist group, did a little figuring, accounted for technology, and concluded that we'd each have to put in four hours weekly to keep the world spinning. Both subtracted profits from the equation—there would be no surplus labor value, just labor value—but along with profit everybody would have to eschew the surplus fruits of the marketplace, especially those that drink up fuel and other resources, such as centrally air-conditioned 10,000-square-foot McMansions and 150-horsepower snowmobiles.

None of us can eschew on our own. I know. I have tried. I drive a small car, heat with wood (in the country), fix the toaster rather than throw it out, eat vegetables instead of animals. All this is important to do, and if lots of people did it, Mother Earth would sigh with relief. But the main effects of personal reductions in consumption are personal. Not shopping may dump you into the happy stream of human intercourse or leave you lonely; deepen your education or make you stupid; deliver you to enlightened bliss or depress you so much you are compelled to start consuming . . . Zoloft. My own experience has been somewhere in between: I've contemplated Nirvana and longed for Zoloft.

One promised Simple Living reward I have gleaned, though, is a heightened consciousness, and not just of the pennies in and pennies out of my change purse. With each purchase elected or forgone, I am reminded of its potential effects on the world's resources and people, however minuscule those effects might be. Consciousness tugs at the sleeve of personal responsibility. It shouts in my ear: *Do something.*

Do something, but what? I could withdraw farther from the marketplace, live like Richard Czaplinski. But even if I wholeheartedly wanted to, I could never withdraw altogether. No matter how far off the grid a person wanders, she still resides in a culture. Human cultures are held together with speech and touch, ritual, religion, and law. These immaterial relations are made of material things. Thing plus relationship equals exchange. Exchange comes in many forms—gift, barter, theft, and, mostly, in the form of flat plastic or colored paper in return for shaped plastic and paper- or plastic-wrapped beef, sugar, sweaters, or software. When I joined Voluntary Simplicity, I worried that I might encounter an authentic self who was a shopper. A committed shopper I may not be, but I am a consumer because I cannot not be one.

Does this mean I should give up and retreat to the malls—or

at least to the wood-paneled shops to buy sandals made of recycled tires and organic blue corn chips?

The answer is yes only if I accept the exclusive role the corporation and, increasingly, the government have cast me in: consumer. If I am a consumer first and last, all I can do to better the world is consume more responsibly—"buy green," invest in socially responsible businesses, and buy less.

The other choice I have is to reject consumer as my sole role and reclaim my other public identity: citizen. During our year without shopping, Paul and I had extra time, energy, and money to act as citizens. We also felt more personally the need to do so. Self-exiled from the shops and eateries, we had no place to hang out but the olde publick square. There we found much that was rich and surprising, but we also discovered that what our nation owns in common is in critically bad shape. Libraries, schools, and bridges are falling down; in 2004, the voting machines broke again, all over the place.

When the very gears of democratic participation grind to a halt and nobody seems willing or able to fix them, it's a sign that tax-cut fever is more than a matter of fiscal conservatism. Our nation's busted budget, and its broken infrastructure, are symptoms of a broken commitment to the *public good*—the things and processes whose universal benefit exceeds the private interests of individuals, and whose value exceeds that of the commodities that can be sold at a profit.

With the public sector in the shop for repairs, anyone seeking pleasure, sustenance, community, and meaning (not to mention health care or education) has nowhere to turn but to private consumption. The public good becomes little more than a dream, and people like Paul and me, galloping over the landscape in search of the un-commercial fulfillments, are Quixotes tilting at Wal-Marts.

Citizenship means changing the whole picture. It means demanding policies and working for an economy and a culture that reject environmental destruction, the exploitation of working people, the privatization of the commons, and the commodification of every desire and satisfaction.

New systems don't have to be invented. Environmentalists and allied economists have been thinking them up for decades, even centuries. One of the most prominent of these people is Herman E. Daly, a University of Maryland public affairs professor, former World Bank senior economist, and coiner of the term "steady-state economy." Such an economy encourages, through tax and regulatory policies, a relatively slow flow of well-made, durable, energy-efficient goods, rather than the breathless production of low-quality, fast-obsolescing, and energy-hungry ones—for example, more bicycles, fewer Hummers. This doesn't mean economic stasis. Daly distinguishes "development" (making things, and life, better) from "growth" (making more things). A development economy, he says, can thrive inside the finite space of the earth's environment. A growth economy, by definition, will inevitably outgrow its home.

Economic policy advances certain priorities. Besides a clean, sustainable environment, the goal of economies in democracies is to give the greatest number of people the greatest degree of happiness. That was Jeremy Bentham's idea when he thought up utilitarianism, a philosophy to which most economists still adhere. But because the fruits of America's economic growth are so badly distributed, increasing wealth has not delivered happiness to an increasing number of people.

Socialists and labor unions address this maldistribution by demanding higher wages and lower taxes for lower-income workers. Juliet Schor agrees that the underpaid need and deserve to be paid and to keep more. But, she has recently argued, simply increasing wages won't reduce the happiness deficit in the U.S. As long as the wealth gap endures, the relentless need to keep up with the Gateses will mean that wages never meet perceived need. Given all our need/desires, more leisure is unlikely to turn the happiness tide either. As I noticed on the mountain trail in Bozeman, leisure is a form of work, requiring tools. Teach a man to fish and he will buy a pair of $400 Simms waders. Then, he'll have to go back to work and stay overtime to pay the bill, and he won't have time to wear them.

It's not just envy or the desire for an unending supply of new things that is bringing us down. The marketplace itself, the things we make and the things we (and our government) choose to spend money on, have a big effect on whether life is good or not. To gauge how an economy is doing on the human-happiness scale, Redefining Progress (the same outfit that came up with Ecological Footprinting) has developed an alternative to the gross domestic product, called the Genuine Progress Indicator. Instead of adding up all the dollars spent in the economy, as the GDP does, the GPI looks at what the dollars are spent on, by whom, and how much they enhance or worsen people's lives; it also assigns values to nonmonetary benefits and costs. So, for instance, the GPI enters in the asset column the value of unremunerated time spent on housework, child care, and volunteering. Deficits include "defensive expenditures" such as hospital bills for car accidents, prison costs, and the "depreciation" of old-growth forests. As you can imagine, America's GPI does not look as rosy as its ever-expanding GDP.

Many European Union countries have achieved a healthier GPI, balancing social benefits with free markets, leisure with productivity. Those economies are growing a bit more slowly than ours—about 2 percent compared with our 3 percent. Europeans are on average 30 percent "poorer" than Americans—they don't have as much disposable income, so they can't shop as much or buy stuff that's as expensive as what we buy. But their relatively lower wages also reflect the fact that fewer people work or they work fewer hours, often by choice. Europeans can choose not to work as much because they don't have to pay for a great deal of what we pay for. The welfare state provides a web of health, housing, education, unemployment, and retirement benefits. In Denmark, the state pays for your funeral. Europeans are not eager to privatize these benefits, and most are willing to pay high taxes for them. Compared with their American counterparts, their material standard of living is lower, but their life satisfaction is higher.

The EU economies have their troubles: high unemployment especially for the unskilled, an aging population—same as us. Although productivity there has grown faster than in the U.S. (in spite of a decrease in average hours worked), that rate is now only holding steady. Recently, some analysts have been warning that pressure from global capitalism will force European workers to give up such long-cherished gains as the thirty-five-hour week and the five-week vacation. But that's not inevitable. No economy is a force of nature; all are the products of human decision-making. "It's a perfectly rational policy to accept lower output for higher welfare," Nicholas Barr, a professor of public economics at the London School of Economics, told the *New York Times* about such decisions in Europe.

In the end, it's a matter of how you, or you collectively as a nation, define prosperity and poverty, abundance and scarcity—a question of what "you," the nation, the culture, desire. This year,

Paul's and my household is a little like Denmark. Neither of us earned a lot, but we both feel prosperous.

I've tacked a headline from the *Onion* to my bulletin board to inspire reordering of my personal and—in my public good–promoting citizenly activities—our national priorities. It reads: "180 Trillion Leisure Hours Lost to Work in 2004."

DECEMBER 28

Every time I go online, the AOL screen reports a higher death toll from the Asian tsunami—18,000 . . . 20,000 . . . 24,000 . . . 57,000 . . . 114,000 . . . 120,000. Millions have lost everything and have nothing with which to replace it. No insurance policies, no bank accounts, no houses or fishing nets, water, or families.

After three days, Bush emerges from his vacation in Crawford, Texas, and pledges $15 million in aid. The U.N.'s relief effort coordinator accuses the rich countries of being "stingy." After a few more days the administration ups the U.S. contribution to $35 million, still $5 million short of what the Bush inauguration will cost. A few days later, the White House pledges $350 million, a smaller share of the GDP than any other developed country's.

I write a check for $50 to Doctors Without Borders. At a bit over one-tenth of 1 percent of my income, I'm not doing much better than the Bush administration. I have given away almost $500 this year to political and charitable causes—a measly 1.2 percent, but still five times what I usually part with in donations. Hyperconscious that money can only be in one place at a time, this year I put my money where my mouth is. Not buying things has made this easy.

But I could increase my contribution tenfold and it would still feel puny. In fact, the waves that drowned South Asia are making this whole project seem puny. Like the waves, the forces that are devastating the victims' lives—poverty, globalization—seem unstoppable, acts of a vengeful god disinheriting the meek, then kicking them in the teeth for good measure. With so much need in the world, how can I be thinking about desire?

Other people may be feeling the same. Clothing, food, and millions of dollars are pouring eastward from the wealthy countries. Like September 11, this disaster has temporarily dampened material desire. At the same time, along with compassion and grief, I wonder if it has opened a space for another desire—a desire for something bigger.

Since Saturday, I've been thinking about Sarah. A generous, empathetic girl born at the dawn of the Reagan era, she has never lived in any but the most cynical, self-protective, and politically pinched of times. Might she figure out how to put her generosity and empathy to effective use? She can't quite imagine finding a halfway-interesting job with a decent wage. My thoughts also turn to Christmas Eve at Plymouth Church and the tears that I could explain only as an envy of faith. And I realize: I don't want faith. As far as I'm concerned, there is far too much blind faith out there; the worst, from Islamic jihadists to Christian anti-abortion assassins, are full of passionate conviction.

But I do want something that religions offer in abundance: the permission to desire wildly, to want the biggest stuff—communion, transcendence, joy, and a freedom that has nothing to do with a choice of checking accounts or E-Z access to anything.

We don't need religion for any of this. Even the modest secular social democracies of the EU have made room for caring about something besides money and things. That they have the room is the result of the hard-nosed, pragmatic efforts of the labor movement. But if pragmatists can create such realities as the weekend, only the loafing likes of Paul Lafargue can dream up, in the first place, the big idea that everyone deserves the time and space, the freedom, as Ellen Willis put it, to wander off the map.

No, we don't need religious faith. But if we are going to desire the big stuff and get it, one kind of blind faith is necessary: the faith that it is possible.

Pace Robert Frank and Juliet Schor, America's aspirations are not rising. They're a lead bob plummeting to zero. We've endured three decades of a political culture of scarcity, which posits no public good beyond private interest. Free markets have displaced free speech; sexual freedom is the right to get breast implants or make a designer baby; security is not a home and health care but a bomb detector scanning your shoes at the airport. For us citizens-turned-consumers, satisfaction is a pair of lime-green shoes, fantasy is a Jaguar XJ8L, and a vision of the future is $1.25 million in the 401(k). We are Bonshe the Silent, the I. M. Peretz character who is so demeaned by his laborer's life that when he gets to Heaven and is offered anything he desires, all he can think of is a hot roll and fresh butter every morning.

Today's Bonshe wants a pecan-raisin multigrain roll from Tribeca Bread slathered with sweet organic butter from Vermont Butter & Cheese Company, and he wants it not just every morning but at midnight, in London, delivered. I'm not denigrating these things. The pleasures of the consumer culture are indeed many and luscious.

And yet, compared with what we might imagine, the desires of the American consumer are paltry.

DECEMBER 31

I call Jonathan to make plans for tonight. He's coming over for New Year's Eve dinner, spaghetti and champagne, the second and last bottle left from last year.

"So tonight's your last night," he says. "What are you going to buy tomorrow?" That's the other question—besides how much money we've saved—that interests our friends. I tell Jonathan I have a list of a half-dozen movies I'd like to rent. Paul misses Q-tips. We both sorely need socks.

"Are you excited?" he asks. He's echoing other people's comments: "I bet you can't wait!" they say. "What a relief!"

Paul and I always laugh in response. Excited, eager, and relieved do not describe how either of us feels. Today, I am calm. Paul is wistful. For him, it's been one of the best of our fourteen years together. We have had a joint project. As Paul and I withdrew from private consumptions this year, we found ourselves more than ever out "in public." But we also became more intimate with the back roads of the places we live and with each other, doing what Paul calls "embracing the ordinary."

This evening, in the hours before Jonathan arrives, we embrace the extraordinary ordinary of New York and for about the twenty-fifth time this year, walk over the Brooklyn Bridge and visit Bruce and Sara.

Bruce and Sara are not friends—not exactly. They are pieces in a public art exhibition in the environs of City Hall. Created by the British artist Julian Opie, the two are amber-colored light emissions, each from an eight-foot-high LED screen erected on one of the pedestals that flank the staircase of the Tweed Courthouse, behind City Hall. The exhibition is paid for with a combination of private and public money. So, in a manner of speaking, was the courthouse, an elegant, enduring public work financed in the late nineteenth century through one of New York's most spectacular government embezzlements.

By the time Paul and I reach Bruce and Sara, the darkness is gathering. The black background of the LED screens has dropped away and the two figures have stepped into space. In trousers and boots, Sara lopes, assured and sexy. Bruce, slender as Sara and a bit more tentative, perhaps a little fey, matches her gait. Paul and I watch them, mesmerized. Are they lovers, friends, strangers? Both empty and alarmingly real-looking, they can accommodate any fantasy.

Like us, Bruce and Sara walk and walk. They carry no wallets, wear no logos. They are not buying or selling anything, cannot be bought. Here in downtown Manhattan, crossroads of commerce and government, shopping and cost-cutting, opulence and home-lessness, this man and woman on the street appear both purpose-ful and casual, at work and at play. The *flâneur*, wrote Walter Benjamin, "takes the concept of marketability itself for a stroll."

It is time to go home and cook dinner. As we turn back toward Brooklyn, Paul lifts a hand and waves to the two light-wave public citizens who have walked beside us through our year without shop-ping. What do they need? Not much (a little funding and their screens cleaned now and then). What do they desire? Anything. Everything. They stride into the imaginary, open to all.

Acknowledgments

All gratitude and no blame is extended to Janice Irvine, Ann Snitow, Prudence Crowther, Paul Cillo, Alison Bechdel, Joy Harris, Leslie Meredith, Judy Halasz, Andrew Paulson, Edith Lewis, Tom Pitoniak, and Tina Peckham.

Index

Index

Index

Index

Home Depot, 185, 187, 214, 219
Home renovation, 21–24
Homeland Security, U.S.
    Department of, 180, 181–82,
    184, 207
Houellebecq, Michel, 60
Household storage, 185–87
Howard, Sandy Buck, 138–39, 149,
    151, 152, 163, 168–71, 230
Hussein, Saddam, 1
Hyde, Lewis, 122
Hyperconsumption, 79–80

Impulsivity, 42
Interest rates, 27
Internet access, 36–37
Intimacy, fear of, 42
Iraq War, 1, 98, 99, 184–85, 189,
    230
Isherwood, Baron, 53, 55, 90

Jefferson, Thomas, 239
John, Sean, 229–30
Jones, Suzanna, 151, 167
Journal of Clinical Psychiatry, 42
Justice, U.S. Department of,
    181–82

Katchor, Ben, 235
Keillor, Garrison, 101
Kentucky Fried Chicken, 99
Kerry, John, 179, 189, 193, 195,
    201
Ketchup Advisory Board, 101
Keynes, John Maynard, 32, 90, 93
Kmart, 219
Krispy Kreme, 97, 98
Kruger, Barbara, 209

Lafargue, Paul, 247, 255
Landfills, 5, 158
Land's End, 219
Lasn, Kalle, 5

Leach, Robin, 79
Lehrer, Brian, 234
Libraries, 59–61, 95–98, 100, 106–7
Lincoln, Abraham, 240
Liquor supplies, 14
Livingston, New York, 149
Luttmer, Erzo F. P., 39–40
Luxury fever, 39

McCarthy, Joseph, 151
McDonald's, 99, 227
McKibben, Bill, 85, 86, 89–90
Madame Bovary (Flaubert), 61
Madonna, 79
Magical thinking, 42
Mai-Mai (Brooklyn), 193–94
Malinowski, Bronislaw, 95, 97
Malthus, Thomas, 32
Maniates, Michael, 82, 85–86, 148
Mapplethorpe, Robert, 104
March for Women's Lives, 81,
    82–83
Market choice, 102–3
Martha Stewart Living, 77
Marx, Karl, 100–101, 199, 231, 247
MaryJanesFarm magazine, 77
Materialism, 19–20, 42
Matrix, 181
Mauss, Marcel, 95, 97, 113, 117,
    237
May, Toni, 163, 164, 168
Meat consumption, 4
Medicaid, 101
Medications, 20
Merkel, Jim, 142–43, 145–48, 164,
    187
"The Metropolis and Mental Life"
    (Simmel), 62
Metropolitan Museum of Art (New
    York City), 74, 99–100
Microsoft, 212
Mill, John Stuart, 39
Moore, Michael, 141

Index

Moral Right, 88
Motor Vehicles Bureau, 101–2
MoveOn, 192, 205
Muir Trail (California), 148
Muir, John, 147–48, 165
Mukerji, Chandra, 197
Murdoch, Rupert, 239
Murray, Bill, 65, 66
Museum of Modern Art (New York City), 100
Museums, 74, 99–100, 176, 177

Narcissism, 42
National Labor Committee for Labor and Human Rights, 230
Nature, return to, 147–48
Naylor, Thomas H., 39
Neoclassical economists, 27–28
Nestle, Marian, 97
New Grub Street (Gissing), 165
New York magazine, 178
New York Post, 207
New York Public Library, 94, 95
New York Times, 79, 98, 149, 207, 209, 220, 252
New York Times Magazine, 94, 213
New Yorker, 29, 99
NEXGEN Tactical & Law Enforcement Supply Inc., 178
Nichols, Bob, 33
Nineteenth century, 36
No More Nice Girls: Countercultural Essays (Willis), 88–89
Noonday Demon: An Atlas of Depression (Solomon), 232
Northern Sun: Products for Progressives, 76–77
Northrop Grumman, 181

Obesity, 97
Office supplies, 13
Oil consumption, 4, 57

Opie, Julian, 256
Organic Living magazine, 77
Organic Professionals ("Oppies"), 149, 172
Organic Style magazine, 77
Outsourcing, 212
Overconsumption, 3–6, 42
Ownership Society, 206–9
Oz, Amos, 205
Ozone layer, 4, 7, 84

Paley, Grace, 33
Paper use, 3, 4, 16
Paris Commune (1870–71), 199
Paris Opera Ballet, 103
Les Particules Elémentaires (Houellebecq), 60
Pepsi, 88
Peretz, I. M., 255
Perfectionism, 42
Pesticides, 3
Pet care, 94
Pharmaceutical industry, 42–43
Phillips, Adam, 93, 94
Photosmart R707 digital camera and 375 printer, 172, 174
Plato, 46–48, 90
Plenty magazine, 77
Plymouth Church of the Pilgrims (Brooklyn), 240–41
Pokémon Center, 177
Population, 4
Postal service, 36–37
Postmodern marketplace, 132
Potlatch, 236
Presidential campaign and election (2004), 175–78, 192–95, 201–2, 203–5, 206–7, 212–13
Princen, Thomas, 7–8
Privatization, 100–105
Property values, 168, 169
Protestant ethic, 247
Proust, Marcel, 47

Index

Index

About the Author

For over twenty-five years, journalist and author Judith Levine has explored the ways history, culture, and politics are expressed in intimate life. She is the author of *Do You Remember Me?: A Father, a Daughter, and a Search for the Self; My Enemy, My Love: Women, Masculinity, and the Dilemmas of Gender;* and *Harmful to Minors: The Perils of Protecting Children from Sex,* which won the 2002 *Los Angeles Times* Book Prize. Levine has contributed articles to dozens of national publications, including *Harper's,* the *Village Voice, O,* and *Salon* and writes a column called "Poli Psy," about emotions in politics, for the Vermont weekly *Seven Days.* She lives in Brooklyn, New York, and Hardwick, Vermont.

A Conversation with Judith Levine

1. What motivated you to write *Not Buying It?*

The idea first occurred to me on a slushy day in New York, a week before Christmas 2003. My feet were wet, my shopping bags were soggy. I'd maxed out my credit card. All around me, folks were in the holiday mood: getting and spending! But I wasn't feeling remotely merry.

I thought back to September 11, 2001, when the president and the mayor were telling us we could defeat the terrorists by going out and buying more stuff. Family, friendship, spirituality, national security—we would get all this from shopping? The idea depressed me.

It angered me, too. Overconsumption is already wreaking havoc on the earth and its people—from global warming to record numbers of personal bankruptcies to the crummy wages of the foreign workers who make the $29 DVDs on sale at Target. We can't keep this up: Environmentalists estimate that if the whole world consumed and discarded at the rate we Americans do, it would take three planets to sustain us.

2. So you decided to do your part by Not Buying It?

Not exactly. Overconsumption is a big political, economic problem. It needs big political solutions: emissions standards, international treaties.

But shopping—my little contribution to global warming—is personal. To understand consumption, one has to investigate feelings about buying stuff. That is, *my* feelings, *my* buying. *My* stuff.

On the theory that you don't think about your water 'til your well is drained, my partner, Paul, and I vowed to go a whole year purchasing nothing but the barest necessities. If I got really thirsty, I reasoned, I might learn something about how and why I quench that thirst.

3. How did the Year Without Shopping change you?

To my surprise, the transformation was not from Consumer to navel-gazing Anti-Consumer. It was from Consumer to Citizen.

The Simple Living gurus promise that, if you stop shopping and "declutter," behind that nest of old tennis rackets at the back of your closet you'll find your Authentic Self. At first, I worried that I'd find my Authentic Self, and she would be a shopper.

But not shopping didn't make me look inward, it pulled me outward. Paul and I had to find fun, stimulation, and meaning out there, with other people—at the library, on the street, in the mountains.

The first thing I noticed was the threadbare condition of the public sphere: libraries closed, trash in the parks, outer-borough subway stations crumbling. I realized that if we weren't pouring money and passion into the private consumption of goods, we could devote a lot more to the public good. That might make us all happier in the long run.

4. Did you long for stuff?

When I stopped shopping, I had a surprising amount of time on my hands. I often felt antsy, directionless, and bored.

That boredom puzzled, even embarrassed, me. Then I read an essay by the psychologist Adam Phillips. He defined boredom as the state of "waiting to desire." The marketplace supplies a zillion names for desire: Kate Spade handbag, eco-friendly Costa Rican adventure travel, General Tso's chicken. But take away those names and you lose a sort of instant goal. You have to invent something to want and map routes to attain it. I didn't crave stuff, but, rather, the ways that stuff organizes desire and, with it, life.

5. What advice do you give people who want to cut back on their consumption?

The first thing to know is, you can't withdraw altogether from the marketplace. Don't try—because you can't.

In every civilization, people relate to each other and

the world through things. In a capitalist society, things—and family life, gifts, culture, and politics—are bought. Our identities are purchased, too. People call my Alain Mikli glasses my "signature" accessory. Alain Mikli signs my name!

Still, there's more to life than shopping. If you wait five minutes, the impulse to buy will probably pass.

6. Are Americans too greedy to stop shopping?

Quite the contrary. Americans don't desire too much. We desire too little. We've been so brainwashed to believe there's not enough to go around that we can't even *imagine* what we might want.

There's a Yiddish story about a downtrodden laborer named Bonshe the Silent. When he gets to Heaven, the angels tell him he can have anything he desires. He thinks for a long time and finally says, "I'd like a hot roll every day." "That's all?" the angels ask. Bonshe shrugs, adding, "With butter."

Instead of bread and butter, we Americans want a two-pound T-bone steak and a glass of champagne. Still, compared with what we could want and *could have*—from the freedom to call any doctor when your kid is sick to time to lie by a lake and dream—consumer desire is a paltry thing.

I say, let's want more.

Printed in the United States
By Bookmasters